RESTORING SMALL FORDS

By

TOMMY SANDHAM

WILLOW PUBLISHING (Magor), Barecroft Common, Magor, Newport, Gwent, NP6 3EB, United Kingdom.

RESTORING SMALL FORDS

British Library Cataloguing In Publication Data

Sandham, Tommy
 Restoring Small Fords.
 I. Title
 629.28722
 ISBN 0 - 9512523 - 6 - 4 *Paperback*

Production and Typesetting by Willow Publishing (Magor), Barecroft Common, Magor, Newport, Gwent, NP6 3EB, United Kingdom.

Cover design by A.R. Doe, The Studio, Llandevaud, Newport, Gwent, NP6 2AE, United Kingdom.

Printed in England by View Publications (Bristol) Ltd, Arnolds Fields Estate, Wickwar, Glos. Gl12 8NP, United Kingdom.

CONTENTS

PAGES

Acknowledgements

BOOKS EVOLVE! *"Restoring Small Fords"* has changed along the way since the original idea in March/April 1991 and the reality in November 1991.

This book would not have been complete without contributions from:

Jill and Mark Bradbury of the 105E Anglia Owners club, Liz and Ray Checkley of the Corsair Owners club, Mike Pratt, of the MK1 Cortina Owners Club, Maureen Salmon of the Ford Classic and Capri Owners Club,
Special thanks to Jim Norman, of the Ford Sidevalve Owners club, and to Jeff Fenton, Bryan Moorcroft and Andy Middlehurst of the Lotus Cortina Register.
Most of the people involved in the owners clubs have full-time jobs as well. This means that they are giving up their valuable leisure time to help other owners. This help is often taken for granted. To all those hard-working people involved in the clubs -- THANK YOU.

Damian Halliwell of Frost Auto Restoration Techniques Ltd, Steve Burton of Burton Power Products Ltd,
Belinda Wilkins for Lotus Cortina engine photographs, and Miles Wilkins for information,

Photographs and enthusiasm were also supplied by (and gratefully received!), Alex Gooding from the Isle of Wight, who describes himself as a Corsair fanatic, Jeremy Tallett for Anglia photographs, Mike Watkins for Classic photographs, and Bert Wiesfeld of the Netherlands for 100E photos at very short notice,

LMC Panels, for making such good panels and allowing me use of their superb illustrations,

Ford Motor Company for allowing use of illustrations from their literature, and The Parts Department, Newport Ford, of Newport, Gwent for FINIS information,

Jeff Clew, for pointing the way when all looked lost!

Jo and Tony Doe for cover design, illustrations and general graphics help, Garth Morgan and his team at View Publications for production and printing, and their support!
To boss-man Dave Furlonger and all at Wordstream of Poole, for typesetting help and being all-round good guys,

Special thanks to Wyn Evans for keeping BEJ 555 C in such good condition that it survived the next 9 years before coming into my hands, and to Cliff Beer who allowed me to rescue the car from oblivion,

Terry Burville who shows me the way when it comes to sheet-metal working, and Derek Thow for one single photograph but mountains of help on the mysteries of computers.

On a sad note, several people were unable to contribute to the book as their businesses were about to close down due to the recession. To them I extend my sympathy and hopes for a brighter future.

If I have missed anyone out I am sorry. The author records with gratitude the work put in by so many people to help this book towards publication.

Finally, to my wife **Susan** and children, **David and Rae** -- thanks for putting up with me and all the problems, both real and imaginary, which occurred during the writing and production of *"Restoring Small Fords."*

INTRODUCTION

People like to have something different -- that's part of human nature. So it is no surprise to find that cars from the 1960s continue to be much sought after by enthusiasts. But it is now over thirty years since the start of the 1960s, so there is a whole new generation of car enthusiasts who never saw Minis, Ford Anglias, Cortinas and Hillman Imps when they were new. They might have seen the odd one now and again as they grew up, but they never lived in the time when these cars were the latest thing, and traffic jams were filled with them!

This new generation of enthusiasts need basic, sound information if they are to tackle a restoration. *"Restoring Small Fords"* provides that much-needed information. It covers the Prefect, Anglia, Cortina, Corsair, Capri and Classic. Owners of the MK2 Cortina will find a lot to interest them too!

In a previous book, entitled *"PANEL CRAFT,"* I covered the subject of car body restoration in some detail. That book was very well received and the format and style has been appreciated by many enthusiasts. This book is written in the same way. I try to assume that you are with me in the workshop, and that I'm explaining something as we go along. It is written specifically with the amateur in mind and it gathers together some thirty years of Ford experience.

Often a large part of the work on an old car is fault-finding. Fixing the things that the last owner couldn't be bothered to repair, installing the correct parts, putting right years of neglect and apathy. This is all covered in *"Restoring Small Fords"*

With labour charges well in excess of twenty pounds per hour, the amateur must do as much work on his old car as possible, otherwise the hobby becomes far too expensive. You can do most things on a car, although there will always be some jobs that are best left to the experts. To describe these specialised jobs, there is a Chapter called "Expert Required".

For example, you can fix almost all electrical faults yourself, but with items such as control boxes, the best solution is

The 1963 Ford Capri provides a distinctive and "different" car to restore. This rebuilt bodyshell is delivered to the workshop for mechanical work to commence. (Photo: Maureen Salmon, Membership Secretary of the Classic & Capri Owners Club).

to prove that the item is definitely faulty and then exchange it for a new or working second-hand one.

On engines, the biggest expense is dismantling, especially if you have to remove the engine from the car first. If you can prove that the fault is in a particular component, then you can save considerable time and money. Yet again, most fault-finding can be done without dismantling the complete engine.

Bodywork is a major problem area. While many mechanical parts are still available for old Fords, either from original stock or re-manufactured components, the position with body panels is less promising. I make no apologies for devoting a large section of the book to body and chassis renovation. If you know what to look for, and are prepared to spend some time actually underneath your vehicle, then you can have many happy years from a small Ford which someone else has abandoned as being "rusted-out".

One point to be emphasised is that you MUST buy the correct workshop manual for your Ford model. *"Restoring Small Fords"* is NOT a workshop manual although I do try to provide as much Key

Information as I can. If possible try and get hold of the official factory manual. This will often include a parts list as well. (If it doesn't, then try to get that too!). These factory manuals are often available in autojumbles or through the owners club. Some clubs offer photocopies of the original manuals.

It needn't cost a fortune either. I currently have three Cortinas and a Capri - their total cost, spread over the last ten years was 350 pounds. That's right, 350 pounds to buy four cars! They needed work -- a lot of work -- but it can all be done by an enthusiastic amateur. Small Fords are cheap to buy, cheap to run and above all great fun! I have had hundreds of happy hours restoring my small Fords.

I wish you happy restoring -- and don't forget to join the relevant owner's club!

Tommy Sandham

MAGOR, September, 1991

Buying a small Ford

RESTORING SMALL FORDS applies to Anglias, Prefects, MK1 Cortinas, Corsairs, Classics and Capris, these being cars produced by Ford of England between 1959 and 1968. Owners, or potential owners of the MK2 Cortina will find plenty to interest them as well! The Corsair V4 engine is NOT covered in this book, but most Corsair information will apply.

Although covering all of the above Fords, this book has a Cortina bias, and I make no apologies for this. It is based on enthusiasm for the car, both from myself and other owners, plus the fact that production figures show that 1,010,090 Cortinas were built in four years while the Anglia reached 1,083,955 units between 1959 and 1967 - a total production life of eight years. The G.T. Cortina and Lotus Cortina also enhanced Ford's sporting image no end, so much so that the Cortina is very fondly remembered from 30 years ago!

There are some enthusiasts who will spend considerable sums of money on a Lotus only to have it lie around their garage for 9 months of the year, while others will spend a quarter of the money on a standard Ford which then provides three or four years of reliable daily service. It was always my ambition to own a Lotus Cortina, but I don't think I will ever achieve that ambition now. The asking prices are too high. However, I now have the next best thing, a 1965 G.T.

Much of the text and photography relates to the 1965 Cortina G.T. which I am currently restoring. Where there is a difference between the various models covered, this is highlighted in the text. However, no book can possibly list all the differences between all the cars.

For those new to the range, there now follows a brief history of the various models.

Brief History

The late 1950s and early 1960s heralded the introduction of many interesting and exciting Ford cars. These included the Ford Anglia, Classic, Capri (the early, twin-headlamp model), the distinctive Corsair and the best-selling Cortina. Before

Key Information

MODEL NUMBERS

Anglia (997cc engine) 105E

Anglia Super (1200cc engine) 123E

Anglia Van (997cc engine) 307E

Anglia Van (1200cc engine) 309E

Prefect (997cc engine) 107E

Consul Classic (1340cc engine) 109E

Consul Classic (1500cc engine) 116E

Consul Capri (1340cc engine) 109E

Consul Capri (1500cc engine) 116E

Consul Corsair (1500cc engine) 120E

Consul Cortina (1200cc engine) 113E

Consul Cortina Super (1500cc engine) 118E

Consul Cortina Lotus (1558cc engine) 125E

Consul Cortina G.T. (1500cc engine) 118E

NOTE: For left-hand drive vehicles add ``1" to the model number, for example 116E becomes 117E etc.

someone says, "What about the Prefect," I'll mention that the basic design of that model had been around since 1953 as the 100E.

The Anglia, Prefect and Squire were phased out in September 1959, when the Popular became available.

The new 105E Anglia became an immediate best-seller after its introduction in September 1959 and it acted as a test bed for many of the mechanical parts for the other cars mentioned. My father won one of the first six 105E Anglias in Scotland in a competition in the Kelvin Hall, Glasgow,

in September 1959, and from that point on, at the tender age of 11, I was a confirmed Ford enthusiast!

Without delving too deeply into the philosophy behind each model, it is worth mentioning a few important design features about these cars. Since the Anglia was first, let's look at it first. Introduced in September 1959, the new Anglia had as its most striking feature the stylishly raked rear window. This was something totally different from the 100E range of Ford cars available until then. The Anglia was initially built with an all-new 997 cc

This 1965 Corsair is completely original, including paintwork. On the bonnet is a trophy for Best Corsair from a recent Corsair Club event. The distinctive line across the front of the car gives it such a sharp appearance that the Corsair was once described as a pedestrian slicer by a motoring magazine. (Photo: Liz and Ray Checkley).

overhead valve motor, but later appeared as a 1200. This replaced the trusty 1172cc side valve unit. The 105E was never fitted with disc brakes as standard, although this conversion has been carried out by many private owners and is extremely easy to do. The improvement is dramatic! Early cars were fitted with a four speed gearbox with synchromesh on gears two, three and four, making selection of first gear while moving an interesting experience. Later cars had an all-synchromesh gearbox.

The Cortina was announced in September 1962 and boasted "big car comfort with small car economy." Initially supplied with the 1200cc engine it was later available with 1500cc motors and a tuned 1500cc G.T. motor.

Much has been written about the Cortina, and it has even had its own "Arena" TV programme. For most people, the Cortina had two distinctive features -- the "ban the bomb" rear light cluster, and the flute running up the bodywork. These were unchanged until the MK2 Cortina was introduced in 1966. Everyone either knows someone who had a Cortina or remembers that their father had one. Most people have a happy Cortina memory. They are firmly embedded in motoring history.

While this was going on the 1340cc Classic and Capri were proving to be a big embarrassment to Ford, who soon found that the Cortina was loved by the motoring public. The Classic was the first Ford car to be sold with front disc brakes, but the distinctive styling (especially the Capri) attracted only a minority.

The Classic lasted only two years, the Capri slightly longer. The Corsair slipped into the model range as the Classic faded away but Capri was never replaced.

Buying a small Ford

Any car you are offered now has survived at least one round in the battle against the elements. Rust and road accidents have whittled away the numbers over the years, so the chances are that anything restorable has either been well protected (by paint and underseal) or has already been repaired.

All Fords of this era suffer much the the same maladies, such as the M.O.T. tester's favourite -- the MacPherson strut top mountings. This can be plated, with the repair panels still available for around eight pounds per side. (Welding extra of course!). Make sure that there is still something left to plate.

Other points to look at are front jacking points, chassis outriggers, rear chassis legs and sills.

Continued on Page 10

CORTINA MK1

Introduced in September 1962 in 1200cc form and known as the 113E. In January 1963 the Super version, 118E, with 1500cc (five main bearing) motor was introduced. Also in January 1963 the Cortina-Lotus 125E was announced. Later, in April 1963 the G.T. Cortina 118E was launched.

Estate cars were introduced in March 1963 in 1200cc and 1500cc options.

In December 1963 an automatic transmission option (Borg Warner 35 type) was offered on all 1500cc models (except the G.T.)

The MK1 Cortina saloon was phased out in September 1965 and the other models were replaced by the MK2 Cortina in October 1966.

Several face-lifts were implemented, including a new dashboard layout with Aeroflow ventilation system for 1965 models.

Some 1,010,090 Cortinas were built between 1962 and September 1966.

PROBLEM AREAS

Rust may be found almost anywhere, but specifically:

Front of front wings round the headlight area, rear of front wings either at the top where the wing runs to a point, or at the bottom of the wing where it joins the inner wing. Rust can also creep either up or down the rear edge of the front wings.

The outer part of the inner wing, just in front of the front outrigger, is a major rust area. This probably starts on the inside and works out. Similarly, the outer part of the inner wing where the front bumper mountings locate is also a certainty for rust.

On the front valance, check both sides where the valance meets the wing. Also, in the middle of the front valance rust can

form in the box section.

Outer sills can rust anywhere, as can rear wheel arches. If the rust is bad on the outer sill, suspect rust damage to the inner sill. Similarly, if the outer wheel arch is rusty, the inner wheel arch will be worse! Where the rear wheel arch meets the floorpan can also rust.

Doors seem to rust first at front or rear corners, then it spreads along the bottom of the door. Front outrigger/jacking points rust first, followed by centre outrigger at the point it meets the inner sill. Rear chassis legs rust from the rear bumper mounting flange forwards.

MacPherson strut towers rust near the top, but generally this occurs long after the top of the inner wings are showing signs of damage. Most cars available now have had the tops of the inner wing plated. This may need to be cut away and replaced again.

Where floor panels rust it is generally caused by a chassis member rusting first, unless carpets are wet in which case rust starts in the car and works outwards.

Occasionally windscreen pillars rust near the junction with the A-post. This can be expensive to pay for and time consuming for the amateur restorer.

Spare wheel wells rust as a matter of course, unless water drainage is properly attended to. Lower rear corners gradually rust away but can be replaced. Lower rear valances tends to go at the right hand side first, and can also rust round the bumper mountings.

Petrol tank tops form the boot floor, so beware wet carpets on top of the tank. This can cause leaking tanks when they are well filled.

Boot floors can rust depending on the carpets fitted and the rubber seal round the boot lid. The floor extension and support panel also rust.

Over the rear axle is a reinforcing section and this must have been designed to trap water! This can be repaired, but can appear daunting to a newcomer to chassis welding!

Bonnets will rust at the leading edge first, given away by pin holes of rust appearing.

CORTINA LOTUS

Announced in January 1963 the Cortina developed by Lotus (also known as the Type 28 Lotus) or Ford 125E was fitted with the 1558cc engine. This consisted of the 1500cc Ford engine and the specially developed Lotus twin overhead cam cylinder head.

Production figures indicate that 2,894 Lotus Cortinas were built between 1963 and 1966.

Andy Middlehurst, the Technical Representative of the Lotus Cortina Register, estimates that some 600 genuine cars are known to the club. He also believes that between 50 and 100 cars are in California alone, and not members of the Register. Many cars have been scrapped, either as a result of accident damage, rally or race damage, or just plain worn out. However, there appears to a large number of these cars not accounted for and hence possible restoration projects -- if they can be located! But beware, there could be at least 100 non-genuine cars around. See, Lotus - Friend or Fraud? in the text. Be sure before you buy.

PROBLEM AREAS

See MK1 Cortina, plus: Battery was housed in the boot. Beware corrosion from spilt acid.

Beware competition wear and tear or outright damage. Beware replicas.

PREFECT 107E

The 100E Anglia and Prefect saloons were introduced in 1953, although only one Prefect was actually built in that year. The 5 cwt. van came in July 1954, the 7 cwt. the following year and this formed the basis of the two estate versions -- the Escort trimmed to Anglia specification, and the Squire built to Prefect specification and originally fitted with wooden side trims. All these models were facelifted from October 1957.

The Anglia, Prefect and Squire were

phased out in September 1959, when the Popular became available. The Escort estate and both van versions continued until April 1961 when the 105E-based models were almost ready. (There was a gap!). The Popular finally gave way in June 1962.

These models are not specifically covered by this book although much of the information given for the 107E will be relevant.

All the above models shared the 1172cc side valve engine and three speed gearbox.

Introduced in October 1959 as the New Prefect 107E, was the old style 100E 4-door body with 997cc overhead valve engine, four speed gearbox and the new Anglia's hypoid rear axle. On this New Prefect the de Luxe specification was standard.

An economy version of the old Anglia 100E was introduced in September 1959 and continued until June 1962. This was designated the Popular 100E.

The Prefect 107E was discontinued in March/May 1961.

Production figures for the 107E show that 38,154 models were built.

Problem Areas

Generally as MK1 Cortina, plus:

The front of the outer sill is very prone to corrosion which spreads from the outer wing (which bolt onto this car). Vertical area of A-panel rusts at the bottom where it meets the inner and outer sills.

ANGLIA 105E

Introduced in September 1959 with 997cc engine, known as 105E. In June 1961 the Ford Thames van with 997cc engine was introduced, known as the 307E. In

October 1961 Anglia Estate introduced with 997cc engine.

Anglia Super 123E with 1200cc engine introduced in October 1962. Also in October 1962 the Thames van was made available with the 1200cc engine, known as the 309E.

October 1962 Anglia de Luxe and Estate car option of 1200cc engine introduced.

In March 1965 Ford dropped the names "Thames" and "Trader" and the van became known as the Ford Anglia Van. The Anglia de Luxe with 1200cc engine was discontinued in September 1965.

All Anglia production ceased in November 1967. Some 1,083,955 Anglias were built between 1959 and 1967.

Problem Areas:

As MK1 Cortina.

CLASSIC / CAPRI

The Classic 315 was introduced in May 1961 with 1340cc engine, and known as the 109E. In January 1962, Capri 335 with 1340cc engine introduced.

In August 1962 both cars available with five-main bearing 1500cc engine, known as 116E. Capri G.T. introduced in February 1963.

Classic 109E models were phased out in August 1962. Classic 116E models phased out October 1963 and were replaced with the Corsair.

Capri 116E phased out June 1964.

Some 128,000 Classic and Capri models were built. Of these approximately 18,000 were Capris plus a further 2,000 Capri G.T. models were made. The remaining 108,000 were Classics.

Problem Areas

All the areas mentioned for the MK1 Cortina, plus:

Headlamp panels, headlamp panel shelf

and sidelamp inner are all prone to severe corrosion. Gutters on the Capri rust due to the large chrome decoration trapping water.

The A-post sometimes rusts on the Capri and this can be put right but involves a fair bit of dismantling and welding.

Horn rings are very scarce, as is all the chromework. Many panels are very difficult to obtain unless an owners club member.

CORSAIR

This car is actually a Cortina variant, in fact a Cortina with a longer wheelbase (8 ft. 1 inch on the Cortina and 8 ft. 5 inches on the Corsair). Not many people seem to realise this, so most of what applies to the Cortina applies to the Corsair.

Introduced as 120E in October 1963 with 1500cc engine. Both standard and G.T. versions were offered.

In December 1963 an automatic transmission option (Borg Warner 35 type) was introduced (not for the G.T.).

The 1500cc "in-line" version was discontinued in October 1965 but replaced with V4 engined version which continued until 1970. Production figures state 137,734 1500cc models were built between 1963 and 1965. In addition 21,857 1500 G.T. models were built in the same period. Of these cars only 311, 2-door 1500s were built (right hand drive), plus 24 left hand drive 2-door models.

From 1965-1970, 135,000 V4 cars of 1700cc and 2000cc were built. V4 2-door cars were for export only and no figures are available.

Problem Areas:

See MK1 Cortina.

Many small Fords seem to develop a rust hole on the vertical section of the inner wing, just in front of the front outrigger. Again a repair patch is available, or can be made quite simply. The spare wheel well will probably have suffered, as the car will have transported a few gallons of rainwater around until the well floor gives way through rust and releases the water! This can be repaired too, but you may have to make up the patch yourself depending on which model you buy.

Have a look under the carpets, where the inner sill meets the floor pan. This can corrode without the owner knowing and can be a bit more costly to put right.

All the engines suffer the same problems, with the 1200 and 1340 needing most attention. One trouble is the crankcase breather which needs to be kept clear, otherwise the crankcase will pressurise and send oil out past the seals. This can be messy.

We've all seen an old Ford leaving a trail of smoke from the breather under the engine. If you opened the bonnet on one of these cars and removed the oil filler cap with the engine still running you would feel the back pressure as the pistons leaked under compression and forced high pressure gas into the crankcase. The good news is it can all be repaired.

The rocker shaft and rockers get noisy in high mileage engines but this is something to be noted rather than worried about.

Rear wheel arches can corrode but repair panels are available.

Doors rust in a fairly predictable pattern. The front wing suffers round the headlamp ring, but much more so at the bottom of the rear of the wing, just in front of the door.

All these rust problems can be cured. The problem is trading time against cost. If you can do all the work, the cost will be very low. If you have to get someone else to do the work the cost rapidly rises until the point is reached where you must ask yourself, "Is it worth it?"

Budget versus Time

As with most things in life, money is the key. Throw five thousand pounds at your Ford Anglia and you can have a full restoration done for you by several specialists. Do it yourself and it will take a lot longer but may only cost one thousand pounds.

You will have to work out a budget for

This 1965 G.T. Cortina is the same one shown on page 77. The difference is approximately 10 years and three different owners. The author is currently restoring this car when not writing books! Owner Wyn Evans kept the car immaculate for eight years before selling it. (Photo: Wyn Evans).

doing the work. How much can you afford? Will the car be worth what you put into it? Do you want to keep the car, or take a profit from it? Decide what you want to do. As with most things the original idea will be different from the final result, but a good idea at the start will be worth a lot when the job gets tedious in the middle of the restoration.

Inspecting a car

Imagine you are going to look at a small Ford offered for sale. I want to give some broad advice about making lists of problems as you choose a car to buy. Don't buy the first car offered unless you are absolutely sure it is what you want and is restorable. Read this section first.

The best plan of action is to take a note pad and pen to the car and start at the front and work towards the back. Write down each and every fault you notice. Don't worry if things look trivial, write everything down and sift through it all later.

Let's take an imaginary look at a second-hand small Ford. I've got my pad and pen, and I'm going to start from the front. The first thing I notice is the badge which I think should be on the radiator grill. It is missing, so I write that down. The near-side indicator lens is cracked, but not too badly. That might be an M.O.T. problem. I'll write that down too. Under

the bumper, the lower part of the front panel is a bit rusty. A closer inspection will show that it is mostly surface rust, where paint is missing. That is jotted down in the book.

Having followed this plan on the front and sides of the car, it is now time to look inside. Okay, the driver's seat is ripped, well not so much ripped, more some stitching has broken. That's very common! That can be fixed quite easily, so I'll jot it down. Now it is time to turn on the ignition and see what engine and electrical faults are present.

I've turned on the sidelights and noticed that the right hand side of the dashboard does not seem to light up very brightly. I suspect that a bulb or bulbs are blown behind the dashboard. Remember that on the Classic/Capri there is a "twist" to the sidelamp switch which allows you to dim the dashboard lights and turn them off, so keep that in mind. Most people can't be bothered to replace blown dashboard bulbs so don't be surprised if some don't work. They do make a big difference to a restored car, though!

Turning on the ignition ONLY (I've not tried to start the car yet) I find the indicators work. I know that because the dashboard lights wink steadily. If there was a problem the light would either stay on steady or flash very quickly. (The correct

Buying a small Ford

Four beautiful Anglias at the show in Tredegar House in Newport, south Wales in September 1991. All members of the enthusiastic Ford 105E Owners Club, the various cars show off their winning plaques from other events. The Anglia was made from 1959 until 1968 and is still a very practical classic today.

flashing rate is between 60 and 120 flashes per minute for the M.O.T. test).

The chrome work round the instruments looks a bit tarnished, but that can be cleaned up with a cotton bud and some cleaning fluid. I'll note that down.

Most things seem to work, including the windscreen wipers. Again, the Classic and Capri have a twist control to increase the speed of the wipers.

Smells a bit in here. I wonder if the carpet is wet. Thought so. A soggy wet carpet and underfelt, covering a rusty floor panel. Looks like the carpet can be dried out and saved, but I might need to weld in a new floor panel. I'll note that down in the book and try and remember to look at the same panel when I'm under the car. I should be able to knock something off the price if I am going to have to spend money having it welded. (Don't tell the owner you can weld! He'll only stick to his original asking price).

Time to try and start the car. It is turning over okay, but is reluctant to start. Right, it started on the fourth try, so it may need attention, or it might be my technique on this particular car. Once the motor has warmed up, I'll blip the throttle a few times and look for smoke from the exhaust. Talking of exhaust, there is a hissing noise, so I now suspect either a leaking exhaust or a leaking inlet manifold gasket.

Time to have a look under the bonnet. Seems like a lot of wet oil around the top of the rocker box. That usually means that there is a lot of back pressure within the engine caused by worn piston rings. It might just be that the crankcase breather is blocked -- I'll hope that is the explanation as it is a lot quicker and cheaper to fix than piston rings!

The battery looks pretty old. There is a lot of horrible white fungus around the terminals and there is a suspect wire dangling from the battery post. Perhaps the owner has had some accessory connected directly to the battery.

I don't want to labour this example, but you should have the idea by now. Note down everything you discover about the car, either problems, or things you need to check later.

While you are making this inspection and compiling an ever-growing list, the current owner is making disapproving noises, wanting to know why you are putting so much effort into what he thinks is a "banger". The answer is that you are going to have to spend a lot of your valuable time working on this car to get it back into a satisfactory state of repair. Whether you are spending 20 pounds, 200 pounds or 2,000 pounds, make a thorough examination of what you are buying. As the old saying goes, "Marry in haste and repent at leisure." Now ask for a test drive.

Which small Ford?

Let's pretend you have the choice of every small Ford in the land. Which one should you go for?

If you fancy an Anglia or Prefect then the choice is narrowed down considerably. The Prefect has the advantage (or disadvantage?) of having four doors to the Anglia's two, but the Anglia was made in 1200cc form, so that is probably the one to look out for -- a 1200cc Super. Remember the estate and van versions.

Cortinas were made in 1200cc and 1500cc versions but the 1200cc had the three bearing crankshaft. If you have the choice, go for the 1500cc example as the extra power makes for a smoother, nicer car to drive.

There is also little to choose between an early or late model, but the later ones have disc brakes, so let's go for one of them. Saloon, Super, Estate, or G.T.? If you want a G.T., then you know what you are looking for and should be prepared to pay a little more, both for the car and for insurance. The car may also have been worked bloody hard at some time in the last thirty years, so have an extra careful look before buying. You don't really want someone's rally car right-off. If you are looking for a Lotus, heed the advice given a few paragraphs ahead!

Cortina Estates are more difficult to find so you may have to look quite hard to find the one you want.

That leaves us with a 1500cc, disc-braked saloon. I much prefer a two-door car as it seems they are simpler to restore. Those two extra doors can add a lot to the bill especially if they are rusty. So why not look for a two door Super, with some extra chrome-work on the side.

The Classic and Capri offer a wide choice. If you fancy the sporting image of the Capri, then look for a 1500cc model. The 1340cc engine is all right if you treat it gently, but the 1500cc engine is so much better.

The Classic was available in two or four door varieties, so take your pick. Look out for column gearchanges on both Classic and Capri as spares for the gearchange linkage are like hen's teeth - very hard to come by.

I know I will take a lot of stick for the following statement, but it is based on ten year's ownership of a Capri. If I had my time over again I would not go near a Capri. Compared to the seven Cortinas I have had, it has been nothing but trouble. It is harder to work on than the Cortina and spares are more difficult to find. However, other people swear by them, so it is a good job everyone is different!

This 1958 Ford Anglia 100E shares much of the 1953 designed bodywork with the later 107E. The 100E uses the reliable 1172cc side valve engine and three speed gearbox. This tidy example was on show at Tredegar House, south Wales in September 1991.

The Corsair is distinctive and available in two door or four door versions. The biggest decision is going to be whether to look for an early one with the 1500cc engine, or a later one with the V4 unit. The choice is yours.

Small Fords are some of the most practical every-day classics ever built. Although scrapyard spare parts are drying up quickly there are still plenty of cheap spares around. Quite why the Anglia and Cortina don't have their own horde of specialist dealers like the Morris Minor is hard to understand. The cars still turn heads, are completely practical even today and are very cheap to run. Why wait?

LOTUS - FRIEND OR FRAUD?

Finding a genuine Lotus Cortina can be a problem. The safest answer is first to check with the Lotus Cortina Register to find out if the car is known to the club, and also to take an expert with you when you look at the car.

The following tips may be helpful when taking an initial look. Mike Pratt, Chairman of the MK1 Cortina Owners Club provided this information in an article in the owners club magazine recently:

a) The Lotus battery sat in the boot. Look for signs of the battery tray being removed from the engine compartment.

b) "Lotus 3A" should be hand-painted on the metal panel below the rear windscreen, under the trim. This could have been painted onto a 2-door G.T. shell.

c) The bodyshell was always white, so look out for signs of a respray hiding another colour.

d) There should be a big nut brazed under the boot floor to locate the spare wheel, which lay on the floor rather than in the well as on standard cars.

e) If there are signs of three small badge holes on the rear wings, suspect a G.T. or Super bodyshell.

This is by no means a complete list. As stated, take an expert with you!

DRIVING A SMALL FORD

I learned to drive in a Cortina 1200 and I remember I had some problems. That was in 1965. I sold my MK1 in 1972 and returned to Cortinas in 1982. The first thing I noticed when getting back behind the wheel, is the size of the steering wheel itself. It feels BIG. However, after ten minutes this feeling disappears and you begin to enjoy the car.

Braking is excellent, even with drum brakes, and unless you tune the engine, you need have no worries about the brakes. If you intend to modify the engine (and they do respond well!) you should fit the later disc brakes.

Steering is difficult to describe. Vague is the wrong word, but it does take a bit of getting used to after driving any other modern car, especially one with rack and pinion steering. There are a number of rubber bushes in the steering mechanisms and if there is any wear, it will show up right away as sloppiness or "play" at the steering wheel.

Gear change is again, well, distinctly Ford. It's an easy box to use but the gear lever has a lot of travelling to do between 1st and 2nd and again between 3rd and 4th. Most early gearboxes on 997cc Anglias and 1340cc Classics and Capris have a "crash" first gear but all later boxes should have synchromesh on first gear. However, I seem to remember a few of the early Cortina 1200s escaped from the factory with early Anglia boxes fitted in September 1962. These were all recalled at the time under a project known (if memory serves) as "Project T".

Seating is comfortable without being sensational, and as with most cars of this era there is little side support. The seat back is relatively flat. Having said that I have done a lot of long distance driving in my Cortina and never had any back aches.

The petrol tanks generally hold around eight gallons, giving a useful cruising range of up to 240 miles, depending on how hard you push the car.

SPECIFICATIONS

One thing you might now be asking

Two well-restored examples of the Ford Capri, again at Tredegar House. These cars attract a lot of interest now, but to Ford they were a bit of a flop. The styling was a bit extreme for the early 1960s and the Cortina was the car that the public bought in large numbers. The Classic and Capri were over-engineered but many of the lessons learnt were incorporated in the Cortina. Available in 1340cc and 1500cc versions the small engined model is never as popular as the 1500.

yourself is, how do I know if such and such should be fitted to my car.

Don't worry. There is a specification for every car. You can find it by looking in the owners workshop manuals. Try and get hold of a copy of the Ford manual. Another book you should try to acquire is the official Parts List. As well as listing all the parts which go into making your car, the Parts List will have large exploded diagrams of how the parts fit together. This can prove very valuable when you are having trouble assembling something, especially for the first time.

Normally, you can purchase second-hand Parts Lists at autojumbles or in second-hand bookshops. They are relatively inexpensive for the run of the mill small Fords, but can cost upwards of 30 to 40 pounds for more exotic vehicles. For example, I bought a Cortina MK1 Parts List with a torn front cover for just 2 pounds -- a similar book for the Lotus Cortina was priced at 30 pounds. Although the Lotus book was in as-new condition, you will see that prices vary considerably depending on the car you have chosen. As mentioned above, these manuals and parts books are freely available from second-hand sources, such as transport bookshops

or autojumbles, so you should have no difficulty finding what you need.

If you are in any real doubt about something, write and ask Ford. Most manufacturers have some sort of customer liaison department, so if you want to know something, write and ask. Ford's address is given in the address section at the end of the book. Remember to state all the details about your vehicle. You will need to know the year of Registration (from the log book or V5 document), the engine and chassis numbers (from the plate attached to the inner wing) and if the problem is related to paint or soft trim you will need to state the paint code or the trim code numbers. It helps to state details like engine size (is yours the 1200cc or the 1500cc) or the version (Super, G.T., Lotus etc.).

Armed with this information Ford should be able to answer the most detailed questions. Remember that most owners clubs have either a spares secretary who usually has a detailed knowledge of the cars, or they might have a technical information officer whose job it is to collect and pass on technical information about the cars.

Chassis Plate

Ford identification plates, or chassis plates, are found on the inner wing, near the battery tray and usually held on by two or four pop rivets. The information they contain describes the main specification of the car. Beware of buying a car where this plate is missing. Find out why the plate is missing. It could be a reason like the top of the inner wing was plated and the chassis plate was thrown away with the old rusty wing. It could also be a more sinister reason (the car may be stolen).

Chassis plate information is quite complex, the format having changed at least three times. **The following information is offered as a guide.** For detailed information refer to the relevant Parts Book.

Pre-1965 identification plates showed the model number, for example 100E or 107E, then the engine number prefixed either 100E (or 105E for the 107E).

In 1962 a new system of ten digit numbering was introduced. The first digits showed the assembly plant, (Z = Dagenham, H = Halewood), the next two the body type, the next letter was the year (A = 1961, B = 1962 etc.). This was followed by the actual vehicle number.

A new style of plate was introduced in January 1965 as follows. (A sample plate is illustrated above).

DRIVE: 1 Means the car is right hand drive. (2 means left hand drive).

ENG: 1 is 1198cc (High Compression) 2 is 1198cc (Low Compression) 3 is 1498cc (High Compression) 4 is 1498cc (Low Compression) 5 is 1498cc G.T.

TRANS: Gives details of the gearbox, where:

1 is floor change, 2 is steering column change, 3 is automatic gearbox, 4 is remote control floor change (as on G.T.)

AXLE: Provides details of rear axle ratio where:

S is standard ratio of 4.125 to 1 for 1198cc Saloons, 3.9 to 1 for 1498cc Saloons and Estate cars, and 4.44 to 1 for 1198cc Estate cars.

1 = 4.44:1, 2 = 4.125:1.

TRIM: This provides the colour and or combination of colours used on seats and carpets. This code is very complex and could fill many pages. Look in the Ford Parts Book.

VEHICLE NUMBER:

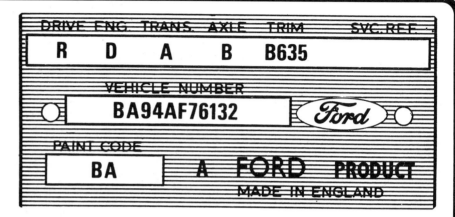

FIRST LETTER: B = Assembled in Britain.

SECOND LETTER A = Dagenham, B = Halewood, C = Langley, D = Southampton.

NEXT TWO NUMBERS: Body and gearchange type, as below:

11 = **Corsair**, 2-door, standard, column change, 12 = Corsair, 4-door, standard, column change, 13 = Corsair, 2-door, de Luxe, column change, 14 = Corsair, 2-door, de Luxe, floor change, 15 = Corsair, 4-door, de Luxe, column change, 16 = Corsair, 4-door, de Luxe, floor change, 17 = Corsair, 2-door, G.T., floor change, 18 = Corsair, 4-door, G.T., floor change,

21 = **Anglia**, 2-door, standard, floor change, 22 = Anglia, 2-door, de Luxe, floor change, (used with 997cc and 1200cc engined versions), 23 = Anglia Estate, standard, floor change, 24 = Anglia Estate de Luxe, floor change, (used with 997cc and 1200cc engine versions),

25 = **Prefect**, 4-door, standard, floor change,

31 to 34 V4 engined Corsair models, (not within scope of this book),

35 = **Corsair**, 2-door, G.T., Export, 36 = Corsair, 4-door, G.T., Export

31 = **Classic**, 2-door, standard, floor change, 32 = Classic, 4-door, standard, floor change, 33 = Classic, 2-door, de Luxe, column change, 34 = Classic, 2-door, de Luxe, floor change, 35 = Classic, 4-door, de Luxe, column change, 36 = Classic, 4-door, de Luxe, floor change,

37 = **Capri**, 2-door coupe, de Luxe, column change, 38 = Capri, 2-door coupe, de Luxe, floor change, 39 = Capri, 2-door coupe, GT, floor change,

71 = **Cortina**, 2-door standard, floor change, 72 = Cortina, 4-door standard, floor change, 73 = Cortina, 2-door de

Luxe, column change, 74 = Cortina, 2-door de Luxe, floor change (also used for LOTUS CORTINA) 75 = Cortina, 4-door de Luxe, column change, 76 = Cortina, 4-door de Luxe floor change, 77 = Cortina, 2-door G.T., 78 = Cortina, 4-door G.T., 81 = Cortina, 2-door Super, column change, 82 = Cortina, 2-door Super, floor change, 83 = Cortina, 4-door Super, column change, 84 = Cortina, 4-door Super, floor change, 86 = Cortina Estate, de Luxe, column change, 87 = Cortina Estate, de Luxe, floor change, 88 = Cortina Estate, Super, column change, 89 = Cortina Estate, Super, floor change.

NEXT LETTER = Year of manufacture, where:

A = 1962, B = 1963, C = 1964, D = 1965, E = 1966, etc.

NEXT LETTER = Month of manufacture. Much too complicated to list here. Refer to vehicle Parts Book.

PAINT CODE. This describes the colour of the paint used on the bodyshell, for example: A = Savoy Black, M = Ambassador Blue, AN = Monza Red, and so on. So when you order paint to have your car re-sprayed you ask for (for example) Ford paint code AN, Monza Red. Any worthwhile paint supplier will recognise the reference code and can mix the paint for you accordingly. For a full list of paint colours for your car refer to the relevant workshop manual and/or Parts Book.

NEXT FIVE NUMBERS. This is the actual number of the vehicle.

If you have an SVC number, it denotes a year of manufacture where a vehicle has been shipped abroad unassembled and put together in another country.

Spares

There should be little difficulty finding mechanical parts for small Fords and many of the body parts are still available. Cortina Estate cars had some fancy woodwork on the side of the body and this might well be an area of difficulty should it need replacing.

Engine parts are freely available as are brake parts. If you have trouble finding any body parts try looking in Practical Classics for specialist dealers.

Steel wings for the Cortina have been re-manufactured by the Owner's Club at around 120 pounds each, but other models are currently not so well catered for. Glass fibre wings are available for most of the small Fords.

The Classic and Capri are probably the worst ones for getting parts for, as there were fewer of them, but against that the owners club's re-manufacturing scheme is probably one of the best around and a complete list of their new steel panels is given at the end of the book.

Mike Watkins and Richard Butterworth rebuilt this Classic and entered it in the 1991 Pirelli Classic Marathon. The car was fully stripped and restored prior to the event. Here the car is admired at the start in London. (Photo: Mike Watkins).

Standards

If you are keen to restore a car to its original condition, how do you decide what its original condition should be? I don't mean that things should be as-new. What I mean is position of badges, differences in dashboard layout between MK1 and MK2, things like that.

The owners club for your particular car is the best place to find out this sort of information. Usually, they have a spares or information officer, who can answer your questions. Don't worry about bothering him -- that is what he is there for. You'll probably make a friend! However, one word of warning. Don't phone these people up at eleven o'clock at night and start asking stupid questions. Phone at a reasonable time and ask if it is convenient to talk. People are helpful, but object to phone calls late at night. I know, because for two years I supplied body panels for the Classic and Capri club. Members thought that I should be up at eleven at night just because they were. I know of several other club secretaries and spare parts officials who have had the same problem.

There is one golden rule which I try to apply to any car I am working on. It is -- If the car was fitted with something when it left the factory, it must work on my car. Let me explain that in more detail.

If the car left the factory with a cigarette lighter on the dashboard, then I will ensure that the cigarette lighter on my car works. I don't smoke, but I don't want to make an exception. If I choose not to have the cigarette lighter, would I have a hole in the dash, or install a dummy lighter or try to find a suitable blanking plate? What would you do?

If you cannot find your answer through the owner's club (which will be a surprise as they are remarkably well informed) write to Ford at the address given under Addresses at the end of the book.

Specific Problems

Gearboxes do tend to leak a little oil at the back, where the prop shaft enters the gearbox. Don't rush out to cure a small oil weep here. A little spilt oil goes a long way and you may replace the gearbox seal with little improvement.

Differentials are alleged to go noisy after a high mileage, but either I have never done enough miles or I have been lucky and never had a differential problem. If you do have a problem, changing the diff is quite easy and is covered in Chapter Four. You may wish to change the diff anyway to get a more suitable final drive ratio. Again this is discussed in Chapter Four.

Engines need to have the breather kept clear otherwise back pressure builds up in the engine and can force oil out all sorts of places. You can usually spot an engine with this sort of problem as it is covered in wet oil -- on the outside!

A noisy rocker gear indicates a high mileage engine which might want expensive attention. To give an idea of current prices a set of pistons will cost around 55 to 60 pounds while a rebore is about 25 pounds and a 9-journal crankshaft re-grind about 25 pounds. See Chapter Nine.

The camshaft is driven by chain and if the tensioner wears out the chain can rattle a bit. This job can be done by removing the radiator and taking off the timing cover. However, replacing the chain on an otherwise worn motor is really a waste of time.

Lotus owners should refer to their specialised workshop manual. Lotus top ends are not covered in this book.

Seats (especially the drivers seat) will generally be torn unless you are spending a lot of money on a top quality car. Torn seats can be fixed by you or there are specialists who can repair a seat for you.

Generally, mechanical problems are much easier to sort out than bodywork problems. Body panels are in much shorter supply then mechanical spares -- with a few exceptions!

Gutters sometimes rust on the Classic Capri but these can be repaired by welding. See Chapter Six. This means some attention with a little bit of body filler and a local repaint job.

Chrome trim on the Capri and Classic is very difficult to find in good condition. The trim on the gutter and especially the bit known as the horseshoe are practically impossible to get new. The best you can

ABOVE: The gutter on the Capri can rust badly due to the chrome strip which covers it. This traps water and the gutter rusts. This one has had a U-shaped section welded onto the roof, followed by a flat piece of steel which will locate the gutter trim.

BELOW: The Lotus Cortina -- admired by many, and owned by the lucky few. This is a late MK1, identified by the grill extending round the sidelights.

hope for is something which is sound enough to be re-plated. There were plans to have these items re-manufactured in stainless steel, but the idea was not pursued.

Headlamp panels rust on the Capri and Classic at a phenomenal rate, but these are available from the club. An interesting point here is that these headlamp panels have been made by at least one supplier for over five years. They are ordered in batches of ten pairs at a time and they sell quickly. It seems every Classic and Capri still in existence must have had at least one new pair of headlamp panels. Mine has had two sets and the second set are now rusting again.

Other difficult bits are the horn ring on the Classic and Capri, and some of the steering bushes are getting scarce. The owners club have recently looked at having horn rings re-manufactured.

The Classic and Capri are well catered for by their owners club, with an expanding range of re-manufactured panels and other components. The parts and panels available from the Classic and Capri club is shown at the end of the book.

Electrics generally do not give much trouble, unless encouraged to do so by ignorant owners. Some of your major problems are going to be caused by botched electrics. None of these cars had a fuse box, so take care to get the electrics safe and sorted. Any small problem rapidly becomes a major problem if there is no fuse to blow. See Chapter Five. Cut wiring looms, joins with Scotchlock connectors and extra switches all make up the mix of botched electrics. Remember, owners take all their best accessories off the car before selling it to you. Look out for live wires which have been cut by pliers and just left hanging. You must make this sort of thing safe.

On column change cars you may have a major problem getting spares for the linkages in the gear change. Floor change cars have no such problems.

Front wings are now becoming scarce although glass fibre ones are available. However my opinions of glass fibre components cannot be printed here! Just be VERY CAREFUL in your selection if you do decide to purchase glass fibre, as they do not fit all that well. Remember when considering glass fibre that the only cars which have bolt-on wings are the Classic, Capri and Prefect -- all the others are welded on. If you cut your old wings away and fit glass fibre you risk weakening the bodyshell.

ABOVE: The Capri and Classic share a problem area, the headlamp panel! This is a very common problem so if you are buying one of these cars take a close look. The owners club re-manufacture these panels so they are available. (Photo: Mike Watkins).

BELOW: The lower, rear of the Cortina wing, showing an advanced case of rust. The door panel may well be repairable, while the sill looks as though it will be happy with a clean-up and repaint. The wing could be saved but it would need a lot of work!

OWNERS' CLUBS

It is time for a moan now about all the ex-members of various clubs who still try to order parts when they do not belong to the club.

I have strong views on this as I used to run the panel side of re-manufacturing for the Classic and Capri club. The number of people who would phone up and were not members was quite astonishing. For the sake of a reasonable membership fee they would lie about membership and complain that they had not received a club magazine for months. When I followed up some of these early complaints I found they had not been paid-up members for two or more years. They are just trying it on at the genuine club-members' expense. They pay each year and get a regular magazine. Money accumulated by the club is ploughed back into the re-manufacture of panels and parts. This costs big money. Up to 1,000 pounds for panel orders was not uncommon. Non-members have no right to abuse the system. The policy of most of the clubs is to sell spares to members only -- and quite right too! Sermon over! Join the appropriate club please.

SAME but DIFFERENT?

Beware. There are many parts which look the same on different cars but are actually very different and cannot be interchanged. I have been caught out on Anglia track control arms, thinking they were Capri while all sorts of other bits and pieces are either half an inch longer or a little bit wider...

Look out for different items on opposite sides of the same car. I have found a car with a G.T. front spring and MacPherson strut on one side, and a standard saloon spring on the other side. The springs are pictured to show the difference.

Also, it is very easy for the previous owner to fit two different leaf springs. Count the number of leaves on each side. Buying new springs can be expensive, but as long as the main leaf is not broken you can have them re-conditioned quite easily. Look through the Yellow Pages for spring reconditioners.

Remember, the car's value has followed a predictable pattern. It cost a lot of money to buy new and was then looked after well. The owner probably cared. After a period of time and several owners who cared less and less it lost value until it reached the point where it was old, out of fashion and

ABOVE: The engine bay of an Anglia receiving some attention. This is the typical state of a car which really needs a good clean up rather than major restoration.

BELOW: The same engine bay after cleaning work is finished. Note the heater and air filter have been re-painted. (Photos: Mark and Jill Bradbury).

worth very little. If it survived this stage (and many don't) and found a good home it will begin to appreciate in value again.

GETTING it HOME

Once you have agreed a price for the purchase of your small Ford, you now need to make the decision about how to get it home. If it is a good running example with a current M.O.T. Certificate then there is no problem. If however, you are buying something which has been lying in a garage for years you have a problem. If you are fully confident about the brakes working, then you may be able to tow the vehicle home. If the car still has steel brake pipes then I would forget that idea straight away and make alternative arrangements.

ABOVE: Only 19 of these Corsair Cabriolet's were ever built. In this rare photograph two of them are caught together. The car on the left is silver and owned by Liz and Ray Checkley of the Corsair Owners Club. The car on the right is red. Both are immaculate! (Photo: Liz and Ray Checkley).

BELOW: We have the technology, we can rebuild him... This Classic looks hopeless but could be worth restoring if the bodyshell is in a reasonable state. Read this book first, though! (Photo: Maureen Salmon).

I remember backing a car out of a garage to drive it home and the first time I pressed the brake it went straight to the floor. Luckily we could push the car back and sort out the problem later. Two to three years is all you can safely expect from steel brake pipes.

I well remember getting my Capri home from its former resting place. Although the distance was only about three miles the journey 'was fraught with danger. We pushed and pulled the old car out of the garage and decided to dismantle the rear brake which was seized. Having done this we tied the car to the towing van and set off home. However on the first hill we discovered that the towing van had a clutch on its last gasp and the weight and drag of the dead Capri finally pushed the clutch past the point of no return. Having got up the hill we carried on home, using the Capri's handbrake to slow down.

Having got the car home we next found that the rear brake we didn't dismantle was now on fire, and the brake drum was red-hot. Having nothing else to hand but a celebration can of beer, we had to use that to cool the hub.

The only other safe solution to getting the car home is a trailer. There are no particular problems involved here, you look in Yellow Pages and find someone who rents out trailers. Remember that if you are not used to towing you will need to take a lot of extra care when driving. Acceleration takes much longer, and braking distances are also increased. If you have not loaded the trailer correctly you run the risk of it snaking. Four wheel, close-coupled trailers can be run at up to 70 mph, but you must decide if it is wise to do this. If you are using a two-wheeled trailer, the speed limit is 50 mph. Remember to take lots of strong ropes to hold the car in place on the trailer. You will probably need two or three helpers at each end, unless the trailer is fitted with a winch, in which case you can load the car yourself.

Beware the loading ramps which may be designed to smash the chassis of a car just as it pivots over the point where the loading ramp meets the trailer. This situation is aggravated if the car has soft tyres. I speak from experience!

I could recount several hair-raising trailer stories, but if you take reasonable care there should be no problem.

KEY INFORMATION

PART NUMBERS

All Fords originally used part numbers which had the following format, for example, 109E 4248, which was the oil seal for the rear axle. Similarly the differential housing gasket was 105E 4035.

In 1971 Ford introduced a new part numbering system known as Finis Codes. ``FINIS''stands for Ford International Numerical System and applies to all Ford parts worldwide.

So the same oil seal is now listed as 1709525, and the gasket 1709393.

All Ford parts departments should have a conversion book which cross-references the old part number with the new code.

Some 1960s parts are still used on Escorts, so may still be available.

OPPOSITE PAGE: Two shots of an ex-works MK1 Lotus Cortina. The history board on the front of the car contains the following information:

"Registered to the Ford Motor Company on 1st June 1965 and used by Vic Elford, KPU 381C also saw service as a press car but competed as a fully prepared rally car in the 1966 Gulf London Rally. It was sold by Ford in 1967 as a trimmed shell to Peter Hilliard who re-equipped the car with a dry sump engine, Minilites etc... and with Leo Bertorelli did various Continental rallies, Coupe des Alpes, San Remo, Geneva and the first ever Lydden Hill rallycross.

It was bought by Chris Sclater in 1969, still in its original colour of Boreham Red, as were most of the KPU series of cars. Sclater proved very competitive in the now-obsolete car, clocking up second overall on the Welsh International that year, and leading the Scottish until crashing end-over-end in a huge accident on stage 28 which resulted in the first of several bodyshell replacements the car was to undergo during its life.

By 1970 David Oliver had bought the car, crashed it, repaired it, and sold it. The car then passed into the hands of a friend of Bryan Moorcroft (1970) and continued to slog on as a club rally car getting more and more tatty, being re-shelled and treated to an engine rebuild in 1974.

By now it was a painter and decorator's van by day and a rally car by night, but 1975 brought another huge accident. The wreck was towed home and stood derelict until 1981 out in the open, being robbed of bits, until it passed into the ownership of Bryan, on his undertaking to one day rebuild it when time and money allowed. This was done between May and November 1986 during evenings after work. The car as you see it still has many of the detail parts to be refitted as time and money permit."

Finding the History

Now that you have acquired your small Ford, you should try to find out if it has any "history." If you have been lucky enough to find an ex-works Lotus Cortina you will have paid a lot of money for it (unless you were very lucky indeed and the last owner did not know what he had!). Mere mortals like you and I will have acquired less spectacular vehicles -- but it is still very worth-while tracking down previous owners as I will now demonstrate.

I bought BEJ 555 C, a four-door 1965 G.T. Cortina MK1 for 200 pounds, which included a pair of new wings valued at 100 pounds each, so I could not really lose on the deal. The choices were I bought the car or it went to the scrapyard. Several things about the car pointed to a competition

history -- like extra holes in the front panel which probably held four big spot-lamps, and the battery in the boot.

I bought the car (what other choice was there?) and registered it with Swansea (DVLC - Driver and Vehicle Licensing Centre, Swansea, SA99 1AR) and when this was done, I wrote and asked for details of all previous owners. (When you get your new V5 document back from DVLC there is a little note which comes with it, and one of the things on this note is that you are free to write to DVLC requesting details of previous owners).

I did this, and two weeks later a bunch of photocopies was returned together with a letter advising me to keep the information as it may be valuable to a subsequent owner!

I looked through phone directories trying

to find the original owner, but could find nothing. Next I wrote to the addresses quoted on the DVLC photocopies. (I addressed the letters to the owner's name plus "or Occupier" in case they had moved away). My return address was also on the back of the envelope in case the address was no longer valid.

Two days later the original owner phoned me up, quite excited that I had his car and that it had survived. During the course of the phone call he offered me the use of original photographs, plus a G.T. cylinder head, Weber carburettor, extractor manifold and the original front seats!

I have traced original owners for three cars and you always learn something to your advantage. At the very least it allows you to build up a picture of the vehicle's use, plus there is always the chance of acquiring some much-needed spare part. I recommend it!

Stripping

Warning. This is the single most important section in the book. Don't dismantle anything yet!

Pulling a car to pieces is great fun. In one ten-hour day you can reduce an almost running car to a pile of bits.

I got my Capri home as described above and tried to get it started. It would not fire up despite a fresh battery and fresh petrol. (We finally found that a valve had rusted in the open position).

At that point I made a fatal mistake and started to strip the car for a rebuild. I often wonder what would have happened if I had got the engine to work. I expect I could have done some limited work and got an M.O.T. Certificate and then carried on the work as a rolling restoration. As it was, I stripped it, and it took three house moves, two new jobs and a divorce before I got it back together again, running and M.O.T. tested. That took nearly ten years!

Don't make the same mistake. It is easy to get carried away with enthusiasm. Any parts you do remove MUST be clearly labelled and put in a bag or a sturdy cardboard box. In five years time will you remember where every screw and washer

ABOVE, AND OPPOSITE PAGE: Three shots of KPU 383C showing the superb detail of this restoration. Note the wire on the petrol cap, and the boot's interior light. In the engine bay note the way the cables and wires are run neatly, plus the bonnet's interior lamp probably made from a number plate lamp.

The car is ex-Roger Clark, used by him in British events during 1966 after winning the 1965 Welsh rally with co-driver Graham Robson.

came from? I couldn't!

Be warned. Every book tells you the same thing, but almost everyone ignores this most important advice and ploughs into the dismantling right away.

Having now bought the car, brought it home and surveyed the situation, it is time to have a look at engines, and that is the subject of the next Chapter.

AS FOUND...

LEFT: *After lying for almost eight years in a sheep stable Bert Wiesfeld from the Netherlands discovered this 100E. It turned out to be better than he expected, although there was still plenty of work to do. Most important, according to Bert is the bodywork. There are very few panels available for the 100E so you must make and repair them yourself. As we all know, this is not easy at first but can be achieved given time and patience.*

The 100E uses the 1172cc sidevalve engine and three speed gearbox. Bert also has a Ford Prefect E93 A.

(Photo: Bert Wiesfeld).

AS FOUND...

RIGHT: *This is KPU 381 C, as shown on page 21, only this time you see the car as it was bought by Bryan Moorcroft. This was in May 1981, and it was not until 1986 that Bryan was able to fully restore the car.*

To be able to take a car in this sort of condition and restore it is a rare gift. We won't all be as lucky as Bryan in finding an ex-works car, but you should always try to achieve the very highest standards possible coupled with your ability.

(Photo: Bryan Moorcroft).

AS FOUND...

LEFT: *Another view of KPU 381 C, again taken in May 1981. Bryan described the car as "wreckage" at this time! The car had stood abandoned for six years at the time of its purchase. It took Bryan almost ten years of nagging to get the previous owner to part with it.*

The engine had to be tracked down as it had been lent to an Escort driver! At times like this you wonder if the car can ever be restored. (Photo: Bryan Moorcroft).

WELL ON THE WAY...

RIGHT: After eleven years off the road KPU 381 C has been restored to a painted bodyshell. The colour is the original Ford Boreham Red, as used on the works rally cars. This is a major milestone in the restoration and worthy of a celebration.

In this shot the hydraulic master cylinders and brake servo have been refitted. The windscreen is in and work is starting on some of the electrics.

Although this is the summer (of 1986) a dry garage is essential for this sort of work.

(Photo: Bryan Moorcroft).

WELL ON THE WAY...

LEFT: Having a hydraulic lift in the garage is a big help! Here the headlamp bowls have been fitted, the regulator box is mounted on the inner wing and some wiring has been installed.

This photo proves that there is no battery tray in the engine bay of a Lotus Cortina. The battery is carried in the boot.

Note Bryan's natty headgear!

(Photo: Bryan Moorcroft).

WELL ON THE WAY...

RIGHT: It is now August 1986 and the car is moving under its own power for the first time in eleven years. Another reason for a celebration.

The driver's door is being re-hung, the passenger door and bonnet are next.

The attention to detail is excellent, with all cabling run neatly and everything looking spotless.

When not working on the Lotus, Bryan runs a service and repair workshop at Nailsea Services, Unit 38, Southfield Trading Estate, Nailsea, Avon, BS19 1JE, telephone 0275 858807.

(Photo: Bryan Moorcroft).

ABOVE and BELOW: Bert Wiesfeld's 100E, showing the rust on the inner wings and at the bottom of the A-post, both weak points on the 100E and 107E. The inner wing can be repaired with a few patches while the bottom of the A-post requires more advanced surgery. In the lower photo the remains of the old sill can be seen under the car. Not a pretty sight. (Photos: Bert Wiesfeld).

Engines

An example of the 1500cc unit installed in a Capri. This one has the Weber 28/36 from the G.T. and also has a G.T. exhaust manifold. The throttle linkage on this carburettor seems to be incorrect. Instead of the "bell-cranked" lever it should have a straight throttle lever.

All cars covered by this book have variants of the 997cc engine, sometimes known as the "Kent" engine. This overhead valve, four cylinder unit first saw the light of day in 1959 in the 105E Anglia. The motor had three main bearings, a point which was to cause some problems as the engine was developed and enlarged.

The 997 was well received, and soon the tuners were at work extracting extra power for racing and rally work. Shortly afterwards Ford lengthened the stroke of the crankshaft to produce the 1198cc unit.

Yet another increase in stroke produced the "notorious" 1340cc engine which was prone to crankshaft whip and broken crankshafts. While it ran it was a bit rough, when compared with the later 1500 unit. This 1340cc unit was fitted to the early Classic and Capri.

Years ago I ran a 1200 Cortina fitted with one of these 1340cc engines which I got second-hand (nobody wanted it!). I took the precaution of fitting main bearing strengthening caps which were then available, and had no problems. However, I tend not to be lead-footed and never ran the engine above 5,000 rpm so did not encourage any problems.

People tend to steer clear of these engines, but perhaps their reputation is worse than the reality. If you are a steady driver with no sporting inclinations then a

ABOVE: The three main bearing engine in all its glory. This unit is from a 1200cc Cortina, but the same engine was also fitted to the Anglia Super. In the final expansion the engine was pushed to 1340cc which was really one step too far. The 1340 has a bad reputation but with care it can provide reliable motoring.

In this photo the centre and rear main bearing caps have had their bolts removed as part of the dismantling process.

LEFT: The 1500cc engine block with most of the ancillary parts removed. For those not familiar with the engine the square hole is for the petrol pump and the round one with the circular clamp is for the distributor. Above the petrol pump mounting is the hole for the crankcase breather. Basically there were two versions of this -- a slim, round one and the later, flat-sided square one.

ABOVE: *The five main bearing 1500cc engine. This motor is smoother, stronger and more capable of being tuned than its three bearing brother. It also formed the basic building block for the 1558cc Lotus engine. (The Lotus version is over-bored to 82.55 mm from the standard 1500's bore of 80.97 mm).*

well maintained 1340cc engine should serve you well. However, the 1340 was only fitted to the Capri and Classic range for a short time.

The main bearing strengthening caps mentioned above were made by several companies, but from an engineering point of view they were not quite right. Some needed the original main bearing cap ground to flatten it. This actually weakened the part you were trying to strengthen. Others used a heavy steel strap with a centre screw and locknut. You tightened the main bearing bolts then nipped up the centre bolt. This again could cause a weakness if over-tightened. Best left alone.

The 1340 was an embarrassment to Ford, especially the early hollow crankshaft versions. A case of a design being pushed just beyond its sensible limit. If you have the later, solid 1340 crankshaft, then in everyday use you are certainly safe to 5,000 rpm. If you want to run above that you must have the crankshaft crack-tested and it is recommended that you have it

KEY INFORMATION

ENGINE	997cc	1198cc	1340cc	1498cc	1558cc
Bore	80.97mm	80.97mm	80.97mm	80.97mm	82.55mm
Stroke	48.41mm	58.17mm	65.07mm	72.74mm	72.74mm
Power	39bhp	48.5bhp	54bhp	59.5bhp	105bhp
C. Ratio	8.9:1	8.7:1	8.5:1	8.3:1★	9.5:1

★ **G.T. Compression Ratio 9:1.**

The Lotus Twin Cam engine installed in a MK1 Cortina. If you turn the book upside down you should be able to read "Big Valve" next to the word Lotus on the cam cover. This indicates a 1970 or later engine. Earlier engines just said "Lotus." Note the brackets bolted to the suspension unit top mountings. On this rally car a strengthening bar is bolted between the brackets to prevent the inner wings trying to meet in the middle when the car is jumped!

"Tuftrided" which is a strengthening process. My recommendation is -- why bother? Either run it very sensibly, (under 5,000 rpm) or buy the 1500cc engine which was the next development from Ford.

The 1500cc engine has five main bearings and is much smoother and much stronger. This engine was fitted in the Cortina, Corsair, Capri and Classic. It can easily be fitted into the Anglia or Prefect, simply by changing the engine mounts on the side of the block.

The 1500 motor was further enhanced by the addition to the range of the G.T. engine which boosted maximum power from 59 to 78 BHP.

While Ford were enlarging their range of engines, Lotus started to develop their own top-end with twin overhead camshafts -- and the rest is history. Initial work was

done on an innocent 997cc 105E Anglia (which does not survive) but finally the production version emerged as an over-bored 1558cc unit. There is a well-documented story about Jim Clark borrowing this Anglia to drive back home to the Borders after a visit to the Lotus factory. Not knowing what was under the bonnet Clark set off and soon found that there was a lot of power available. After seeing off a Jaguar at well over 100mph, Clark lifted the Anglia's bonnet to see the now familiar two camshaft covers stamped "Lotus."

Success followed success for the Ford race and rally cars, and anyone who has seen photos of the great Jim Clark cornering on three wheels (the technique for racing a Lotus Cortina) will never forget it. For those interested in a much more detailed history of the Cortina, see

Graham Robson's "The Sporting Fords, Volume 1, Cortinas."

For Lotus Twin Cam owners there is a superb book called "Lotus Twin Cam Engine" by Miles Wilkins. This costs around 20 pounds but contains over 100 pages devoted entirely to rebuilding this superb engine.

This range of small Ford engines is generally very reliable. I have covered well in excess of 150,000 miles in various cars with only one major problem. The cam followers broke up on one engine and the resultant mess looked like someone had taken a sledge hammer to the engine. It was a total right-off.

Basic Engine Theory

Engine faults can be many and various,

and a badly running engine can spoil even the most exciting car. To be able to fault-find on an engine, a basic understanding of what is happening is essential.

An engine goes through four stages to produce power. These are known as Induction, Compression, Burning and Exhaust; these are the technical names. I'll now give you a simpler set of words to remember, and these will relate to what is discussed later in the chapter. The words are suck, squeeze, power and blow.

The engine sucks in a mixture of petrol vapour and air. The mixture has to be within certain limits of a petrol to air ratio. Outside these limits the engine will either not run, or run badly.

The second stage consists of squeezing this mixture of air and petrol. In the average car engine the mixture is compressed to about 1/9th of its original volume. This is technically known as the compression ratio.

The third stage is the power-producing stage. The compressed mixture is made to burn by a spark produced across the terminals of a spark plug. This spark causes the mixture to BURN. Note the word burn. The mixture does not EXPLODE as some people believe. There is a fault condition which causes the mixture to explode, but a correctly running engine BURNS the air-petrol mixture. This burning causes the hot petrol-air mixture to expand, and this expansion pushes the piston down the cylinder and produces the power. The four cylinder Ford engine has four such pistons and cylinders arranged to produce power in sequence.

The final stage consists of getting rid of the burnt gas - the exhaust, or blow.

So there you have it, the Four-Stroke cycle. Engine faults can be caused by any one of these four stages going wrong. How can we locate these faults, and more importantly can we do so without dismantling the engine? The most useful device is the compression tester.

COMPRESSION TESTER

Let's now look at a way to find out if there are any faults inside an engine - WITHOUT dismantling anything. We use a device known as a compression-tester.

You can buy these testers from several manufacturers (the High Street motoring shops usually have them) and there is little to choose between various models. The secret is being able to interpret the results.

The rear of the 1500cc engine, showing the core plug in the centre of the back of the casting. The two other core plugs can be seen on the left side of the block. It pays to replace core plugs when you recondition an engine. (The core plugs are in the same place on the three bearing engines).

The compression tester being used to diagnose a Volvo engine. This tool can locate problems without you having to dismantle the engine first.

A reground 1500 crank complete with new big end and main bearings. The two half moon items in the middle of the photograph are crankshaft thrust washers, used to control the endfloat of the crankshaft. Refer to the workshop manual for fitting details.

Basically the compression tester consists of some sort of dial, which will be calibrated in good old pounds per square inch or kilograms per square centimetre. The other parts of the tester consist of a threaded end which you screw into the spark plug hole. There will probably be some sort of release valve to bleed out the compressed air which maintains the pressure reading. This is how you use it:

Remove all the spark plugs. You'll need to have a battery in the car as you have to turn the engine over on the starter-motor to get a reading on the tester. Screw the end of the tester into the front plug hole. When it is in properly, make sure your hands are clear of the fan blades, then press the starter solenoid. Turn the engine over for about 10 seconds. The dial should rise steadily, then remain at a certain reading. As a rough guide you will be looking for around 140 - 150 lbs per square inch (19.32 - 20.7 Kg sq/m) from a Ford engine. (Refer to the workshop manual). The important thing to look for is not a high reading -

rather that all four cylinders should read the same! Note down the cylinder number on a scrap of paper, then the pressure reading next to it. Repeat the process for the other three cylinders.

Interpreting the results:

Four readings, all within 10 lbs sq/in (1.38 Kg sq/m) of each other -- a sound engine.

Three readings within 10 lbs, (1.38 Kg sq/m) plus a low reading -- a faulty cylinder. (see below).

Two good cylinders, plus two low pressure cylinders next to each other -- indicates a blown head gasket or two faulty cylinders.

Some people say that if all the cylinders are within 20 lbs sq/in (2.76 Kg sq/m) of each other then all is well. All I can say is that if the engine is healthy they will all be within 10 pounds. A fault tends to show up

quite dramatically on the tester.

Having the above information, you can perform a further test on a low pressure cylinder to establish if the piston rings or the valves are faulty. Add a small amount of engine oil to the cylinder. I use a pipette for this, but a bit of plastic windscreen washer tube will do. About two inches of oil in this type of plastic pipe will be about right. Perform the test again. If the pressure rises, perhaps by 20 lbs sq/m (2.76 Kg sq/m), then rings are broken. (The oil is forming a temporary seal - thus raising the pressure). If the reading does not rise, then suspect the valves. A faulty inlet valve often gives itself away by spitting back through the carburettor.

Don't be afraid of the compression tester. It is easy to use and the results are pretty accurate. I have diagnosed dozens of engines over the years without once getting the diagnosis wrong.

One last word. Some people say turn the engine with the throttle fully open. I do it with the throttle shut, simply because it is easier to do single-handed. The important thing is, do ALL the cylinders the same way!

Inlet Valve Faults

There are two kinds of valve fitted in every cylinder head - the inlet valve and the exhaust valve. Exotic racing engines may have more than one of each, but the principle remains the same. A fault in an inlet valve produces different symptoms from an exhaust valve fault.

An inlet valve fault shows up as a general loss of power, but the biggest clue is spitting back through the carburettor.

When the piston rises on the compression stroke, both valves need to be closed so that compression can be achieved. If the inlet valve is leaking, then that compression will try to escape, and the escape route is through the inlet valve. In extreme cases, the mixture could be ignited in the carburettor mouth, causing damage.

Don't try and "tune away" a leaking valve. I've known people take their cars to mobile tuners, who charge them around 30 pounds, and when they're finished the basic fault is still there. Borrow or buy a compression tester and prove the fault for yourself!

Exhaust Valve Faults

An exhaust valve fault often shows up as a cough! The engine will probably still start quite easily and run, but there will be a power loss, and depending on how severe the damage is, the engine may run roughly. Remember that valves depend on their contact with the valve seat to get rid of heat, so a damaged valve is not going to get rid of as much heat as an undamaged one, so the risk of further damage is increased. Having said that, I noticed one engine cough at about 70 mph and immediately thought of a valve problem. I continued my journey (another 150 miles) and was able to use the compression tester to prove the problem. A new valve was bought but it was another week before I was able to fit it.

I have had cars where a much smaller valve had been fitted and it sank very deeply into the valve seat. This causes all sorts of rough running and poor starting and is the sort of thing which is done to "old bangers" to keep them running. You,

KEY INFORMATION

Valve sizes: 997cc, 1200cc, 1340cc engines

Head diameter : Inlet 1.262 - 1.272 inches
Exhaust : 1.183 - 1.193 inches

Valve sizes 1500cc engine

Head diameter: Inlet 1.432 - 1.442 inches
Exhaust: 1.183 - 1.193 inches

Valve sizes 1500cc GT engine

Head diameter : Inlet 1.405 - 1.415 inches
Exhaust : 1.24 - 1.25 inches

NOTE: IMPORTANT! Do __NOT__ grind-in the Inlet Valves!

On the left and weighing in at 14lbs is the 105E Anglia flywheel used on 997 and 1200cc engines. On the right, at 18lbs is the 1500cc engine's flywheel. The lighter Anglia flywheel can be used on the big engine for increased acceleration.

as the new enthusiastic owner, must expect these problems, diagnose them and repair them.

Piston Faults

Unless you are very unlucky and have a piston seizure, or a piston breaks the most common fault will be a broken piston ring. This can be detected with the compression tester as described above. The only cure is to replace the rings. This means dismantling the engine, and having done this you may decide to carry out full reconditioning with a rebore and new pistons.

RIGHT: Always use new gaskets when building an engine. Gaskets are available from motor factors, the specialist dealers listed at the back of this book and from autojumbles. Follow instructions on the packet regarding use of jointing compounds. Remember that the manifold gasket is different for the G.T. cars. A torque wrench is essential when building an engine. These can be hired from tool hire shops if you do not own one.

LEFT: Placing the big end cap onto the connecting rod. The main bearings have been properly tightened with a torque wrench and the crankshaft frequently rotated to ensure smooth turning. If the crankshaft sticks or is tight do not go any further until you have found the cause of the problem. This, and the other photos on this page and the facing page are of a Lotus unit being rebuilt by Lotus specialist Miles Wilkins.

(Photo: Belinda Wilkins)

RIGHT: The cork strip oil seal on the front of the sump can be troublesome to fit. Use jointing compound and ensure that the seal is well located into its groove. As shown here, gentle tapping with a hammer will aid location.

The seal at the rear of the sump must be cut with a very sharp knife so that it is 1/32 inch above the flange face. The seal must then be well oiled before placing the sump in position. Tightening the sump bolts will compress that extra 1/32 inch to provide an oil-tight seal.

It is worth taking a lot of trouble to get the seals correctly fitted.

(photo: Belinda Wilkins).

BOILLOT le gagnant sur voiture PEUGEOT
carburateur CLAUDEL
magnéto BOSCH – roues RUDGE-WHITWORTH

The
Automobile   **The Grand Prix of the French Automobile Club, 1912.**
Boillot wins the epic race driving a Peugeot.

PARIS-MADRID 1911

Vedrines le gagnant sur monoplan Morane-Borel

moteur Gnome, magnetis Bosch, helice Chauviere –

Vedrines pilots his Morane-Borel monoplane to a
famous victory in the Paris-Madrid air race of 1911.

LEFT: Before fitting the sump pan make sure that everything is correctly fitted and all bolts are correctly tightened with a torque wrench. Use a new cork gasket and use jointing compound to ensure an oil-tight seal. Again this photo is of a Lotus engine, but the same care should be taken on a humble 997 unit.

Care taken at this stage will reward you for many years.

(Photo: Belinda Wilkins)

RIGHT: Carefully lower the sump pan onto the block. As you lower the sump it will make contact with the spring-loaded oil filter on the oil pump pickup. Gently push the sump down onto the block and insert a few sump bolts. Tighten the bolts a little bit at a time until all are tightened to 8 lb ft. This tightening may need to be repeated a few times as the gasket compresses. It is essential to get a good oil-tight seal between the sump and block.

(photo: Belinda Wilkins).

LEFT: Having successfully completed the bottom end of the engine, it is now time to fit the cylinder head.

Get hold of a couple of spare cylinder head bolts and cut the heads off. Cut a slot in the head end and screw the bolts into diagonally opposite holes in the block.

Using these locating studs first install the cylinder head gasket, followed by the cylinder head.

Fit a couple of "real" cylinder head bolts and then use a screwdriver to remove the dummy bolts.

(Photo: Belinda Wilkins).

If a piston seizes, say for lack of oil, then generally the engine will not turn over on the starter. If the engine is left to cool, then the seized piston might free itself from the cylinder bore, but by that time the damage has been done and reconditioning is the only answer.

A broken piston will probably have broken rings, and will probably have dropped some metal into the sump. This could then be carried right round the engine in the oil, doing damage as it goes. One quick test for damage is to drain the oil and look for bright pieces of metal pouring out with the oil. Stick your finger into the sump plug hole and you may find metal in amongst the sludge. Be careful not to cut your finger, either on the broken engine/piston fragments or on the threads of the sump plug hole. Stripping and reconditioning the engine is the only answer. A magnetic sump plug is helpful for picking up the little bits of metal caused by wear and tear.

Bearings

Most of the engines use steel-backed white metal type bearings which are perfectly satisfactory for general running.

The G.T. engines use steel-backed copper/lead or lead/bronze bearings which are much more expensive. If you have a G.T. engine, then you should fit the copper/lead bearings to ensure conforming to the standard of the engine.

However, if you decide to tune a standard engine then you must make a decision about bearings. If the unit is going to be used for competition, then the choice is obvious, fit the copper/lead bearings. If however, you just want a faster shopping car, then you will quite happily get away with the softer white metal bearing shells. If in doubt ask your local engine reconditioning expert.

G.T. Pistons

As with main bearing shells, the G.T. engines have stronger pistons. If you have a G.T. motor then you should fit the correct pistons for that engine. However, a standard engine which is slightly tuned will be quite happy with the standard pistons. Only if you are using the motor for competition purposes do you need the heavier pistons. Again, if in doubt, ask your supplier, or a Ford tuning specialist.

Poor Starting

Poor starting can be caused by any one or more of a hundred different things. Let's narrow the field down a little bit and consider mechanical things which can cause poor starting. (Electrical problems are covered in the Chapter on Electrics).

As we said at the start of the Chapter, the engine relies on Induction, Compression, Power and Exhaust. Let's look at these in turn.

Induction consists of the piston descending in the bore and causing a partial vacuum. The inlet valve and carburettor try to fill this vacuum by supplying a heavy mixture of air and petrol vapour.

If too much air is drawn in, or it is drawn

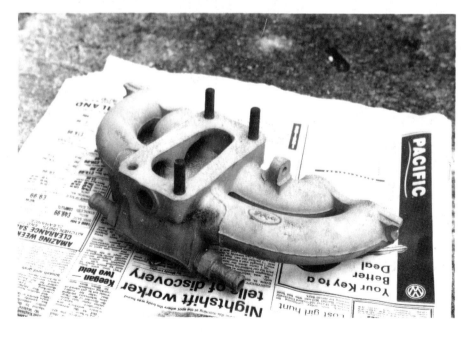

TOP, LEFT: The Weber 28/36 carburettor fully overhauled and ready for fitting. This twin choke unit can have chokes and jets changed to suit the engine and the state of tune.

LOWER, LEFT: The Weber sits on an alloy, water-heated manifold. This one is genuine Ford, but there are several other manifolds available which look very similar. The fourth stud had still to be re-fitted when this shot was taken.

in through the wrong hole, the car may not start.

Also, if air is restricted, such as by a blocked air filter, then not enough air is drawn in and again the engine will not start.

If in doubt, remove the air filter and see if the engine starts any better without it. It will do no harm to run an engine without an air filter. If the car does run better, then find out what is wrong with the filter or its housing.

Too much air could be drawn in by a leak in the inlet manifold. Air would be drawn in, but it would be downstream of the carburettor and would tend to weaken the mixture. Too weak a mixture and the engine docs not start.

Poor Tickover

Poor slow running problems generally stem from leaking induction or leaking exhaust. There can be other causes, for example, if the ignition is timed wrongly, the slow running may be poor, but so will the acceleration.

If the inlet manifold is leaking the engine will draw in extra air through the leak and cause erratic running. The clue here is to listen for a hissing sound. You might also find that the inlet manifold is loose on its mountings!

I have found that the G.T. inlet manifold is difficult to tighten to the head, because access to one of the studs is restricted. The first stud (top stud, from the front of the engine) between the inlet and exhaust manifolds is very close to the inlet manifold and if you don't get this tightened properly the gasket will leak. It is difficult to get a 1/2 inch drive socket onto this and you will have to devise your own way of tightening this stud.

Lack of Power

On the standard 1500cc engines there is an economy valve diaphragm in the carburettor. This is used to control the amount of air going through the carburettor and it relies on being intact with no holes in it.

If, through wear or ingress of dirt, a tiny pin hole develops in this diaphragm you will get strange behaviour from the engine. It might start all right, but lack power. Hills you used to romp up in top gear will now need a change to third. If you have good hearing you might hear a high pitched whistle from the carburettor.

When re-fitting main bearing caps make sure you fit them the correct way round! The arrow points the way to the front of the engine, hence the "F."

ABOVE, LEFT: The Zenith carburettor fitted to the 1500cc engine. This unit has a long life and requires little attention. An economy diaphragm may cause problems if a leak develops in the diaphragm material.

LEFT: The G.T. cylinder head can be identified by the water outlet pipe on the thermostat housing, and the two locating rings on the two outer inlet tracts. There is also a difference in height between the G.T. and standard heads.

ABOVE: The standard cylinder head has one hole in the thermostat housing for the water temperature sensor unit.

Having eliminated all the obvious things you now need to look in the carburettor. Remove the three screws holding the cover over the diaphragm. Take the diaphragm out, taking great care not to lose the small coil spring.

Hold the diaphragm up to the light and look for minute pin holes. If you find one fit a new diaphragm, the results will be dramatic. If you are entirely happy with the condition of the diaphragm, then refit it and look elsewhere for the problem.

I have been caught by this diaphragm on two occasions. On one, the power loss was dramatic, and when the new diaphragm was fitted the return to full power was also dramatic. On the other occasion the symptoms were just erratic running.

Cooling Faults

Cooling faults are usually only one thing -- leaks. You could have a broken or slipping fan belt which would cause the water pump to run less efficiently, but generally the small Fords are well cooled,

and in some circumstances over-cooled.

Look for leaks from the radiator, from the water pump and from the heater. If there is a lot of froth in the top of the radiator when you open it look out for a blown cylinder head gasket. This will try to pressurise the water system and at the same time add gasses from the combustion chamber. A steady loss of water, and when you top it up it appears dirty or frothy is a sure sign of a cylinder head gasket problem. You may also be down on power too!

Most small Fords are over-cooled, that is, they tend to run cooler than they should. Some people remove the fan blades with no ill effects. Simply undo the four bolts holding the fan blades to the front of the water pump, remove the blade unit, and re-fit the four bolts.

I have done this on a brand new, tight, 1500cc engine, in summer and have had no problems. The snag is, there is less margin for overheating. If, for example you get stuck in a traffic jam, then you will find

that the engine will get much hotter, quicker. However if your mileage is just to and from work the chances of finding a 10-mile jam are that much less unless you live in London, in which case do not remove the fan blades!

One compromise might be to remove one set of blades, as export cars and G.T. cars are fitted with two sets of blades.

Lubrication Faults

Oil is the only thing between your bearings and the crankshaft. If the oil goes, so do the bearings.

The quickest way to check that oil is circulating is to remove the oil filler cap, start the engine and look for a steady stream of oil coming out of the holes on each rocker. No oil means a problem!

Remember, if you have just had the engine rebuilt and are starting it for the first time, it will take some 20 to 30 seconds for the oil pump to fill and then pump oil through all the oilways within the engine. For this reason I always run the engine with the spark plugs out to get the oil flowing. See later in this Chapter.

Similarly, when you replace the oil filter (either type) it will take up to 20 seconds for the new filter to fill with oil. During that time period your oil pressure light will stay on. If it stays on longer than 30 seconds you may have a problem.

The oil filter and the oil should be changed every 5,000 miles.

Engine Reconditioning

Having decided that there is a problem requiring attention, or that your motor is tired, you can dismantle it and recondition it. I must again insist that you buy the relevant owners workshop manual for your car as the information contained is quite specific to your model. The information given here must be general for all the engines in the range.

Removing The Sump

Very often you will want to remove the sump to inspect the main bearing shells or to replace them. If you find that the manual says "remove the engine" there may be an alternative to expensive hydraulic hoists or a lot of sweaty manual effort.

Consider lowering the suspension, which undoubtedly is the reason you cannot get at the sump.

This technique has been described in some workshop manuals, but does not appear in the official Ford workshop manuals.

Normally, four bolts hold the engine crossmember to the chassis. If these bolts were removed, the crossmember would try to fall, thus leaving extra space between the crossmember and the sump.

The correct way to tackle this is not to just remove the bolts, but to make up or acquire some longer bolts. They need to be about three inches long (or a bit longer if you can get them).

If your car still has the cardboard-type sump shield, remove the four screws holding this to the chassis. The reason I say if is that most of the cars I have seen have long since had this item thrown away.

Remove the two front bolts holding the crossmember to the chassis, and fit the two longer bolts. Then slowly jack up the car to allow you access to the sump. When you have access, put another jack under the engine. You really want this to be in some out of the way place, such as under the crankshaft pulley at the front of the engine.

KEY INFORMATION

ENGINE Torque Wrench Settings

Main Bearing Caps	55 - 60 lb ft / 7.60 - 8.29 kg m
Big End Bearing Caps	20 - 25 lb ft / 2.76 - 3.46 kg m
Flywheel bolts	45 - 50 lb ft / 6.22 - 6.91 kg m
Crankshaft Pulley	24 - 28 lb ft / 3.32 - 3.87 kg m
Cylinder head bolts	65 - 70 lb ft / 8.98 - 9.67 kg m
Manifold nuts	12 - 15 lb ft / 1.66 - 2.07 kg m
Manifold nuts G.T.	15 - 18 lb ft / 2.07 - 2.49 kg m
C/shaft rear oil seal carrier	12 - 15 lb ft / 1.66 - 2.07 kg m
Oil pump	12 - 15 lb ft / 1.66 - 2.07 kg m
Oil pump to filter bolt	12 - 15 lb ft / 1.66 - 2.07 kg m
Rocker shaft/Cylinder head	17 - 22 lb ft / 2.35 - 3.04 kg m
Rocker adjustment bolt	10 - 14 lb ft / 1.38 - 1.93 kg m
Sump bolts	7 - 8 lb ft / 0.97 - 1.11 kg m
Sump drain plug	20 - 25 lb ft /2.76 - 3.46 kg m
Camshaft sprocket	12 - 15 lb ft / 1.66 - 2.07 kg m
Camshaft Thrust Plate	2.5 - 3.5 lb ft / 0.35 - 0.45 kg m
Timing Cover bolts	5 -7 lb ft / 0.69 - 0.97 kg m
Spark Plugs	24 - 28 lb ft / 3.32 - 3.87 kg m
Exhaust manifold / downpipe	7 - 10 lb ft /0.97 - 1.38 kg m
Rocker cover set screws	2.5 - 3.5 lb ft / 0.35 - 0.48 kg m
Generator bracket to block	20 - 25 lb ft / 2.76 - 3.46 kg m

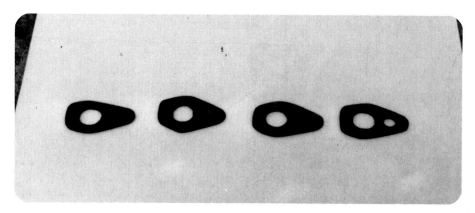

If fitting a skimmed head or a G.T. head to a standard engine you might need to fit spacers under the rocker shaft supports in order to get good valve adjustment. Shorter pushrods are an alternative answer. Note that the front spacer has a hole for the oil supply. This is VITAL if you want the engine to run longer than a few minutes...

Next remove the bolts holding the engine to the crossmember. The engine is still supported by the jack.

Remove the two rear crossmember bolts. You will find that the crossmember will try to sink under its weight plus the action of the front springs, and it will allow you to remove the sump retaining bolts and get the sump off from the bottom.

When you refit the sump use a sealer on the gasket. I have also found that the sump retaining bolts tend to work loose. Not enough to cause any problem, but when I check them I always find them less tight than I expect. This can easily be cured by using some sort of "Locktite" product which will help to bind the threads of the bolts to their holes. There should then be no further problem.

Flywheel

On the flywheel there is a starter ring. This is just a large gear wheel which is engaged by the small gear wheel on the end of the electric starter motor. When the motor is turned, it drives the large gear wheel and so revolves the engine.

This ring gear can wear and has to be replaced. The first problem is to remove the old ring gear. To get at it you have to either remove the engine, or remove the gearbox, because the flywheel and starter ring are at the point where the engine meets the gearbox.

Having got the flywheel off the engine, the next step is to match the existing ring gear with the one supplied by the main dealer or motor factor. Make sure it has the same number of teeth as the old one. There are two ways to check this. First you can count them. This is more difficult than you

might think, so the second way is my preference. Simply lay the new ring gear on top of the old one. If all the teeth line up then you have an identical item. If one ring gear has one or more teeth different (either greater or fewer teeth) this will show up by the teeth not lining up. If you are still in doubt, try counting! Normally, you should have 110 teeth.

Talking of teeth, remember to check that you have the correct starter motor pinion fitted. One tooth too many or too little and you will cause excessive wear and expensive and time-consuming repairs on the flywheel ring gear.

To remove the old ring gear I use a sharp chisel. Chisel through the ring gear taking care not to damage the flywheel. When you have severed the ring, it is quite a simple matter to lever the old gear off with a couple of screwdrivers.

Before trying to fit the new ring gear make absolutely sure that the flywheel circumference is clean. Use a wire brush, or wash it with petrol. It must be very clean to aid the fitting of the new ring gear.

You must also make sure that the ring gear is going to go on the same way as it came off. In other words can you fit the teeth facing the wrong way round? Make sure of this point before you go any further.

The next step is tricky, and if you do not have the equipment (or the knowledge) please pass the job onto a garage. You need to heat the ring gear to 400 degrees F (240 degrees C) either in an oven, or more usually by playing a welding torch around it. Do NOT exceed this temperature or you may damage the temper of the ring gear and hasten rapid wear.

Support the ring on some bricks and

keep the torch moving. Do not concentrate too much heat at any given point. You must ensure an even spread of heat.

You can assist this process by cooling the flywheel, perhaps by putting it into the fridge for a couple of hours, but normally the job can be done by heating the ring gear.

When you are sure the ring gear is hot enough, place it on the shoulder of the flywheel, and it should drop into place with just some slight assistance from a mallet. If it seems tight and does not drop into place then you have probably not got it hot enough. I would advise spending extra time heating it prior to trying to fit it. As you try to fit it it cools, and you then have to re-start the heating process again.

When it is finally located, make sure it butts evenly against the flywheel. Double check this point before deciding the job is complete. Remember it is very hot, so leave it for half an hour to cool before re-fitting the flywheel to the engine.

When refitting, make sure the locking tabs fitted to the bolts are in useable condition. If not they must be replaced as you do not want to run the risk of them coming loose.

Fitting a ring gear is quite a tricky job, so if you are in any doubt leave it to an expert.

Flywheel Weights

Two flywheels are used on this range of car. Normally, you should fit the correct one for the car, but there are occasions when you might want to use the other one.

The lighter flywheel weighs approximately 14 lbs (1.93 Kg) and the heavier

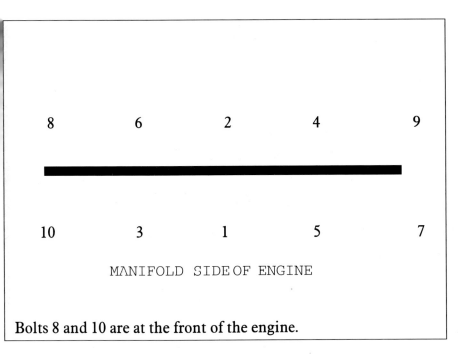

```
8          6          2          4          9

██████████████████████████████████████████████

10         3          1          5          7
```

MANIFOLD SIDE OF ENGINE

Bolts 8 and 10 are at the front of the engine.

Cylinder head tightening is very important. Head bolts must be done up evenly and gradually and in the order shown above. Final torque must be 65-70 lb ft. After 500 miles you should check the bolts again with the torque wrench to allow any bedding in.

LEFT: The diaphragm on the Zenith carburettor shown dismantled. The paper gaskets and a new diaphragm come in a kit which costs a couple of pounds. It can be an amazing cure for a sick engine!

version 18 lbs (2.48 Kg). If you are tuning a 1500cc unit you may wish to consider fitting the lighter flywheel. While this will aid acceleration it may make gearchanging slightly more difficult and make the car less easy in traffic.

Engine Modification

As mentioned at the beginning of the chapter, this range of overhead valve engines respond well to tuning. If yours is not a G.T. engine then you can fit the G.T. camshaft, G.T. cylinder head and four-branch exhaust manifold and get quite a significant increase in power.

If you want to go for something even more powerful, you will have to turn to one of the established tuning organisations for help. You can buy stage one, two or three cylinder heads for these cars. Stage one is generally reckoned to be an improved road head, while stage two is a very fast road or rally head, while a stage three is an out and out racing head and has no place on a road car.

As with cylinder heads there is a range of camshafts available from mild road to full race. Don't pick the wrong one or your car will become a misery to drive on the road.

Carburation is usually taken care of by Weber. The 28/36 is quite good enough for a fast road car. The next step up is the Weber type 40 DCOE as used by the Lotus Cortina.

Push Rods

If you fit a shorter G.T. head, or have your cylinder head skimmed then fitted to a standard engine, you may have trouble adjusting the rockers. The push rods will be too long. There are two recognised methods of overcoming this: buy special shorter push rods or fit four spacers under the four rocker shaft pillars.

Beware the second choice. While perfectly acceptable to fit a big washer, the oil is fed to the rocker shaft via a drilled oilway in the front rocker pedestal. If you fit a washer you will block the oil. You MUST arrange for a suitable hole to be drilled in the washer, then ENSURE that the oil hole lines up properly. If you don't then a seized rocker shaft will be your reward. You can just about get away without this mod on the 1500cc block. The rocker adjustment screw will be almost completely loosened off but you can get the correct adjustment. However, the rockers will not be at their most efficient operating angle.

Cylinder Heads

The heights of the cylinder heads vary, as described above, with the G.T. head being shorter in height. This means when you come to fit the cylinder head bolts, they may "bottom" in their threaded holes. You can either shorten the existing bolts or get hold of a set of 1200cc or 1500cc G.T. bolts which are shorter.

Cylinder heads can generally be skimmed up to 80 thou to increase the compression ratio. This is usually done in conjunction with other cylinder head mods such as opening up the inlet and exhaust ports and re-shaping the combustion chambers.

I have had about four or five heads skimmed this amount. On one occasion the head cracked between the second and third combustion chambers. The head is then only fit for scrap. So if you are modifying a head, work out how much you need to have it skimmed, then have it skimmed, then start work on the rest of the head.

When dismantling valves and springs I usually find that the valve collets have frozen to the valve stem. You set up the spring compressor and the whole valve cap and collet assembly does not compress. A

An early oil pump with four bolts holding the pump cover on. This pump also shows the old steel filter housing which, incidentally, hold a bit more oil than the later type. The pump on the right is the later type as fitted to Escorts and uses a disposable oil filter cartridge. Oil pressure from either pump should be 35 - 40 lb sq inch.

sharp tap on the valve spring cap with a hammer usually loosens the collets and allows the spring to be compressed. I only warn you because the first time this happened to me I bent the spring compressor!

Note that the manifold gaskets are different between standard and G.T. engines. The G.T. one is black while the standard one is a silvery colour and has an uneven looking surface.

Main Bearing Caps

I have had problems on several occasions with main bearing caps which I could not identify. If you didn't know, the main

This cylinder head is in the process of being modified. The inlet ports have been opened up slightly with a grinding wheel, and the exhaust ports have simply been cleaned up. The next stage involves modifying the combustion chamber. The author modifies heads using an electric power drill and a selection of grinding stones. This takes a long time to achieve the desired result but gives you more time to avoid making a mistake!

bearing caps MUST be replaced in the same position they were removed from. This is due to the fact that when the engine is actually being made, the main bearing caps are fitted to the block and the caps and block are Line Bored. This means that if the caps are put back in their proper places then the crankshaft will run smooth and true.

Some caps have little lumps on them. One lump means one, two lumps means two and so on. The front cap can always be identified as it has the stud protruding from it. The stud carries the timing chain tensioner.

The centre cap usually has CENTRE stamped on it, and often the rear has REAR. This leaves identifying the remaining caps as a problem. Take care to label your caps otherwise you run the risk of having a rough-running engine and new bearings being required after a low mileage.

Main bearing caps must be clean before assembly. This does not just mean clean of oil or dirt, but also of carbon deposits. I once had an engine which was extremely tight when I assembled the crankshaft and bearings. Finding the crank tight to turn I loosened off one cap after another trying to find the culprit. I couldn't. Finally I took the crank to the re-conditioner and asked advice. He looked at my main bearing caps, picked up a piece of emery paper and proceeded to clean the bearing surface of the cap. Giving me a ticking off, he told me to clean all the surfaces till they shine before assembling again. Needless to say the engine build went normally after that.

Connecting Rods

Connecting rods almost always have the numbers stamped on BOTH HALVES of the big end. This means you should always refit cap 1 to connecting rod 1 and so on. Don't mix. Where an engine has a replacement connecting rod make sure the rod and its cap have the same number, otherwise you will run into tight bearing problems and a rough engine.

Some connecting rod caps have a number stamped on them as well as a number of dots centre-punched on. This is confusing. Make sure you mark the caps as you dismantle. Incidentally, it is NOT recommended that you punch an identification, or file a groove in the cap. Both of these weakens the cap. Try a marker pen, some paint, or use the original Ford markings.

ABOVE: On the left is the smaller sump as fitted to 997cc to 1340cc engines. The larger sump on the right can be identified by the bulges on the sides. If using an engine for competition you may want to weld in some baffles to prevent oil surging forward on heavy braking and starving the pump.

Sumps and Oil Capacity

In November 1964 a change was made which added 1 pint to the capacity of the sump. The mod? The dipstick was shortened! Check the part number on your dipstick. It should be 105E 6752 B.

On the small Ford engines there are basically two sizes of sump. The 997cc and 1200cc engines use the 4-1/2 pint sump identified by having straight sides, while the 1500cc engines used the 6-pint sump which bulges on both sides. Refer to the photograph.

Two types of oil filter were used. The early type consists of a steel canister, into which is put a paper-type oil filter. This arrangement actually gives you about a quarter of a pint of extra oil in circulation than the second type.

The second or later type consists of an oil filter cartridge which you buy and screw onto the oil pump. When the oil filter is changed, the whole cartridge is removed and a new one fitted.

Some people like to fit the old, steel oil filter but the choice is yours.

Note that if you have the old style steel filter, there is a rubber O-ring which fits into a groove in the oil pump. I once made a mistake and fitted the new ring without removing the old one. This can have messy results as a lot of oil then gets past the imperfect seal. Prise the old O-ring out with a small pointed screwdriver, and wipe some fresh oil on the new one before pushing it into the groove.

ABOVE: Two different lengths of cylinder head bolt. If you need shorter bolts you can cut the long ones down with a hacksaw, but you need to make a tidy job of the ends. It may be better to consider buying the correct bolts or fit a spacer.

Crankcase Breathers

There are two types of crankcase breather assembly fitted to these engines. The early type is the small, round cylinder type. This is a tube containing wire wool which allows fumes to pass out down the breather pipe, while keeping oil in.

The second, more efficient type consists of a small, rectangular box breather. This also contains wire wool which acts as a filter, but there is an empty space above the wire wool which helps to prevent this filter clogging up.

Both of these can be cleaned out with petrol and left to dry. If possible acquire the later type.

CAMSHAFTS

Three camshafts are used on this range of engines. One was used on very early 105E units. The other two are more commonly found in service. These camshafts are detailed in the Key Information table opposite.

VALVES

Valve head sizes vary depending on the engine. Also, if you are tuning an engine and wish to fit larger valves you may find one suitable from one of the larger engines. The valve size information is given in the Key Information table on page 33.

NOTE: The inlet valve has a diffused aluminium coating on the head to increase resistance to wear and high temperatures. This face must NOT be ground-in using grinding paste. Instead use an old, or dummy valve to grind-in the valve seat. The exhaust valve can be ground-in in the normal way.

CORE PLUGS

There are three core plugs on the small Ford engine block. Two of them are accessible in service, being located on the left hand side of the engine, looking at it from the front. The third core plug is located on the rear of the engine block, and to gain access to it requires either engine removal or gearbox removal.

Fit new core plugs whenever you rebuild your engine. On two occasions I have had the front core plug let go due to rust. I now try and paint the core plug on both sides before I fit it. I don't expect this helps much due to the harsh conditions on the inside face of the core plug (boiling water plus anti-freeze) but it makes me feel happier about it.

The rear core plug has a slightly happier time as its outer face is protected from rust by a film of oil always present on the rear of engine blocks.

Some authorities on these engines recommend using a jointing compound on core plugs. This helps to form a good tight seal.

Remember that the purpose of a core plug is to blow out if the water freezes. In doing so it acts as a fuse and saves damage

New pistons, oiled piston pin and serviceable connecting rods ready to be installed in a rebored cylinder block. Pistons don't often give trouble, especially if you keep the oil level right! Pistons rings have been known to break but this is often in a high mileage engine which may have been mistreated at some time.

to the engine block.

If your core plug does leak due to rust, learn from my experience -- a lump of chewing gum got me the final 30 miles home!

Core plug sets cost under a fiver and are worth renewing as part of an overhaul.

Oil Pumps

Expect 35 - 40 lbs/sq in (2.46 - 2.81 kgm sq/m) oil pressure during normal running and practically nothing on tickover. Since only the G.T. cars have an oil pressure gauge this might be difficult to check!

Remember that if the green oil pressure light goes out you might only have seven or eight pounds per square inch of oil pressure which is not enough and may result in damage. If in doubt, look for oil coming out the rocker shaft when the engine is running. This is usually a good

guide. If no oil is coming out after ten seconds, switch off and find the problem.

Two types of oil pump were originally fitted and they are completely interchangeable. One type is called the eccentric bi-rotor and the other is the sliding vane type. Both of these can be identified by four bolts holding a flat, square, plate onto the side of the pump. Refer to the Workshop Manual for overhaul details of these pumps.

Sometimes you will find a later Escort oil pump is fitted. This can be identified by three bolts holding a triangular plate on the side of the pump. This type of pump will only accept the disposable oil cartridge type of filter.

Oil Leak Elimination

When building an engine use high quality jointing compounds on gaskets. Pay particular attention to getting a good seal on the front cork oil seal which is located on the bottom of the front timing cover. Make sure this is well coated with jointing compound and that the cork is well tapped down into its groove. Wipe off excess jointing compound after doing up the bolts with a torque wrench. Similarly, the rear sump oil seal can be a pig to get right. You may have to cut this seal with a sharp knife to get the right length. Refer to the photos and captions for information.

Look at it this way -- get the job right now, which might take ten minutes more, OR get it wrong and remove the oil-covered engine in three weeks time to do the job again.

Gearbox Shield

That curse of the Ford engine, the "Cover, Flywheel Housing" part number 109E 6382, known to you and I as that troublesome plate which goes between the engine and gearbox, MUST be fitted. I don't care what anyone else says. It is there for a reason and can be fitted without too many difficulties. Look in Chapter Four for easy fitting instructions.

Initial Firing Up

When you build an engine and get ready to run it for the first time, spin it over on the starter for a time *without* the plugs in.

This accomplishes several things. It gets petrol into the carburettor and hence into the combustion chamber and secondly it gets oil circulating through the engine. It gives the battery a much easier life, especially on a tight, new engine. Once everything is circulating nicely, fit the plugs and the motor should fire on the first turn of the starter key.

Front Exhaust Downpipe

If you have a 1200 Cortina and fit a new shiny 1500cc engine, you will find that most things fit straight back on. One problem you will encounter is that the 1200cc exhaust pipe (the downpipe) is shorter than the 1500cc downpipe. If you fit the 1200cc pipe you will find it bangs on the floor of the car and becomes very annoying. The only real answer is to fit the 1500cc downpipe.

Exhaust systems

One problem facing restorers of small Fords is the exhaust system. You can't just walk into one of the high street suppliers

---

Key Information

CAMSHAFT DETAILS

105E camshaft fitted to very early 997cc engines.
Inlet opens 10 degrees BTDC , closes 50 degrees ABDC
Exhaust opens 44 degrees BBDC, closes 10 degrees ATDC
Valve lift Inlet 0.289 inches (7.341 mm) Exhaust 0.290 inches (7.366).

109E camshaft fitted to 997cc, 1200cc, 1340cc and 1500cc non-G.T. cars. Identified by band of white paint.
Inlet opens 17 degrees BTDC, closes 51 degrees ABDC
Exhaust opens 51 degrees BBDC, closes 17 degrees ATDC
Valve lift Inlet 0.315 inches (8.001 mm) Exhaust 0.319 inches (8.103 mm).

116E camshaft fitted to G.T. cars. Identified by 116E stamped on rear end of camshaft.
Inlet opens 27 degrees BTDC, closes 65 degrees ABDC
Exhaust opens 65 degrees BBDC, closes 27 degrees ATDC
Valve lift Inlet 0.344 inches (8.727 mm) Exhaust 0.335 inches (8.519 mm).

---

and buy a system off the shelf. Sources include the owners club or via the specialist outlets advertised in the monthly magazines.

There is one other option open to the restorer - the stainless steel system. This option can mean spending up to four times the cost of a mild steel system, but they come with a "Lifetime Guarantee" and if you intend to keep the car for some time are well worth considering.

Mild steel systems rust from the inside, where acids from the car exhaust gases eat into the steel, and from the outside as salt, dirt and water make their attack. Some protection can be offered by carefully painting the system with a heat resistant paint, but at best you may get three years from a system instead of two. The only long term option is stainless steel.

For the ordinary driver who wants to restore his car once then enjoy it for years to come, stainless is the answer. See the Addresses section at the end of the book.

Conclusion

The small Ford range of engines are hard-working, reliable and have a long life. Take care to change the oil at regular intervals and you should have no problems. The motors were designed at the time motorways were introduced and are generally quite happy to cruise at 70 mph without problem. Don't be afraid to drive yours as it was designed to be driven. All too often I see small Fords driven around as if they are going to break at any minute! Think of their rally heritage and enjoy your car.

Now that the power unit is sorted out it is time to look at some of the other parts which make up the restored Ford. In the next chapter we look at suspension, steering and brakes.

Suspension, Brakes & Steering

The MacPherson strut and disc brakes. Discs were fitted to Cortinas, (most of them!), Classics, Capris and Corsairs as standard and grafted into many an Anglia and Prefect as a worthwhile modification. They provide reliable stopping power and give little trouble. New discs are still available from some sources, but even rusty ones can be restored by having them skimmed in a lathe.

The steering assembly on your small Ford consists of a number of flexible rubber and metal joints which are prone to wear. Normally, these are quite cheap to replace, as and when they wear out, but if you decide to renew all the steering components at once as part of your restoration you are going to face quite a hefty bill.

Let's look at the items a bit at a time, starting with the steering box.

Steering Box

I am not going to tell you how to overhaul your steering box. That subject belongs in the manufacturer's Workshop Manual. Instead I am going to direct your attention to a favourite subject of mine -- saving money.

I was quoted 140 pounds to rebuild or overhaul the steering box on my Capri. The problem was that the M.O.T. tester had failed the car due to excess oil around the steering box.

I did not wish to spend 140 pounds on the overhaul, or lose the use of the car for several weeks while the box was away being repaired. I decided there must be an alternative. There was!

Once I cleaned all the oil off the steering box with Gunk and a hosepipe, I checked all the bolts to ensure that they were tight.

There was one loose bolt on top of the steering box but I decided that it was not so loose as to cause an oil leak. Time to go underneath the car.

I cleaned off the bottom part of the steering box and then got a loan of a two-legged puller to remove the steering arm from the steering box shaft.

Once this was off I could see what the problem was. There is an oil seal at the bottom of the steering box. I decided to take a chance and force it out with a small screwdriver. (This made it completely unsuitable to be re-installed).

Every oil seal has three groups of numbers on it. They indicate the shaft

A rather oily-looking steering box on a Cortina. Boxes are pretty reliable and if they do wear can be adjusted to compensate. Make sure that the three bolts holding the steering box to the chassis are tight, and that there are no cracks in the chassis behind the box.

diameter intended to go through the seal, the outside diameter of the seal housing and the width of the seal. Armed with this information you can look through the available seal catalogues and match the sizes.

I took the oil seal to an oil seal shop (yes, there are such places - look in the Yellow Pages) and they were able to match the seal exactly.

The seal cost under two pounds and was fitted in five minutes. That little exercise saved me 138 pounds and kept my car on the road.

It is not always possible to avoid a major overhaul on a part like a steering box. They do wear with use. But I want to emphasise that you always look for the simple things first!

Another problem on a steering box is the play in the steering box shaft. This is controlled by shims between the top of the steering box and the shaft. The workshop manual provides all the necessary instructions to adjust these shims. Remember, these are the sort of jobs that have probably never been done since the day the car left the factory. You may be lucky and not have any problems, but if you are very unlucky

The steering box on the G.T. cars has an extra steel stud sticking out from the side, just above the bottom, rear bolt hole. This stud provides the pivot point for the dashboard mounted handbrake. This box has been cleaned and checked over ready for installation.

you face the choice of having the steering box overhauled or try to find a second-hand replacement in better condition than your own.

STEERING COLUMN

If you are looking for a second hand steering box and steering column, beware the little differences which can spell disaster later in your restoration.

On some steering boxes there is a steel pin used for a handbrake lever. This is needed on all cars with the handbrake mounted under the dashboard. The lever on the steering box reverses the direction of the handbrake cable (remember you are pulling the handbrake cable towards the back of the car to pull it on) and acts as a lever, multiplying the effort or leverage. Anyway, make sure the steering box you buy has this lever arrangement on it, otherwise your only choice will be to fit a floor mounted handbrake.

At the top of the steering column may be two little mounting brackets. These are used to mount the electrics, encased in a plastic box. Different cars have different mounting brackets. If you can't get exactly what you want and have to choose a second best steering column you could have the correct brackets made up and welded in place using your old steering column as a model. Beware burning the felt bush at the top of the column if you have to weld brackets onto the column. This bush is discussed in the next few paragraphs.

Felt Bush

At the top of the steering column, inside the steering tube is a felt bush. This is about two inches long by an inch wide. It is supposed to be soaked with heavy grease, but one of my cars failed an M.O.T. test due to play in the top of the steering column, caused by this bush being squeezed flat and dried out.

Remove the steering wheel and any electrical switches, direction indicators in the way. Look down the steering column and you will see the top of this felt bush. Using a pair of long-nosed pliers, gently grip this felt seal and pull it out. Remember it is made of felt, so is not all that strong. If you grip it with the pliers and tug it out you could tear a piece out of it. I believe they are still available, but a bit scarce. You could always make one if you could get hold of some felt of the correct thickness.

Having got the old bush out (it comes out in a flat sheet, not a tube) get a little tin, such as a tobacco tin and put some heavy grease into it.

Apply some heat to the tin such as from a blowlamp. The idea is to melt the grease -- not boil it. When there is enough melted grease in the bottom of the tin, drop the felt bush into the grease. You may need to

A MacPherson strut, reconditioned, resprayed and ready for a new spring to be fitted. The spring shown turned out to be a cut-down racing spring which was no use on a road car. Another example of thinking you had found the correct part and being wrong! Note the clamps retaining the spring. These are essential for safety.

push it down into the grease to make sure it gets thoroughly soaked. Don't use your fingers because you can receive a painful burn from melted grease.

When you are satisfied that the felt is saturated, (and this may take some time to achieve), refit it to the top of the steering column and check for play.

The swollen bush should have taken up a lot of play and the whole steering assembly should be improved, both in smoothness and reduced play.

Steering Wheel

Various steering wheels were fitted to this range of cars, but one problem which seems to occur is cracking of the plastic where the spokes meet the steering wheel boss. This need not be a serious problem, but is well worth looking at if you suspect the car has been in an accident.

If you do find cracks you can still use the wheel, but you could always look out for a better one at an autojumble or in a scrapyard.

Wood rim steering wheels were fitted to the Lotus Cortinas, but genuine steering wheels cost as much as I pay for a complete car, so be prepared to pay if you need to replace that type of wheel.

MacPherson Struts

This is the name given to the front suspension units fitted to millions of Ford cars. They are normally hard wearing and reliable. When they do fail, they tend to leak and the M.O.T. tester then fails the car.

Refer to the workshop manual for information about removing the complete strut from the car.

When the complete strut unit is removed from the car, you next need a special tool to remove the spring safely.

There are ways to remove the spring without a spring clamp, but I am NOT going to describe them. Beg, borrow or buy a spring clamp. They are still available from motor factors or accessory dealers. They cost about 10 pounds and could save you from serious injury.

Fit the clamps over as many coils as possible. This is shown in the photographs. When the clamp end is properly located (they are angled, so make sure the angle is correct and that you have not fitted them upside down) tighten the clamp with a spanner. As you tighten the clamps, being sure to tighten each clamp equally, the spring will get shorter. When the spring reaches a certain point, the spring's top mounting may become loose.

At this point, undo the big nut at the top of the strut. As you loosen the nut, you should feel the assembly become free in your hand. If the spring is still applying pressure to the top seat and shroud assembly then you need to tighten the clamp a bit more.

When the nut is loosened off, remove it. The top mounting should then come off freely, leaving the spring to be lifted off the damper body, but still under the control of the clamp.

You next have the problem of removing the clamps from the spring so that you can work on the other strut. If you intend to leave the spring compressed, make sure that no one can interfere with the clamp. If

The spring clamps in place on the front coil spring. Note that the jaws on the clamps are angled, to match the coiling of the spring. Do NOT fit them the wrong way round. A compressed spring is dangerous, and must be treated with respect.

it were dropped on the ground for example, it is just possible that the clamp could release the spring with disastrous results.

The strut then needs to have the brake assembly removed -- either drum or disk. If drum, read the next paragraph. If disc, then you need to undo the two bolts which hold the calliper onto the suspension leg. If the car has been lying around for some time then the disk brake pads may be held in by rust and spiders' webs. It helps to remove the pads first. When the calliper is unbolted, remove it from the disk.

Next, remove the big nut which is found in amongst the grease after you prise off the dust cover. Remove the split pin holding the nut, followed by the nut itself. Take care with the thread on this nut, especially if you have a Classic or Capri. The nut threads on these cars is quite fine and nowhere near as sturdy as on the other small Fords. It is also very difficult to get a new one if you strip the threads. The owners club is probably the only source of these parts. You could get someone to make one up on a lathe if they have the necessary skill.

When the strut is completely dismantled, I recommend that you hand it in to the local motor factors for overhaul. They will probably send it away to be done. The owners club may also offer this service, but remember that a strut is quite a heavy item so you will incur postage costs. If you can't find anyone to do the job, then the owners club may be your only choice.

Re-assembling the strut is the opposite of the above dismantling sequence. Remember to clean all the top mountings and if necessary replace the rubber top mounting if it is perished. Once again your owners club may be the only source of these parts as they are now becoming scarce. Many clubs are re-manufacturing these items.

A couple of points to note. Make sure both units are the same! If you are only re-conditioning one, make very sure that the other is up to the job. Two different units will produce a very strange ride, and could become very dangerous if one was strong and the other weak. If in doubt recondition BOTH units at the same time. Remember, that these units also affect the steering and the balance of the wheels. If the struts are worn you very often get a characteristic wheel wobble between 40 and 50 mph. Sometimes this is caused by wheels being out of balance, but very often it is due to a MacPherson strut problem.

FRONT SPRINGS

There are several sizes of front spring. For example the 1200/1500 Cortina spring's free length is 12.25 inches, the G.T. is 10 inches and the Lotus 11.75 inches. Check in the workshop manual to ensure that you have the correct length of spring. Don't mix spring lengths on different sides of the car. Coil springs can be reconditioned. Look in the Yellow Pages and phone around!

STEERING BUSHES

In all the steering set-ups rubber bushes with steel studs embedded in them are used for the steering joints. These wear out gradually and usually give some warning when they need to be replaced. Play or looseness will be noticed at the steering wheel. On one occasion I had a stud come adrift from the rubber bush. The steering became extremely vague, and very danger-ous. I was only a mile from home so I crept home in second gear!

Bushes are available from the dealers listed at the back of the book.

Classic and Capris have idler arm bushes which are probably only available through the owners club. The Anglia club can supply most of the required bushes for the Anglia range.

Wheels

Various wheels were fitted to this range of cars, and again it is very easy to look at two wheels and not see the differences between them. All of them were 13 inches in diameter, but they varied in width.

Starting with the widest wheels, these were the 5-1/2 J wheels fitted to the Lotus Cortina. Generally speaking these are the widest wheels which can be fitted to any other small Ford without fitting wheel spacers. However, DON'T take my word for it. This is a vital safety item so check that there is at least 1/2 inch between the tyre wall and the MacPherson strut. Remember that tyres flex as they are cornered, so that half inch or more is vital to safety.

The G.T. cars and most of the non-G.T. cars had 4 J wheels as standard. As stated above, many will have inherited wider wheels over the years. Favourites were 4-1/2 J or 5-1/2 J. Some earlier cars had slightly narrower wheels. It would pay to get this detail correct if you wished to

Two different sizes of spring. The unfortunate thing about this photo is that they both came from the same car! This sort of difference can be very dangerous, but must also be expected from a 25 year old car which may have been run into the ground at some time during its life.

exhibit the car in shows. My Cortina Parts Book indicates that early 1198cc Cortinas had wheels 3-5/8 inch wide. Also, look at the relationship between the centre part of the wheel and the rim. Some wheels have more off-set than others. I have several different types of wheel lying around, some with wide spaces between the hub and rim, others with very narrow spaces.

If this is important to you as a detail, then pay attention to this point. If you just like to drive the car and are not too worried about the detail, then just make sure you have four wheels all the same!

WHEEL SPACERS

These are alloy plates fitted between the wheel and the brake drum or disc assem-bly. They are used either to increase the car's track to improve roadholding, or as part of a conversion for example when fitting disc brakes and wider wheels to an Anglia.

They are available in various thicknesses. Refer to the Address section at the end of

the book. They do tend to put an extra load on wheel bearings, so don't overdo the thickness of these spacers.

Disc Brakes

Can you imagine a steel disc, like a dinner plate - only made of steel? Now think of it turning. If you now put your thumb and forefinger on either side of the edge of the disc, you have visualised the disc brake. If you now squeeze your thumb and forefinger against the spinning disc, you have activated your disc brake. The friction between your fingers and the disc will try and slow the disc. That, simply is the principle of the disc brake. You could argue that a bicycle wheel is a disc brake, as it works on the same principle.

On a car it is little different. There is a steel disc, probably about 9-1/2 inches in diameter, and it is connected to the wheel. In fact the wheel bolts directly onto the disc. There is an axle in the middle of the disc, and the disc rotates round this axle. Mounted to one side of the disc is an assembly known as a calliper. That is the assembly demonstrated by your thumb and forefinger. Instead of pressing a thumb against the disc, the calliper presses a disc brake pad- a special pad of friction material which is what does the actual braking. The assembly is arranged so that a pad is pressed against each side of the disc, just like the thumb and forefinger example.

Anglia Disc Brake Conversion

This conversion, often done to the 105E and 123E Anglias, is also easy to do on the 100E and 107E.

You'll need the MacPherson struts, springs and disc brakes and callipers from a Classic or Capri. You should also fit the top mounting from the 100E or 105E as appropriate.

Usually the Classic track control arm is used. Being longer it gives some negative camber and this in itself improves the handling of the car. Anglia 105Es can use their original road wheels, but the 100E uses a different stud spacing so the 100E wheels need to be replaced with 105E wheels on the front. This unfortunately means that you will have to carry two spare wheels, one for the front and one for the rear.

It is very simple to carry out this conversion. Just remove your old suspension units with drum brakes, refit the new Classic and Capri struts with 100E or 105E top mountings and get some new brake pipes and hoses to connect the disc brakes into your braking circuit. Bleed the brakes, sort out the wheels and off you go. Instant brakes.

Drum Brakes

Drum brakes were fitted on the front of the Anglia, 107E, and early Cortinas. These brakes are quite powerful and reliable. They work on the principle of two friction shoes being moved by the action of the brake pedal and forced against the inside of the brake drum.

There are two snail cam adjusters, one for each brake shoe. I recall I had a bit of trouble with these snail cams in the early 1960s on my father's first Cortina. The cams tended to become detached from the stud which went through the brake backplate. This might just have been due to a bungling teenager, but it may be a weakness in the design. The early ones consisted of a stud, spring and snail cam. The stud was pushed through the back-

Re-manufactured suspension top mounts are available from the MK1 Cortina Owners' Club. On original mountings the rubber may become detached from the steel, leading to an insecure mounting.

Bottom ball joints for the Cortina. These bolt onto the bottom of the MacPherson strut and if they wear can be an M.O.T. failure. They are available from several sources.

plate, the coil spring slipped over it and the snail cam then peined in place on the end of the stud. This then used to slip in service, making brake adjustment a nightmare. The situation was aggravated by trying to force the stud backwards, and forcing it hard against the brake shoe. This is really a point to be noted rather than worried about.

REMOVING REAR BRAKE DRUMS

On paper, removing the rear brake drums looks very simple. In practice, a mixture of rust, brake dust, spiders' webs and dirt usually means that it takes a bit of effort to get the drums off.

Note that there is a small set-screw holding the drum onto the half-shaft. I'm not quite sure why it is there, but Ford fitted it so I always try and find one to re-fit. Most other owners don't seem to bother so you may have to search around to find a suitable screw.

Remove the road wheel and make sure the car is supported by an axle stand. Nothing else will do. Next back off the square-headed brake shoe adjuster on the brake backplate. Get this nice and loose as

The track control arm on the Cortina comes in two varieties. The one shown above is known as the "cast" or heavy duty type, while the other is known as the welded, or mild steel type. This second type can rust on more neglected cars. Most of the other small Fords use a cast type of control arm.

A rear brake hub on a neglected car. The white on the hub is spiders' webs! This hub could prove quite difficult to remove. See text.

This is the rear brake assembly on the Capri. Note that the hydraulic cylinder is double-acting, that is it has two pistons. A close look at the left side of the photo shows two rubber dust covers protecting the pistons. The brake shoe retaining clips are the coil spring (finger skinning) type! See the text for an explanation.

you will need all the help you can get to remove the drum.

Having removed the set-screw (if it does not want to shift you will have to use an impact screwdriver, or chisel it off), try and tap the edge of the drum with a mallet to see if it wants to come off.

The chances are it will be stuck firmly in place. Try two screwdrivers, inserted between the drum and the backplate, and at opposite sides of the drum. If this levering does not work, try a spot of penetrating oil at the seam where the centre of the hub meets the half shaft.

If all else fails you will have to start getting tough. If you can find a large enough two or three legged puller then you should be successful in removing the drum. If not patience and a small hammer and block of hard wood should start to ease the drum off.

Once it is off, clean up all the surfaces with either a wire brush (on the outside) and some clean emery paper on the inside, braking surface. If the drums are badly scored you will have to have them skimmed. See Chapter Nine. The only

alternative is to find some new or good second-hand drums.

Brake Shoe Retaining Clips

I've found two different types of brake shoe retaining clips. These are the springs which hold the brake shoes against the backplate, while allowing enough movement when the brakes are applied.

There is the coil-spring type which consists of a small coil spring and two cups, one for each end of the spring. There is also a steel pin with two ears on it. The pin is pushed through the backplate, from the outside and the cup, spring and cup fitted over the ears. The top cup is twisted 90 degrees to locate and hold the pin in place. I don't like this type of clip as it needs a lot of finger pressure to squeeze the coil spring. You can do it with pliers and have no problems, but I much prefer the second

type of clip. This type uses a V-shaped spring clip and a pin. The clip is squeezed together and the pin fitted. The ears on the pin recess into a groove in the clip. Note that if you are mixing both types of clip that the pins are of different lengths!

This preference is purely a personal thing. The memory of a few skinned fingers lasts a long time!

Brake Pipes

Brake pipes were originally made of mild steel, and only lasted a few years before they rusted out. Nowadays, you can purchase a set of copper brake pipes, made to measure for your car. Fit them and forget about rusty brake pipes. Automec are the people to get in touch with. See the Addresses section at the end of the book.

In conjuction with copper pipes you may wish to consider silicone brake fluid.

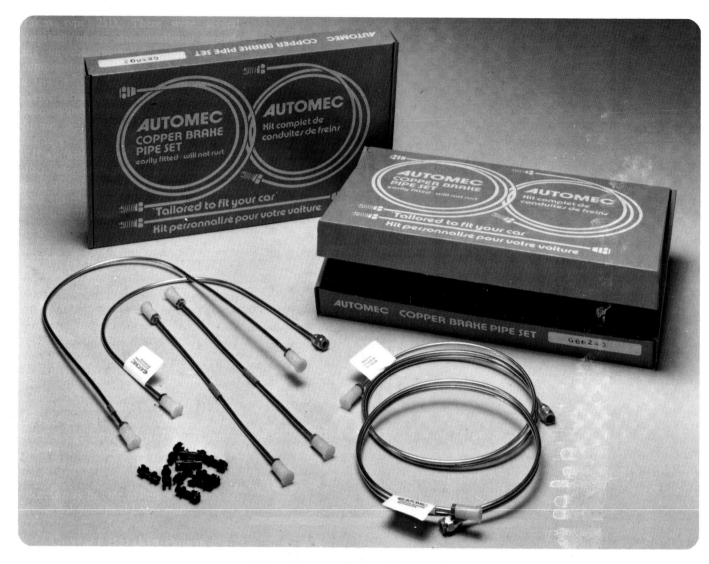

Front Brake Drums

To remove a front brake drum, first loosen the wheel nuts slightly, then jack up the car and support it with an axle stand.

Remove the road wheel. Next remove the grease cap on the end of the spindle. This can be levered off with a small screwdriver. When this is off, you will need to wipe away the grease which should be there! If there is no grease then the last owner did not do his maintenance properly.

With the grease wiped away, unbend the split pin and remove it with a pair of pliers. Next remove the big nut. This may be loose enough to turn by finger only, if not use a spanner. When the nut is off, remove the washer, and then wiggle the drum about. It should come off quite easily.

Refitting is just the reverse of dismantling. Refer to the workshop manual for details of how to adjust the play in the bearings.

Automec's copper brake pipe sets are so good you wondered what you did before they were thought of. They really are everything they claim to be -- easy to fit, made to measure for your car and above all else -- they do not corrode! I have used them on three of my cars with total satisfaction.

Bottom Ball Joints

Bottom ball joints vary in design depending on the model. You may find that repair kits are available for some models, while others require new ball joint assemblies. Assembly is quite straightforward, so refer to the owners club first to acquire your spare, then to the workshop manual for instructions.

Track Rod Ends

Track rod ends wear out after a while and have to be replaced. While spares are still available I have noticed that the prices have been rising quite steeply over the last year or so. It may be that they are starting to get a little bit scarce.

The biggest problem about replacing a track rod end is breaking the taper between the stud and the steering arm.

Undo the nut from the track rod end stud. On some early ones there was a split pin through a hole drilled in the stud. Later ones used a Nyloc-type nut for security.

If you have a wedge-type device to break tapers, then use it. I remember hammering away on the stud with a big hammer trying to force the taper back down the hole -- usually to little avail. The answer is quite simple. With the nut removed, get two hammers. Hold the head of one against the steering part through which the stud goes. With the other hammer, hit the opposite side of the steering part. The idea is that

the shock jars or breaks the taper and the stud will come loose. This sounds implausible I know but it does seem to work well.

Loosen the clamp nuts which hold the track rod end in the track rod. You may need some force, some heat or some lubricant to loosen the threads in the track rod. Remember that one has a left-handed thread and the other is right-handed.

When reassembling track rod ends sometimes the action of tightening the nut will turn the stud. Push the stud firmly into the hole. If this does not do the trick then get tough with it. Either jack the stud into the hole using a small bottle jack, or lever it into the hole with a tyre lever. Make sure it is firmly tightened to the recommended torque.

Master Cylinder Overhaul

The details in the following section apply equally well to the different sizes of brake master cylinder and clutch master cylinder fitted to small Fords.

Buy a new set of seals for your master cylinder. The size of the cylinder is written on the outside of the fluid reservoir. It might be 0.75 inches or 0.50 inches Only when you have the correct parts and a supply of clean methylated spirits do you go on with this procedure.

First remove the master cylinder from the car. This involves disconnecting it from the brake or clutch pedal, then disconnecting the hydraulic pipe, then unbolting the master cylinder from the vehicle bulkhead.

With the master cylinder on the bench, drain off any remaining hydraulic fluid. Pump the operating lever a couple of times to get rid of any fluid still in the cylinder. Make sure the fluid is directed to a safe

place, not into your eyes or on your clothing.

Remove the rubber boot over the end of the cylinder where the pushrod fits.

Using a pair of long-nosed pliers, squeeze the circlip and disengage it from its position in the bore of the cylinder. If long nose pliers are not available, then a couple of small screwdrivers will do the job just as well.

Next comes the tricky bit. Trying to remove the piston and valve assembly. Make sure that the end of the cylinder is clean and well lubricated with a smear of clean brake fluid. Next, pump the assembly in and out a few times, trying to encourage it to pop out on the return stroke. After a few tries at this it usually comes out a little way, allowing the long nosed pliers to grip it. Persevere with this until you get it out.

Slide the spring back from the piston seal, and with a very small bladed screwdriver, bend the spring retainer tag out to allow the two assemblies to be disconnected. There is normally a diagram with the seal kit so refer to this or the accompanying photographs for guidance.

Slide the piston seal off the piston and put to one side. Slide the valve spacer and shim off the valve stem.

Next wash all the parts in methylated spirits. There is no point taking it all apart just to re-fit the old rubber seals, so get the new set ready to fit.

Fit the new piston seal onto the piston with the seal lips facing AWAY from the brake pedal.

Fit the valve seal to the valve stem with the lip towards the front of the valve.

Replace the shim washer on the valve

stem together with the seal spacer so that the legs of the spacer are towards the valve seal. Be sure that the shim is fitted concentrically on the rear shoulder of the valve stem so that its convex face abuts the shoulder flange.

Fit the spring over the valve stem. Fit the spring retainer onto the end of the return spring.

Compress the spring and nudge the tab on the spring retainer into its locked position on the piston.

Dip the assembly in clean hydraulic fluid and insert the assembly into the master cylinder bore. Take care not to damage or force-fit the seals.

Refit the pushrod and circlip. ENSURE that the circlip is secure in its retaining groove in the cylinder. Failure to do so could result in the pushrod becoming detached from the master cylinder with very serious results.

Refit the rubber boot.

Take care to follow any specific instructions from the manufacturer of the repair kit.

Refit the master cylinder, reconnect the hydraulic pipe and bleed as necessary, see "Bleeding" later in this Chapter.

Slave cylinders can also be overhauled but are very easy to do. The hardest part (I have found!) is getting the circlip off the clutch slave cylinder.

BRAKE HOSES

If you find that you can press the brake pedal and it feels firm but there is something not quite right about it, try making a controlled emergency stop in a quiet piece of road. You may find that some of the wheels might lock up, but others don't. Putting all these symptoms together, suspect bulging brake hoses.

The flexible brake hose must bend and flex for years on end, put up with freezing conditions outside, and get very hot inside if the the brakes are used heavily. Add to that it must withstand extremely high pressures from within, and you are left marvelling that they ever work at all.

If you suspect the brake hoses, try this simple check first. Get someone to press the brake pedal, while you lie on the ground and feel the hose as the pressure is applied from the pedal. The hose should not move, distort or bulge. If it does it must be replaced.

You may find that it tries to twist. This too is a sign of weakness and the hose must

ABOVE: The Girling master cylinder with the piston assembly removed. Repair kits are available for these master cylinders which were fitted in different sizes depending on the model and year.

BELOW: The piston assembly broken down. Workshop manuals provide all the necessary information and there are usually some instructions in the repair kit.

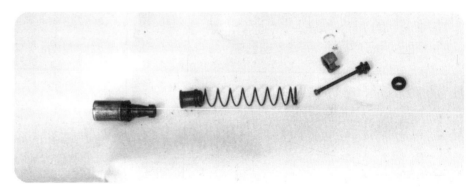

be replaced.

If you are in any doubt about what you are looking for, repeat the above test on a car with fault-free brakes. The hoses will not bulge, distort or twist. Once you have felt a hose distort under pressure you will know what to look for.

I had this particular problem on a car I was rebuilding. I had fitted brand new hoses and bled out the system. The trouble was, the rebuild took so long that by the time the car got an M.O.T and got on the road, the hoses must have perished. As the weeks went by after the M.O.T. the brakes got worse and worse. Of course, sod's law being what it is, I replaced everything else first before I found the problem in the brake hoses.

You may encounter a similar problem with a hydraulic clutch, although the

Transmission

This Chapter contains general information about the gearbox, clutch, propeller shaft and back axle. There is also information about overhauling associated components such as clutch operating systems and universal joints.

Clutch problems

Clutch problems can be split into two simple categories -- either the clutch slips, or it has another fault such as juddering or snatching. In both cases the answer is to replace rather than repair. The only exception to this may be a slipping clutch which is very badly adjusted. Before you hand over your 40 or 50 pounds for new clutch parts, carefully check the adjustment mechanism. Generally this calls for a clearance of 1/10 inch (2.5mm) between the large adjusting nut on the slave cylinder pushrod, and the clutch release arm. Follow the instructions in the workshop manual.

Clutch slip

Very often a clutch will wear very slowly and gradually, and the first time you notice a problem is when you are going up a familiar hill and the engine starts to increase revolutions without the car going faster. Put another way, the engine revs and does not drive the car along. If you ease off the throttle you will very often get drive again. The first time this happens you will either miss it altogether, or start trying to get it to happen again, a bit like something you can't quite believe so you repeat it!

When you are convinced that the clutch is slipping you normally have a few hundred miles before the car becomes totally un-driveable. Start making arrangements for a replacement clutch!

Seized Clutch

This is the term often given to a clutch which has not been operated for a long time, for example on a car which has been lying abandoned in a garage for years. When you come to try to move the car you will find that the clutch plate will be stuck

Looking into the gearbox bellhousing you can see the clutch operating arm and the sleeve which locates the release bearing, which is also known as the thrust bearing. Note the little springs on the operating arm. They must be fitted correctly otherwise the operating arm will not operate. I speak from experience...

to the driven plate. All your efforts to free it off will come to nothing. Bump starting the car in gear and then trying to free the clutch by pressing the brake and clutch may release some clutches. You can also try jacking up the car, getting the car running in first gear then dropping it off the jack so that the wheels hit the road hard. This sometimes works although it is a bit drastic and needs to be done with care.

If the worst comes to the worst you will have to remove the gearbox (or the engine) and either replace the clutch with a new one or fettle the old one.

Other clutch problems

Other clutch problems either relate to slipping, juddering, or sticking (not disengaging properly). If you have checked the adjustment, checked the hydraulics and checked that the clutch operating arm is

moving when you depress the pedal, there is little choice left but to remove engine or gearbox and replace the clutch.

Flywheel Skimming

If you let the clutch continue to slip you may wear away all the friction material and get down to the rivets. These are the rivets that fasten the friction material to the clutch assembly. Normally the rivets are countersunk -- that is, they are below the level of the surface of the friction material. When the material wears the rivet may grind against the face of the flywheel. This can cause scoring and in extreme cases can mean a new flywheel is needed.

If your flywheel is lightly scored you may be able to have the surface skimmed in an engine reconditioning shop. This is a job for experts because special, expensive equipment must be used. See Flywheel

Skimming in Chapter Nine.

DROPPING THE GEARBOX

On some models this is quite a straight-forward procedure. Disconnect the gear-lever from the gearbox. Go underneath (the car being safely propped up on axle stands ONLY), disconnect the speedometer drive gear and remove the prop shaft. Disconnect the operating mechanism's hydraulic pipe. Disconnect the battery and remove the starter motor. Undo all the bolts holding the bell housing to the engine and hey presto the box needs a pull backwards and it will fall onto the floor. Of course, you should make suitable arrangements to support it!

That was the easy (Cortina) version. Now read on for the Classic and Capri version. I have never taken the box out of an Anglia or Corsair, so cannot comment. I have taken the box out of my Capri on a number of occasions, and each time it has degenerated into a swearing competition, me versus the Capri.

This is what you do. Disconnect the battery and remove the starter motor. This will involve you needing double jointed fingers as there is a handbrake linkage in the way whichever way you tackle it.

Remove the gearchange lever from the top of the box. My Capri had a G.T. type centre console and a remote gearchange unit. So remove the centre console taking care to disconnect any electrical wiring rather than pull it out because you forgot it was connected. (I had a clock on the centre console..!)

Try to remove the four bolts holding the remote gearchange unit to the top of the box. On my car three can be undone from the top quite easily with a ratchet and extension bar, but the fourth has to be undone a millimetre at a time from underneath using a ring spanner.

This done, disconnect the hydraulics from the slave cylinder. Next remove the speedometer cable from the side of the gearbox. I use a long slim ring spanner and this is then no problem. Remove the prop shaft.

You now need to examine the gearbox crossmember and its relationship with the exhaust system. The crossmember is not straight, it has a concave (up-the-way) bulge to accommodate the exhaust pipe. If like me you have the G.T.'s four branch manifold you can then disconnect the manifold from the front pipe.

This is the flywheel end of the crankshaft. In the hole in the centre of the crankshaft is a bronze bearing. The end of the gearbox main-shaft locates with this bearing. Later gearboxes used a needle-roller bearing. You must make sure that your gearbox matches the bearing. If you have changed gearboxes, or had a crankshaft reground, make sure that the gearbox is a firm fit in the bearing. If you use the wrong bearing the geabox shaft will whip about and cause a lot of vibration.

Next remove the bolts holding the gearbox to the crossmember. Jack up the back of the gearbox to support it and then remove the four bolts holding the crossmember to the chassis. With a bit of wiggling about you should be able to remove the crossmember from the car without totally destroying the exhaust system.

With all this now free, pull back on the gearbox and it should fall gently onto the garage floor, or more correctly onto some form of wooden support which you and your assistant should have provided for it!

It can only be pulled back so far, as the bellhousing will come into contact with the transmission tunnel part of the bodyshell. There is also the petrol pipe and brake pipe to be looked out for otherwise the gearbox will damage them. Take care.

Installing is the reverse of dismantling, but again is not as easy as the Cortina.

COVER - FLYWHEEL HOUSING

And now a word or two about the single most-hated part on the Cortina, Anglia, Capri, Classic and Corsair -- the metal plate which goes between the engine and gear-box. Known as the Cover, (flywheel housing), from the Ford Parts Book, there must have been more swearing uttered over this little plate than any other component on the car.

It can be SO SIMPLE to fit if you tackle it this way:

With the engine parted from the gearbox, locate the plate onto the engine block. There are two dowels on the engine block which locate with holes on the metal plate. If the plate is twisted or distorted, straighten it with a mallet or hammer!

Once located on the two dowels, TIE IT IN PLACE with some strong sail-makers' twine. Ordinary thread is not strong enough. Put a couple of loops through the hole and through the metal plate. Tie it firmly and cut off the excess. Now fit the engine to the gearbox, or vice versa.

This method has always worked for me. I would never, ever consider running a car without this metal shield in place. I know a lot of people do so, but they are taking a risk with their flywheel, clutch and starter motor gear. If the plate is missing the gearbox bellhousing acts as a funnel and scoops up all the water, dirt, grit and so on, thrown at it by the wheels.

There are several dodges which you can do with this plate. You can cut it in half horizontally and just fit the bottom bit. I know some people have done this, but there is a slight problem in that the joint face between engine and gearbox will not be exactly parallel, so some stress may be put on both assemblies.

So the next alternative is to cut it in half and fit both bits, the cutting in half simplifying the fitting operation.

Follow the advice given above and you should have few problems.

Master cylinder

The clutch master cylinder is the device which transmits the pressure applied by your foot to the movement in the clutch operating lever. As you press the clutch pedal, fluid is forced through a steel, copper or plastic pipe to the clutch slave cylinder. The slave cylinder converts hydraulic (fluid) pressure into movement and causes the clutch lever to move.

Leakage of fluid in either the master or slave cylinder will cause the clutch to drag. You think you have pressed the pedal all the way down, but the clutch still refuses to release. The only cure is to replace the rubber seals in the cylinder (the cheap alternative) OR to replace the whole master or slave cylinder (the expensive alternative).

Overhaul of the master cylinder is discussed in Chapter Three.

Removing half-shafts

If you discover that your final drive is faulty, or you want to change the final drive ratio, you will have to remove the half-shaft from each side of the differential.

Very often the workshop manual will advise the use of a slide hammer or similar device. If you don't have such a tool, and most people don't, here is a hint which might get you out of trouble. Get hold of a spare wheel. You are going to have to hit it

RIGHT: Two versions of the flywheel housing cover. The top one is the standard item, while the bottom one has been cut with a hacksaw to aid fitting. This may cause distortion between engine and gearbox. See test for details.

KEY INFORMATION

Final Drive Ratios

Ford differential units are available in the following ratios:

GEAR RATIO	NUMBER OF TEETH (Pinion/Crownwheel)
4.44:1	(9/40 teeth)
4.125:1	(8/33 teeth)
3.9:1	(10/39 teeth)
3.77:1	(9/34 teeth)

If in doubt, count the teeth!

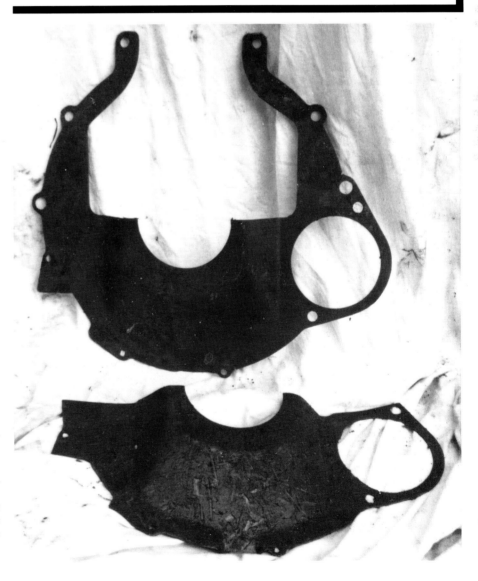

with a hammer, so don't use the real spare wheel from the boot. Get hold of a bent or damaged wheel.

Next, fit the wheel onto the half shaft -- but facing the wrong way. Put two wheel nuts on to secure it. The reason for turning it the wrong way, is to get it to stick out, and away from the half-shaft. This gives you more room to work in.

If you are worried about damaging the wheel use a piece of timber to spread the blows. Hold the timber against the inside edge of the wheel, and hit it hard with a hammer. Turn the wheel and hit it again. By turning the wheel and moving your hitting position round the circumference of the wheel you should be able to remove most half-shafts.

Final Drives

Final drives, often known as the differential or simply the diff are designed to suit all-round driving conditions. In an old car, say 20 to 25 years old, you might find that the final drive ratio is a little on the low side for motorway driving. There is a reason for that. There were very few motorways then, and most driving consisted of start and stop, rather than flat-out. (Remember when the first motorway was opened -- was it really as long ago as 1959? -- may cars literally blew-up with sustained high speed driving. They simply were not designed for it).

All this is leading up to the subject of changing your final drive ratio to suit your driving conditions. You may have a 90 mph G.T., but are unwilling ever to do 90 mph either because it is illegal to drive at more than 70 mph, or that your car is simply too precious to risk at that speed. Perhaps your car, being geared to achieve 90 mph would be better suited to reach just 80 mph. This would involve lowering the final drive ratio.

Changing the final drive

To change the differential unit, jack up both rear wheels and fit axle stands. Remove the road wheels. Remove the brake drums. Remove the four bolts holding each half-shaft to the axle housing. Then remove the half shafts. They do not have to be pulled all the way out, just about six inches or so.

Underneath the car, remove the four bolts holding the differential unit to the prop shaft. Next remove the eight bolts located round the circumference of the

ABOVE: You need to remove the half-shafts before you can change the final drive unit. Use a socket pushed through the holes in the end of the half-shaft.

BELOW: A close up of a final drive unit. The number of teeth on the big gear wheel (known as the crown-wheel) is usually stamped on the crown-wheel. If in doubt, count the teeth. Lower your final drive ratio for faster acceleration, raise it for higher top speed.

differential unit. When the bolts are loosened off, stick an old basin under the differential as one and a half pints of heavy dirty black oil should flow out. If there is no oil, or just a little drop then you have extra problems!

Remove the differential unit from the front of the housing. It is not particularly heavy, but you should be aware of the weight before you wrench it out. Try to keep it off the ground otherwise all sorts of dirt will stick to the gears.

Remember to scrape the remains of the old gasket off the housing, clean up all the surfaces, then install the new unit using a fresh paper gasket. They are still available from Ford main dealers and only cost 50 pence or so.

Very often the differential unit will have a little metal tag attached to one of the eight bolts holding the unit to the axle casing. This tells you what ratio is fitted. However, a mixture of salt, dirt, water and time usually make this little plate unreadable. It might be worth trying to clean it with some emery paper. But if in doubt remove the differential unit and count the teeth.

When you have changed the final drive ratio, remember to change your speedometer drive gear to ensure correct speedometer accuracy.

SPEEDOMETER DRIVE GEARS

Refer to the Key Information table for details of speedometer driven gears.

FINAL DRIVE OIL SEAL

With the propeller shaft removed, devise some means of holding the drive flange while you remove the drive flange nut. How do you hold the flange? Well, there is a special tool (one for the standard diff and one for the G.T. which has a different flange size) but you are unlikely to have this.

If you fit two nuts and bolts to two adjacent holes in the drive flange you should be able to wedge a flat tyre lever between the bolts and secure it that way.

Undo the drive flange nut. Pull the pinion flange off (you may need to use two tyre levers to help it off) and next remove the oil seal. If necessary remove the old seal with a couple of sharp screwdrivers. Remember that you have the new seal in your hand, or at least you should have before attempting the job, so you do not need to remove the old one in an undamaged condition.

Clean up the seal's housing and insert the new seal. Tap it into position as gently as possible so as not to encourage any distortion leading to future oil leaks.

Fit the drive flange and its retaining nut and tighten it until there is a very slight end float on the pinion shaft. The official figure is 2 - 5 thousandth of an inch. Another way to test this is to measure the pull required to turn the pinion shaft against the oil seal's resistance. A fisherman's scale may do this job. When you know this figure add the pre-load figure of 9 to 11 lbs/ inch (0.14 to 0.127 kg/ m) to arrive at the final torque figure.

The poor man's way to do this job is to note how much torque is required to

Speedometer Drive Gears

If you change the final drive ratio on your car there is one job which everyone overlooks. The speedometer will not be accurate any more. The way to correct this is to change the speedometer drive gear in the gearbox.

Speedometer Driven Gear Teeth	Colour
22	Natural
23	Black
24	Green
25	Blue

This is the rear end of the engine block. If you look closely you can see the two locating dowels on the two lower (outer) holes on the block. These dowels are used to locate the cover, flywheel housing, as described in the text. Don't take a short-cut here. Always fit this cover plate.

remove the drive nut, then re-torque it to the same or slightly more. Remember that the torque required to undo a nut is not the same as that required to do it up. For example if a nut is torqued up to a reading of 20 lbs inch then a bit less will be required to undo it.

Half Shaft Oil Seal

With the half shaft removed, use a small chisel or screwdriver to chisel out the old seal. Clean up the seal's housing and offer up the new seal. This job is described in the workshop manual as requiring a special tool to insert the seal without distorting it. In reality you should take a lot of care to get the new seal in without damaging or distorting it, but in real life the job is quickly done by tapping it in with a large socket and a light hammer.

Column Gear Change

Column gearchanges use lots of joints and bushes which are very hard to replace, as spares for these have all but dried up. I believe the Classic is probably the worst off for spares, but the owners club may be able to help. Don't scrap the car if you can't get spares. Fit a floor mounted gear change while you continue to search for spare parts.

Gearboxes

There are several different gearboxes fitted to this range of cars. All are four-speed, except the old three-speed boxes fitted to the 100E range.

The early four-speed ones did not have synchromesh on first gear and you had to use double-declutching to get from second to first while moving.

This technique is all but forgotten, so I would not even consider restoring an early gearbox. If you are so keen on originality, then you may do so, and I believe most of the spares required are still available.

Later boxes had all-synchromesh gears and were very reliable and hard wearing.

One company did advertise kits for home restorers to tackle gearbox restorations, but they failed to respond to my enquiries.

If you have not tackled a gearbox rebuild before, then my advice is, beware. Read the workshop manual and decide if you are still confident about tackling it. There are plenty of businesses offering replacement gearboxes, and second-hand ones are still plentiful. My advice is to get on with something else and put the gearbox out to

Often mentioned throughout this book, this is the official Ford workshop manual. If you are looking round a second-hand bookshop or at an autojumble you should keep your eyes open for one. In it you will find all the mechanical information. What you will NOT find is all the detailed bodywork restoration information given in "Restoring Small Fords", and my previous book, "Panel Craft".

an expert, or buy second-hand.

Later boxes, known as the 2000E gearbox contained a much better selection of ratios than early boxes, and these are much in demand. These were fitted to Corsairs and Lotus Cortinas. You should be able to fit a Corsair 2000E box to your car with few modifications. Make sure you fit the correct length of prop shaft, as this varies from model to model.

Automatic Transmission

The small Fords used the Borg Warner type 35 automatic transmission unit. I last drove an automatic Ford in 1966 so cannot recall much about it. However the same unit is fitted to the Volvo 140 series of cars and I had one of those for two years. If the gearbox is working there is no problem other than to top up with transmission fluid. It is a sound, well-proven unit which gives long service. If the gearbox develops any sort of fault I would not even consider trying to overhaul it at home. Take the box out and let a specialist deal with it. There are a few adjustments which can be made. Yet again, read the workshop manual

thoroughly then decide if you are confident enough to tackle the adjustments.

A disabled friend of mine has a Capri with column change and he finds difficulty in pressing the clutch pedal. He has often thought of fitting an automatic gearbox to his Capri. As far as I can tell the main problem areas will be mounting the gear selector, which may mean having to modify the hole in the transmission tunnel, and arranging a kick-down mechanism. The kick-down feature allows you to depress

OPPOSITE PAGE: An exploded view of the gearbox as fitted to the Corsair. If you read the workshop manual you will find that a number of special tools are needed to rebuild a gearbox. There may be ways round these problem areas, but my advice is to have the gearbox rebuilt by a professional, while you get on with something else. Early boxes had no synchromesh on first gear, while later boxes -- often known as the 2000E gearbox -- had a superb set of ratios which were used in the Lotus Cortina.

(Illustration courtesy of Ford Motor Company).

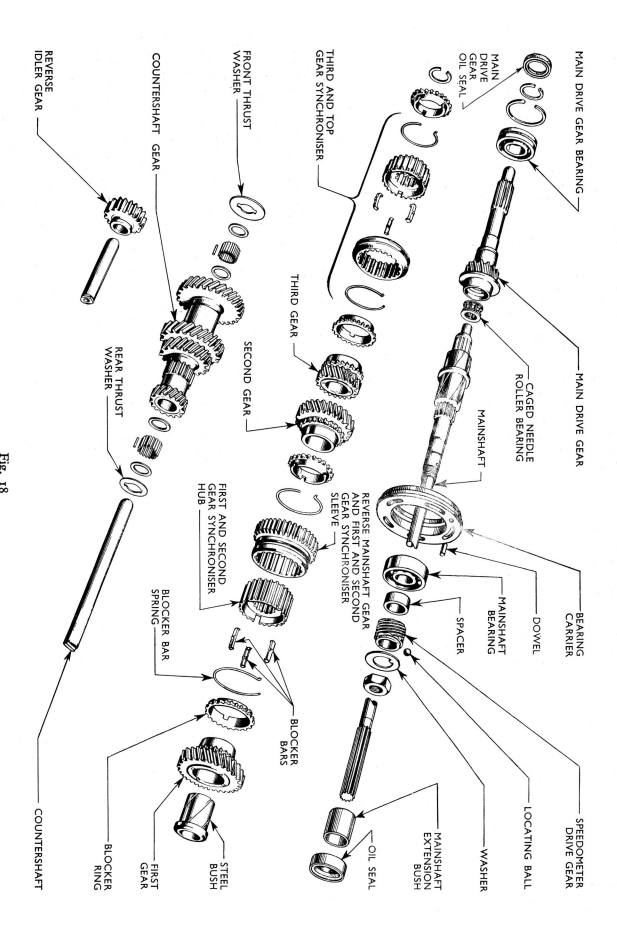

Fig. 18
Exploded View of Gearbox (Interior)

REVERSE IDLER GEAR

COUNTERSHAFT GEAR

FRONT THRUST WASHER

THIRD AND TOP GEAR SYNCHRONISER

MAIN DRIVE GEAR OIL SEAL

MAIN DRIVE GEAR BEARING

MAIN DRIVE GEAR

CAGED NEEDLE ROLLER BEARING

THIRD GEAR

SECOND GEAR

REAR THRUST WASHER

FIRST AND SECOND GEAR SYNCHRONISER HUB

REVERSE MAINSHAFT GEAR AND FIRST AND SECOND GEAR SYNCHRONISER SLEEVE

MAINSHAFT

BEARING CARRIER

MAINSHAFT BEARING

DOWEL

SPACER

WASHER

LOCATING BALL

SPEEDOMETER DRIVE GEAR

BLOCKER BAR SPRING

BLOCKER BARS

COUNTERSHAFT

BLOCKER RING

FIRST GEAR

STEEL BUSH

OIL SEAL

MAINSHAFT EXTENSION BUSH

the accelerator pedal sharply at which point the automatic gearbox will change down to a lower ratio. This is used, for example, when overtaking.

Talking of Volvos, I recall in the mid-1960s that someone built a Cortina with an 1800cc Volvo engine which was used for autocross. It provided better than Lotus performance for less money, and being a Volvo required little attention while giving a long reliable life. (The 1800 B18 Volvo unit is outwardly the same as the later B20, 2 litre unit. Does this suggest anything to you?).

Oil Leaks

One of the things you have to decide is, "What is an oil leak?" How much oil is a leak? The reason for this question is that you can spend hours and pounds replacing seals only to arrive back at the position you started from. There are some things which always leak. For example, I always expect to find some wet oil at the rear of the gearbox where the prop shaft meets the gearbox. Similarly, There is very often some oil seepage at the drive side of the differential unit. Neither of these is serious, but you have to make a judgement as to which really requires attention and which you just live with.

Propeller Shaft Bearings

Originally I was going to refer you to a workshop manual for this subject, then I remembered all the problems I have had over the years. The books make it out to be easy but I have rarely done the job without one or more problems cropping up.

When you remove the prop shaft from the differential mounting flange by removing the four bolts, ensure that you mark both surfaces so that the shaft can be refitted in the same position. The only problem with this is that the previous owner may not have bothered with this so the shaft could have been refitted in one of two positions. Let me explain. The four bolt holes are not equidistant. They are arranged in two groups of two, and the mating shaft can only go on one of two ways.

Anyway, do mark the flanges as you take them off. It will help if a problem occurs later.

Next, the books say, Remove the circlips. My shafts are usually rusty and very often the circlip is seized in its groove. A wash with either paraffin or a spray with WD40

ABOVE: The final drive unit as you have never seen it before! The car is on its side... The drive flange is different on G.T. cars but otherwise final drives can be swapped easily. There is an oil seal behind the drive flange which can be replaced by removing the flange. A torque wrench is essential for this operation.

RIGHT: You'll need two of these kits when overhauling the drive shaft (or prop shaft). These are the universal joints which should be easy to replace but which can catch you out if you are unlucky. Refer to text. Faulty or worn universal joints can make a car very unpleasant to drive due to vibration. Kits only cost about seven or eight pounds each and should only take a few hours to fit.

may be needed to free them. Once they are free, remove them with circlip pliers or two very small electricians screwdrivers. One screwdriver forces an end out of the groove, the other then forces some more of the clip out of the groove and the clip will finally break or spring out. Either way you do not want it as you will be fitting new ones which are part of the repair kit.

Next remove the bearings from the main shaft. If you have a vice, try pushing one bearing cap in as far as it will go. The opposite bearing cap will be pushed out, but you need some sort of tube with a diameter wider than the bearing cap, located against the opposite jaw of the vice. This will let one bearing cap come out. You will then be able to pull it out completely by gripping it with a Mole wrench or large pliers.

Whatever way the book tells you to do it, the object of the exercise is to get the X - shaped bearing (known as the spider trunnion) and the four bearing caps out of the positions they are.currently in. You can use a vice or a hammer and drift. What you must NOT do is damage any of the bearing housings on the propeller shaft or the driving flange.

When all the bearing caps are out, clean up all the surfaces with a fine grade of emery paper. Make sure they are clean and rust free and the surfaces are free from burrs, as this will aid the refitting process considerably.

Next comes a tricky bit. Open the packet with the new universal joint in, and remove the bearing caps carefully. They should each contain some grease which will help to keep the needle roller bearings in place. Look into the cap to see the needle roller bearings. They should all be standing vertically with no spaces or gaps between them. Apply some more grease to each bearing.

Place the spider trunnion into the drive flange yokes. Line up one bearing cap with its mounting flange and push it into position. Some books say tap it into place. This will risk dislodging all those little needle roller bearings, so don't tap it into place! Use the vice again and keeping one leg of the the spider in the bearing cap, fit the bearing cap to the drive flange.

Repeat this process on the opposite bearing cap. Both bearing caps should be pushed into position so that the circlips can be fitted into their respective grooves. If the bearing caps won't go this deep, then suspect that a needle roller has come adrift and is preventing the assembly fitting into place. Dismantle and start again, assuming you can get your needle rollers under control. On at least two occasions in the last twenty years I have had to throw away a kit and buy another one.

Having fitted the drive flanges first, now offer the assembly to the propeller shaft proper. Repeat the above process, taking extreme care not to breathe too heavily and dislodge these needle rollers.

Once all are in place, fit the new circlips. If one or more do not want to seat, tap the flanges with a wooden mallet until all the circlips can be seated. If one cannot be seated, suspect a needle roller has gone walkabout.

Refit the propshaft to the car, following

TOP PHOTO: *The speedometer drive gear and its alloy housing. Take care when fitting or removing the housing not to damage the rubber O-ring. Various drive gears are available, see Key Information.*

MIDDLE PHOTO: *My 2000E gearbox shown with the bellhousing removed. It will be handed over to a transmission specialist for attention. That way I get a good job done, get a year's guarantee, while I do something else.*

LOWER PHOTO: *This is the remote gear change unit as fitted to G.T. cars. It can be fitted to other cars but may foul the floor-mounted handbrake lever.*

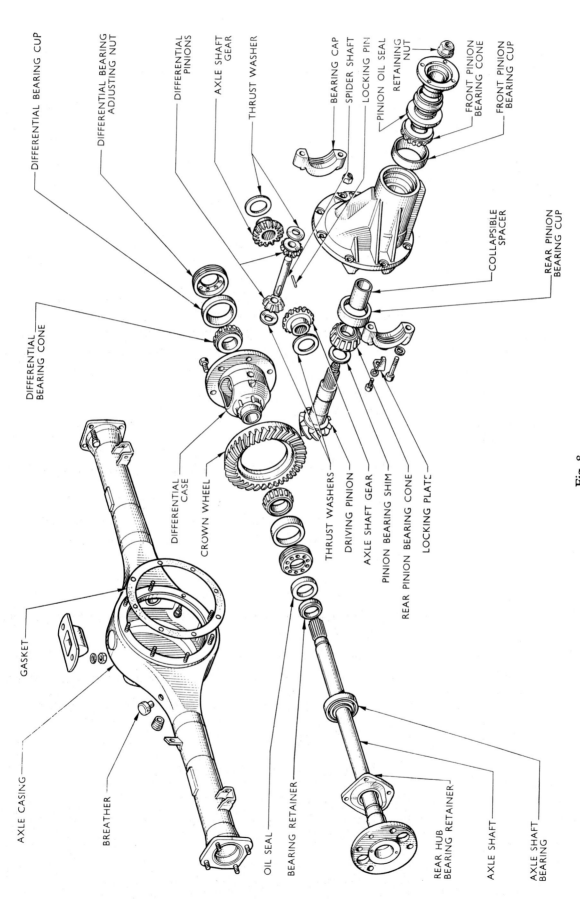

DIFFERENTIAL BEARING CUP

DIFFERENTIAL BEARING ADJUSTING NUT

DIFFERENTIAL PINIONS

AXLE SHAFT GEAR

THRUST WASHER

BEARING CAP

SPIDER SHAFT

LOCKING PIN

PINION OIL SEAL

RETAINING NUT

FRONT PINION BEARING CONE

FRONT PINION BEARING CUP

COLLAPSIBLE SPACER

REAR PINION BEARING CUP

DIFFERENTIAL BEARING CONE

DIFFERENTIAL CASE

CROWN WHEEL

THRUST WASHERS

DRIVING PINION

AXLE SHAFT GEAR

PINION BEARING SHIM

REAR PINION BEARING CONE

LOCKING PLATE

GASKET

AXLE CASING

BREATHER

OIL SEAL

BEARING RETAINER

REAR HUB BEARING RETAINER

AXLE SHAFT

AXLE SHAFT BEARING

Fig. 8

Rear Axle—Exploded View

the marks made on dismantling.

Just to recap. Dismantle the shaft so that the front and rear bits are removed first. Next remove the spider trunnion from both ends of the shaft. On re-assembling fit the spiders to the drive flange and driven flanges first, then fit these assemblies to the prop shaft.

If I have made heavy work of this I apologise. I know it is supposed to be quite easy to do, but I have had many occasions when I could have thrown the prop shaft and all the needle rollers into the nearest canal! It can be done quite easily, but if things go wrong -- they really do go wrong!

Conclusion

Various items, such as master cylinders were discussed under brakes, so are not repeated in this chapter.

Now that your gearbox, clutch and transmission is overhauled, you are ready to start thinking about getting the vehicle running again, especially if the engine is also restored or overhauled.

Don't rush things at this stage. It will be all too easy to rush ahead and spoil the whole project. It is very tempting to throw the rest of the bits back together to get the car running again. Don't be tempted.

OPPOSITE PAGE: The exploded view of the rear axle. The crown wheel and pinion assembly determine the final drive ration, for example 4.125 to 1. If you want to change this you change the entire final drive unit as described in the text. Gaskets and oil seals are still freely available. These units are reliable and give long life. Make sure you top up with the correct oil after changing the diff.

(Illustration courtesy of Ford Motor Company).

RIGHT: A pair of new oils seals for the rear axle. These should be fitted with a special tool to ensure correct alignment, however they can often be tapped into position with a large socket. They are quite cheap to replace.

TRANSMISSION Torque Wrench Settings

Flywheel to crankshaft bolts 45 - 50 lb ft / 6.22 - 6.91 kg m
Clutch to flywheel 12 - 15 lb ft / 1.66 - 2.07 kg m
Clutch bellhousing to gearbox 40 - 45 lb ft / 5.53 - 6.22 kg m
Gearbox drain & filler plugs 25 - 30 lb ft / 3.46 - 4.15 kg m
Gearbox extension to gearbox 20 - 25 lb ft / 2.76 - 3.46 kg m
Gear lever housing 15 - 18 lb ft / 2.07 - 2.49 kg m
Gearbox top cover 15 - 18 lb ft / 2.07 - 2.49 kg m
Mainshaft retaining nut 20 - 25 lb ft / 2.76 - 3.46 kg m
Clutch slave cylinder bleed nipple 5 - 7 lb ft / 0.7 - 1.0 kg m
Prop shaft to diff pinion flange 15 - 18 lb ft / 2.07 - 2.49 kg m
Diff carrier to axle housing 15 - 18 lb ft / 2.07 - 2.49 kg m
Rear axle filler plug 25 - 30 lb ft / 3.46 - 4.15 kg m
Universal joint to drive pinion 15 - 18 lb ft / 2.07 - 2.49 kg m
Differential housing to rear axle 15 - 18 lb ft / 2.07 - 2.49 kg m
Crown wheel to diff case bolts 30 - 35 lb ft / 4.15 - 4.75 kg m
Diff bearing locking plate bolts 12 - 15 lb ft / 1.66 - 2.07 kg m
Bearing cap bolts 45 - 50 lb ft / 6.22 - 6.91 kg m
Axle shaft bearing retaining nuts 15 - 18 lb ft / 2.07 - 2.49 kg m

AUTOMATIC TRANSMISSION Torque Wrench Settings

Drive plate to crankshaft 45 lb ft / 6.2 kg m
Filler tube connector adapter to case 25 lb ft / 3.46 kg m
Filler tube to connector sleeve nut 18 lb ft / 2.49 kg m
Oil pan drain plug 12 lb ft / 1.6 kg m
Pressure take-off point plug 5 lb ft / 0.6 kg m
Starter inhibitor switch locknut 5 lb ft / 0.6 kg m
Support crossmember to transmission casing 12 lb ft / 1.6 kg m
Torque converter to drive plate 40 lb ft / 5.5 kg m
Transmission casing to converter housing 9 lb ft / 1.2 kg m

Electrics

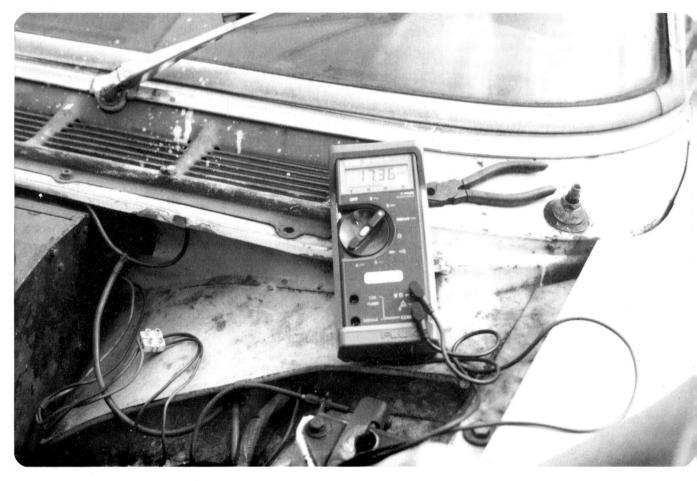

The multi-meter is the ideal tool for finding electrical problems. Here the meter is being used to test the output of a dynamo. If you do not have a multi-meter you can do a lot of testing with just a test lamp. Electrical problems are often self-inflicted so make sure you get all the electrics sorted on your restoration.

In this chapter, we are going to look at the subject which puts most people off right away -- electrics. DON'T PANIC!

In the next few paragraphs, I'll show you a way to visualise electricity which will make it all seem so simple, you'll wonder what all the fuss was about. Let me start off by stating that there are only three possible electrical faults!

These are:

1) Disconnection,
2) Short Circuit,
3) Earth contact.

Right, as promised, the simple way to think about electricity. Think of a garden hose with water flowing through it. If you can create a mental picture of a garden hose, with water flowing through it and spraying out the other end, you can master the electrics in your small Ford.

The minimum requirements for an electrical circuit are two wires, (one the feed and one the return) a battery, and a load, which in our case is the electrical device we want to power from our battery. Just to keep things simple, we will imagine you have a light bulb on the end of your wires.

If you connect one wire to each side or terminal of the battery, and the other end of each wire to the sides or terminals of the lampholder, the lamp will light up. In our garden hose example, you have the water flowing through the pipe (where the water is the electricity and the pipe is the wire).

Whilst that is settling down in your mind, let's look at the first fault listed above. The disconnection.

In the garden hose idea, imagine the gardener puts his spade through the hose. He cuts right through it. Water can no longer reach the end you want it at, to water the flowers, but the water is reaching the end where it was cut. Keep that in mind, it will help a lot later.

Time for fault number two, the short circuit. Again, look at the garden hose. You are watering your flowers again, when someone parks their car right on the hose. The flow of water is stopped immediately. The water is still in the hose, but it cannot go anywhere. If the pressure is high enough, it may force the hose to come away from the tap to which it is fitted. Then there is no water in the pipe. This is like a fuse blowing if the pressure gets too high. A fuse melts or blows if the electrical pressure in the circuit gets too high. We will come back to that later.

Let's have a quick look at the third fault, which is probably the most difficult to locate, the earth contact.

Yet again, you are watering the flowers. This time, someone jabs the hose with a garden fork and puts a hole in it. The water pressure at the watering end drops, as some water escapes through the hole created by the fork. Your water energy is leaking away. Similarly, if an electrical wire gets damaged, and the insulation gets broken, some electricity can leak out and make contact with metal parts of the car, or alternatively make contact with wet carpets or wet mud in the boot. We will look at these faults later on.

Simple Testing

You can carry out a lot of simple tests with either a multi-meter or a test lamp. The test lamp is described below, while the multi-meter is discussed in Dynamo Testing later in this Chapter.

Most testing consists of two things. Test for a voltage, and secondly test for an earth or return path. Armed with this basic information you can test almost all the electrical circuits on your small Ford.

You can test any electric circuit in your car with one piece of equipment. It is simple to make, and will cost you less than a pound for the bits. You need about six feet of insulated wire. You want some sort of 12 volt bulb holder, which can be bought in Woolworth, and two small crocodile clips. This device relies on you having a car battery to supply the energy. If your car is a dead, lifeless hulk without a battery, you will need a small battery such as a 4-1/2 volt flat torch battery. In this case, you would then fit a 4-1/2 volt bulb in the holder.

Cut the wire into two lengths. One length needs to be say, four feet long, with the other length about a foot or so. Connect a crocodile clip to one end of each length of wire.

Connect the other two ends to the terminals of the bulb holder. Fit the bulb.

The first thing you must do with any test equipment, is ensure that it works. Now that sounds so simple, but I know people

This test lamp can be made up by anyone who can connect a crocodile clip to a piece of wire! I have been using this same test lamp for nearly 15 years and it only took five minutes to make. The bulbholder is a dashboard bulbholder from a Volvo. You can buy something similar in the High Street motoring shops.

who used to spend hours looking for faults on telephone equipment using faulty test gear. As soon as help was called, the next engineer to arrive used his test equipment, and found that the first man's test kit was faulty.

The simple test for your tester, is to connect one crocodile clip to one terminal of the car battery. Now touch the other crocodile clip to the other terminal of the battery. The bulb should light. Success!

If for some reason it does not, check that the crocodile clip has attached firmly onto a CLEAN part of the terminal. The quick easy way to check that is to move it. If all else fails, try a new bulb.

Now let's try fault finding on a real problem. Both the rear lights of your car will not light up. (Not the brake lights, the rear marker lights.)

Just a quick tip here. If both of the rear lights are out, have a look at the number-plate lamp. Is it lit? If it is, it may save you a lot of time in locating the fault.

If we assume that both rear lights do not light up, first look at the front side-lights. Do they light up when you switch them on? They do? Good! That means the fault is towards the rear of the car.

Go to the rear of the car and open the boot. Look for the wires going to the rear lights. You will probably find two or three wires entering the lamp assembly at each

side of the car.

From the wiring diagram, you will know that the light wires are coloured Red. Look for a red wire, and then look for a connector.

Having found a connector, disconnect the red wires from the connector. Now attach one of your crocodile clips to a good earth - which means clip it to a metal part of the body. In the boot you will find screws holding the lamp assembly to the body. They make good earths.

Next, touch the other crocodile clip to the red wire coming from the front of the car. The lamp in the lamp holder should light up. That means that electricity for the lights is reaching that point. As a confirmation, switch off the lights. Repeat the test with the bulb. This time the bulb should not light, as the power is switched off.

Replace the red wires in the connector, making sure of a nice tight fit. Try the lights again. If they now work it means that the connector was dirty, causing a disconnection. If they still do not work, trace the wires along the boot, until you come to another connector. Aha, this one is disconnected. Push the wires back in, and the lamps light.

It is wise at this point to try to find out why the connector became disconnected. It might just have been a bad connection, lying there for years waiting to be found.

CHAPTER FIVE

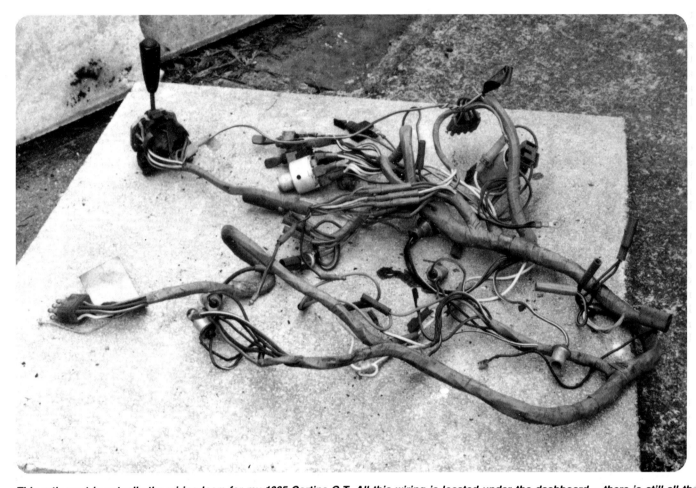

This rat's nest is actually the wiring loom for my 1965 Cortina G.T. All this wiring is located under the dashboard -- there is still all the wiring which extends into the engine compartment and the wiring which runs towards the back of the car. These wires are actually the veins and arteries of the car.

Or it could have been a heavy package dropped into the boot which somehow tugged on the wires, pulling them apart at the connector. Anyway, you have now found your first fault using the bulb tester!

If you have some knowledge of electrics, you may also want to use a volt-meter or multi-meter. There are many types of these, one is shown in the illustration. For the moment, I will show you how to locate faults using just the wire, bulb and crocodile clips.

We have already looked at a typical lighting fault in the early part of this chapter. If one light fails, the first thing to check is the bulb. It is always recommended that you carry spare bulbs, but I have never met anyone who does!

If a new bulb does not cure the problem, check the wiring, connectors and finally the bulb holder.

Battery Faults

Battery faults can show up in many forms. A battery which you have had for years, may suddenly give up one cold morning as you try to start the car. Or the deterioration may be gradual. I also found on one car that the clock started to become very erratic. This pointed me to a faulty battery - eventually!

Check the following things, then consider getting professional advice:

Are the connections to the battery clean and bright? Or are they loose and covered with a white fungus? Disconnect the battery terminals from the wires and clean off the fungus with warm water and a cloth. When they are clean, rub the terminals with a little piece of sandpaper, to make the connection shiny. (An old nail-file can often be useful for this).

Having cleaned the terminals, reconnect the cables to the battery. When they are on nice and tight, rub some grease or Vaseline over the terminal to keep out moisture.

This sort of fault will suddenly appear some damp morning when the ignition lights will come on okay, but as soon as you turn the starter, the lights go out and the starter does not turn. You may also hear a sharp little cracking noise from the battery. That is the current sparking across the damp terminals, between the battery and its connecting cable.

A quick, get-you-going tip is to grab the cables on the battery and either twist them or move them. This is often enough to scratch or disturb the bad connection and improve it enough to get you started. You'll soon have to give it the attention it needs, though!

If you have check all the obvious battery things like connections, then I would advise you to get the battery checked at a service station or garage. The mechanic will use a tester which he clips onto the battery terminals and he will make a note of the reading. He'll probably ask you to start to engine, as the heavy load caused by the starter motor will make another, lower reading show up on the tester. He might then advise that you need a new battery. The problem could be the dynamo or alternator not charging the battery, but these can also be tested. Don't be put off by a reluctant mechanic. Go somewhere else and get your dynamo checked before buying a new battery which you may not really need.

There is very little that can be done for old batteries. I would advise you to shop around for a good discount and get a new battery. There's nothing like it. The improved starting will make it seem you have a new car.

Small Fords generally had the choice of two batteries, the normal capacity one quoted at 38 amp hours, and the heavy-duty type quoted at 51 amp hours. What does amp hours mean? Put simply, it is a rating of how long a battery will maintain a load of one amp. The higher the amp hour rating the more power available from the battery.

This the main wiring connector on the Cortina's bulkhead. As fitted in the factory there is a locking arrangement to prevent the wiring becoming disconnected. On this car the lock is broken and a plastic cable tie is used to fasten the two halves of the connector together.

Dynamo Options

There are two Lucas dynamos used on this range of cars. The 22 amp output version, known as the C40, and the heavy duty or high output version called the C40L. This one has an output of 25 amps.

Both of these dynamos are driven by a fan belt at 1.5 times the engine speed. (If you have an automatic transmission car the dynamo is driven at 1.8 times engine speed).

Ford intended that you have a heavy duty battery and a different regulator if the C40L dynamo was fitted.

If you have heavy electrical requirements on your car, for example some spotlamps which need a lot of power, then you might want to consider fitting the heavier dynamo, regulator box and a heavy duty battery. There is always an alternator conversion!

In July, 1966 Ford produced a Service Letter for 1500cc automatic transmission cars. This is worth outlining here.

It was found that many automatics used in the town ran their batteries down due to inadequate charging. The solution was to fit a smaller pulley on the dynamo. The standard, UK, plastic pulley was numbered 105E 10130 A. This was replaced by 105E 10130 B, a steel pulley which can be identified by spot welds round the pulley hub. A different fan belt was then required.

If you have a similar problem it may be worth looking at your dynamo pulley.

There was a warning given at the bottom of the Service Letter. If this smaller pulley was fitted to manual transmission cars, or to G.T. cars, then there was a risk of the generator being over-revved if high engine speeds were sustained. If you keep this warning in mind it might be a cheap way to solve a flat battery problem on a stop-start, town car.

Dynamos

Dynamos sit there, next to the engine for year after year, suffering all the heat and spray and rarely giving trouble. If they do give trouble, the first symptom you notice is probably that the red ignition warning light comes on while you are driving.

To put things simply, there is a box called a Regulator which manages the electricity from the dynamo. If the dynamo fails, then there is still electricity around, in the car battery. The Regulator is now out of balance, and makes the red lamp come on on the dashboard.

A get-you-home tip: If the red light comes on suddenly, it may be that the fan belt has broken. Do NOT switch off the engine yet, but carefully look at the engine to see if the fan blades are turning. If they are stopped you should be able to see the fan belt either broken or missing. At this point you should have a running engine and a fully charged battery. You can get home within a reasonable distance, but the

engine may overheat if you drive too hard. After all, the fan is driven by the fan belt.

If the fan belt is still connected, it means a dynamo fault. A good battery will probably keep an engine supplied with electricity for at least an hour. I have had this happen on a motorway, just as it was getting dark. I managed to drive for about an hour and quarter, with some lights on, and reached my destination. What is the cause of the problem? Usually it is the carbon brushes in the dynamo. The last time I bought a pair they were 80 pence - so this gives you an idea of the scale of the problem.

Once again, don't part with ready-cash for a new dynamo unless you are sure that a 80 pence set of brushes won't cure your existing problem. Most workshop manuals show you how to change brushes. It means taking the dynamo off the car, and it is a bit fiddly, but it can be done. I've done it many times over the years. One dynamo I have, likes to have new bushes about once a year. There must be some roughness on the surface the brush touches, but I cannot find it, and it does not cause me any worries. When the brush starts to wear out, the red light starts to flicker.

To test a dynamo, you need a multi-meter which can read 30 volts. Any cheap meter will do this job, as you will normally either get the reading you want, or no reading at all.

Before testing the dynamo, check the two cables connected to the rear of the dynamo. Gently pull on the spade connectors to ensure that they are firmly soldered or crimped to the cable. Any loose connection here will play havoc with the charging circuit.

Repeat the check at the other end of these cables which is at the voltage control box. This may be under the glove box on may small Fords, or mounted on the nearside inner wing, in the engine bay.

WARNING: The following procedure involves working in the engine bay with the engine running. Ensure there is no loose clothing and keep your hands and the connections to the test meter clear of the fan blades. Have an assistant available to switch the engine on and off.

Disconnect both cables from the connections at the back of the dynamo.

Set the meter to 30 volts DC.

Connect one lead from the meter to the chassis or bodywork. Ensure a good electrical connection is made.

Connect the other lead of the test meter to BOTH terminals on the dynamo. You might need to twist a bit of wire around both terminals before connecting the lead from the test equipment.

Start the engine and let it tick over. A reading of between 20 and 24 volts should be seen on the meter. This will vary depending on engine speed, but as a guide at about 750 rpm you should see about 15 volts, rising to over 24 volts at about 1,000 rpm. There is no need to rev the engine above 1,000 rpm when testing a dynamo. If the voltage reading is not present there is a fault.

A reading of about 1 volt indicates a field winding fault.

Confirm a field winding fault in the dynamo as follows;

Set the multi-meter to OHMS and measure the resistance between the field winding terminal F and the dynamo body. Make sure you get a good connection between the multi-meter probe and the dynamo body. The resistance reading should be 6.2 ohms. If the reading is different from this suspect that the insulated coils are touching the dynamo body OR that the field coils are disconnected.

There is really nothing you can do about that except replace the dynamo.

If the reading is 4 or 5 volts the armature windings may be faulty.

If the reading is zero then either a

A new dynamo end plate, showing the brush holders and the little coil springs which hold the brushes in place. Dynamos can be brought back to life for about a pound for a new set of brushes. You will also find, if buying a reconditioned dynamo, that the C40L heavy duty dynamo is much more expensive than the more common C40.

dynamo brush is completely broken or there is some break in the testing circuit. Repeat the test.

If there is definitely no voltage reading then the dynamo needs new brushes or must be replaced.

If the reading is within the ranges indicated (15 - 30 volts) but you still suspect a problem in the charging circuit, test the voltage at the control box end of the F and D cables. (Remember to replace the F and D cables to the dynamo). If the voltage is other than 15 - 30 volts then there is a problem in the wiring loom.

There are several tests which the restorer can do on the regulator box. There is even a special tool which you may be able to get hold of to adjust the regulator. A word of warning though. While testing the dynamo output is well within the scope of the average restorer, I believe the regulator is best left to an expert. It may be a more reliable option to simply replace the regulator with a new one. For example, regulator boxes for the MK1 Cortina are listed at just over 16 pounds from one specialist dealer. For that sort of money it is not worth the bother of acquiring a voltmeter, reading the workshop manual and trying out your new skill on your car's electrical system. A bad mistake could cost you a boiled battery, or you may succeed in

removing all charge to the battery. My advice? Test the dynamo and leave the regulator to experts or buy a new one.

Replacing dynamo brushes

Remove the dynamo from the car by removing the two bolts holding the ends of the dynamo to the engine bracket, and the single bolt which is used to tension the fan belt.

Clean any excess dirt or oil from the casing with a rag. Using a large flat bladed screwdriver, loosen and remove the long screws which can be found on the dynamo backplate.

When these screws are pulled out, the backplate can be removed, revealing the dynamo brushes. There are two of them and they should each be in a brush holder. The brushes are made of carbon. Uncoil the coil spring which pushes the brush against the armature. Trace the wire from the carbon brush to the terminal and undo the screw. Remove the brush and examine it.

There is little point in putting it all back together again with old brushes, so fit new brushes. Clean the armature with very fine emery paper. If there are signs of scoring or other damage you will either have to seek professional help, or buy a replacement dynamo or armature.

Install the new brushes. Take care to get the coil springs installed the correct way. Refit the screw over the end of the generator brush and tighten it.

Now, holding the brushes in their holders, gently offer up the backplate to the armature. This may take a few attempts to get right, but when you get all the angles right it will slip on. Check that the brushes are being pushed against the armature by the springs.

When you are happy that all is well, locate the backplate against the main body of the dynamo. There is a little groove and lump to help locate things properly. When located insert the long screws and after a bit of fiddling about to find the holes, tighten the screws.

Refit the dynamo to the car and tension the fan belt.

Starter Motors

Starter motors are bolted onto the engine where they receive all the dirt and spray from the road wheels, they get virtually no maintenance and are only thought about when they give trouble.

If there is a problem with your starter circuit, remember that you can by-pass part of the circuit by placing a heavy insulated screwdriver between the exposed terminals of the starter solenoid. This is the round metal thing mounted on the inner wing, usually close to the battery. This is NOT a test for the fainthearted as there could be a big spark. But it is a valid test and mechanics may do this to quickly locate a starter motor problem.

Later cars used a square starter solenoid, but the principle is the same.

If your starter does not turn when you turn the ignition key but turns freely when you short out the solenoid, then look to the solenoid for the solution.

If you do have to remove the starter motor, you MUST disconnect the battery before you do. If you accidentally cause a short circuit by a spanner touching the starter motor lead and the chassis you could receive severe burns. Extremely heavy currents flow for the short period of time that the starter is connected, so don't take any chances -- disconnect the battery.

If you are not confident about testing a starter motor, then take it from the car and go to a garage or auto electrician.

In any case you can probably get a reconditioned starter from one of the leading high street motoring discount

A brand new pair of front sidelamps for the late type MK1 Cortina. (The early cars had oval lamps). These will be fitted to my G.T. New lamps are still available for many small Fords. Some have weak points and require attention even when new. Front sidelamps tend to rot away very quickly, so some work is required to keep the water out.

shops. Very often it does not pay to repair a starter. A new set of brushes may only cost a pound or two, but while the motor is off the car it makes sense to examine the bendix and replace it if worn. The bendix is the common name given to the starter motor pinion -- the little gear on the end of the shaft. It engages with the ring gear on the flywheel and causes the engine to turn.

Windscreen Wiper Motors

Several types of wiper motor are fitted to these cars. They share one thing in common, they are difficult to get out of the car if they give trouble. Fortunately, they don't often give trouble. If they do, check the wiring in case a connector has come loose, and if this is not the problem then you will have to replace the wiper motor with another one, either new (if you can get it) or more probably a second hand one.

Make sure the wiper arms are located on their spindles properly. If they are not correctly fitted then the wiper blade could be forced against the screen's rubber surround which will cause extra strain on the motor.

Classics and Capris have a twist switch built into the wiper switch. When you twist this it controls the speed of the wiper motor. This was a fore-runner of two-speed wipers!

Heater Motors

Yet again heater motors don't seem to give much trouble. If you do have a problem check the wiring and especially the two speed switch which is fitted to many of them. This switches a resistance into the circuit on low speed, and removes the resistance when high speed is selected. If this resistance component becomes open-circuit then the heater motor will not work on low.

You may need to change the whole motor assembly rather than the complete heater assembly if the motor goes faulty.

If you have never thought about how a heater works, then it consists simply of a small radiator connected to your cooling system and a fan blows air through the radiator. Heat is transferred from the radiator to the air and the car gets heated. As with engine radiators, this heater radiator could develop a leak or become blocked. So remember to think in terms of a water-filled radiator when thinking of a heater. If a problem develops, you can always by-pass the heater by re-routing one of the heater hoses. This will get you out of trouble until you can fix the problem.

Ignition

If an ignition coil develops a fault or becomes suspect, replace it. Don't mess about. There is nothing you can do for coils as they are sealed units. They may be oil-filled so if you find a mysterious oil leak it could be the coil. (You could always borrow a good coil from your mate's car to prove the fault). Make sure you get the correct coil for your car.

The starter solenoid sometimes gives trouble. Bad starting or no action from the starter motor is the most obvious symptom. Once again there is nothing you can do but replace it.

Ignition Faults

Ignition faults are often the most exasperating to find. One minute the electrics work perfectly, the next minute the problem appears.

One thing to look out for is the little rubber covers which go over the ends of some HT (ignition) leads. In the example I am thinking of, the rubber cover was on the coil. The car was getting harder and harder to start. Everything seemed to be correctly set up and I could not find the problem. After days of trying, I started to swap each item, one at a time until the car started easily. The only thing I found wrong was that little rubber cap. As soon as I took it off the problem vanished. When I tried to find out why it was causing a fault, all I found was that it had become dry and brittle. I suspected that it was somehow shorting- out the HT lead to earth.

On another occasion I had a 1500cc Cortina which would not run above 30 mph. It started well but just refused to run above 30. Unfortunately, I only discovered this problem heading back to Glasgow after a visit to Kent, some 420 miles. I used the A1 in those days and well remember limping off at Scotch Corner knowing if the beast kept going I had hours and hours still to drive. The problem? The condenser in the distributor.

This device dampens the sparking which occurs each time the points open. If you had no condenser the contact breaker points would wear out very quickly. If the condenser goes open circuit, then no serious problem - the points just burn out but you get fair warning. If it goes short-circuit the car won't start as there is a short circuit right across the contact breaker points. However if the condenser partly breaks down, when you apply an electrical load to it, it causes intermittent faults and misfires, like I had.

It pays to fit a new one every year or so. Also if you buy a car which has been lying in a garage for years and years, the condenser may break down after a few hours. This is due to its construction and the way it behaves if there is no electricity applied to it for a long period of time. Basically, it dries out and goes faulty.

Spark Plug Problems

It goes without saying that if an engine has four cylinders it should have four identical spark plugs fitted. Yes? Well, not always so. Your new banger may be running very roughly, and only need a new set of plugs to put it right.

I bought a Ford Cortina MK1 a number of years ago. I knew it needed work, but one of the first faults I was able to cure was by removing the four DIFFERENT types of spark plug the previous owner had fitted, and installing a new set of Champions.

The four old plugs were in various stages of disrepair. Dirty, oily, wide gaps, worn electrodes, they would have looked more at home in a spark plug company's black museum. Actually they would have had to go to three museums, as they were of three different makes as well!

The previous owner had tried to get the engine sorted out and one of the things he tried was fitting another set of plugs. Unfortunately all he had available were some old plugs lying around his garage. He fitted them and did not cure the problem. Then he sold the car to me. The problem? Well, it was a burnt valve. No amount of plug changing is going to sort that out!

More recently, one of my cars would not run cleanly at 30-35 mph. It coughed so much it jarred right through the transmission. Above 40 mph it was smooth as silk. After hours of effort, I finally found the problem in the new set of spark plugs I had installed just before the fault started. After gapping the plugs, I must have knocked one of them against the cylinder head as I installed it. That one was gapped at about 5 thou, while the rest were correctly gapped at 25 thou. That was the problem.

I tackled this problem by trying to re-create the engine speed at which the problem occurred. Turning up the engine tickover speed brought the problem on. Once I had got the engine coughing at a certain speed I removed one sparking plug at a time until I removed a spark plug lead and nothing happened. (When I removed a

good plug lead that cylinder stopped firing and the engine stopped). When I removed the bad lead nothing additional happened, so that had to be the problem cylinder. Once I pulled out the spark plug the problem became obvious. But then problems are always obvious once you have found the solution!

Before we leave plugs it is as well to remember that the wrong grade of plug can have a serious affect on an engine. For example if you fit the wrong grade of plug you might find that the engine will not start. Many years ago I had a car which was running well. We removed the good Champion N5 plugs which were correct for that model, and fitted a set of N3s. The car then became impossible to start. As soon as we re-fitted the N5s the engine started first turn as it had done before. The reason we took the plugs out was to try to help a friend who was diagnosing a problem with his engine. More modern plugs have a wider tolerance than their older brothers, but it pays to make sure you have the correct plugs fitted.

In October 1966 Ford issued Service Letter number 25 advising that spark plug gaps on 1200cc and 1500cc non-G.T. engines should be set between 0.020 to 0.024 inches to aid cold starting. New spark plugs are generally gapped at 0.025 so the gap would need to be closed very slightly to meet the revised requirements. The gaps on G.T. engines are 0.023 to 0.028 inches.

Distributor

The distributor fitted to most of the small Fords covered by this book was the

OPPOSITE PAGE: The wiring diagram for the MK1 Cortina G.T. If you have no experience of wiring diagrams, try tracing the dotted line of the pass lamp at the top of the diagram, back to the ignition switch. This gives a complete circuit with voltage supplied at the ignition switch, through the pass lamp switch to the pass lamp itself and then to earth (the car's bodywork).

Having done this, notice that the W (white) wire has a connector close to the ignition switch. If, for example, this was disconnected then the lamp would not light.

I find Ford wiring diagrams quite straightforward, so spend a little time trying to get to know the wiring. It will pay dividends.

(Illustration by courtesy of the Ford Motor Company).

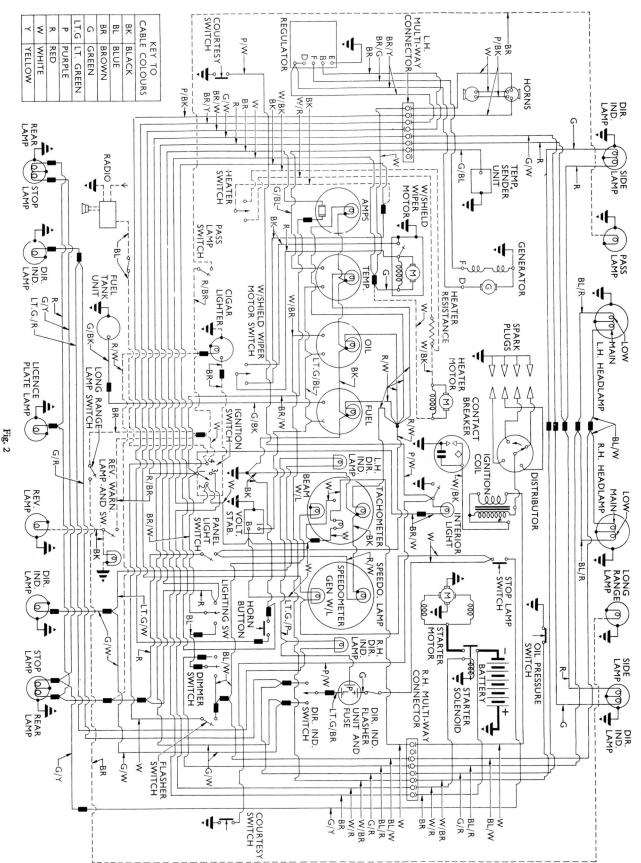

Fig. 2
Wiring Diagram, G.T. cars only

Lucas type 25D. There were several variations on the basic distributor depending on the engine size, high or low compression versions, or if the engine was a G.T. or not. Make sure you have the correct advance/retard weights, springs and vacuum unit for your car. It is all to easy to fit any old distributor to keep a banger running!

If you have a serious problem with your distributor then new ones are still available from various sources. You can also have your distributor reconditioned. However, at around 70 pounds it seems an expensive item.

It is worth noting that the same distributor was fitted to many of the British Leyland range of cars of the same period. The main difference was that on the Ford the distributor was driven by a skew gear, while on the BMC cars there was a drive pin or dog fitted instead of a gear.

I remember once buying a new skew gear and finding that the necessary hole was not drilled in the gear. I drilled the hole and fitted the skew gear, installed the distributor to the car and drove away. Within a few days the skew gear split in half, wrecking a lot of the engine with it. I would never again drill this hole. I would prefer to acquire a new or good second-hand distributor.

Lucas may be able to help with spares or advice. Ask your local Lucas agent.

CONTACT BREAKER POINTS

Contact breaker points used to be available in one-piece units and two-piece units. It does not realy matter which you fit. Points are so cheap that it is rarely worth the bother of flattening out any hills and valleys in them. Points should be changed every 10,000 miles at the same time as you replace the spark plugs. It also makes sense to replace the capacitor or condensor at the same time.

I recall that if you intended to use your car for competition then the Mini Cooper points were rated as heavy duty and these will fit the Lucas distributor without any modification.

CONCLUSION

Get your electrics sorted out and they will give you no problems. Make a hash of it an you will have nothing but trouble!

KEY INFORMATION

Ignition system

Firing order:
1 - 2 - 4 - 3. (Number 1 is the cylinder nearest the radiator!)
1 - 3 - 4 - 2 LOTUS ENGINE ONLY.

Ignition timing (Initial)

997cc engine 10 degrees Before Top Dead Centre,
1200cc engine 6 degrees Before Top Dead Centre,
1340cc engine 6 degrees Before Top Dead Centre,
1500cc engine 8 degrees Before Top Dead Centre,
1500cc G.T. engine 10 degrees Before Top Dead Centre
1558cc Lotus engine 14 degrees Before Top Dead Centre (approx)

Spark plugs, Gap 23 - 28 thou . (Refer to text for details)

Points gap 14 - 16 thou .

RIGHT: Using the multi-meter to detect the position at which the contact breaker points open. With the meter set up and switched on, the distributor is rotated slowly until the points open.

In this photo the distributor is correctly installed, with the vacuum unit parallel to the engine block, and the rotor arm pointing at one o'clock.

If you do not have a meter, use the test lamp described earlier in the chapter. This is used in conjunction with the car's own battery.

If you use the meter, it has its own internal battery so does not want the car's battery to be connected.

Body and Chassis

You won't all be starting from such a dismantled state, but doing the restoration this way ensures that everything gets looked at. This is the author's 1965 Cortina G.T. the day it was delivered! Progress has been made. Here, young David checks over the basic structure!

One of the biggest problems you will encounter when restoring a small Ford of 1960s vintage is the number of body panels needed. If you were to compare a bodyshell of the early 1950s with one from the 1960s you would find a vast difference in the actual number of panels used to make up the shell. In order to carry out your small Ford restoration properly, you will have to repair, replace or make many new body panels or parts of panels. So I make no apologies for devoting a large section of this book to body and chassis renovation. This section shows you some of the things you can do.

At this point I will again recommend my previous book, *"Panel Craft"* which deals exclusively with the restoration of body panels. It is written with the beginner in mind and is available from the publisher of this book. Although suitable for almost all types of cars, there is a large Ford Cortina content which makes it the natural companion to this book.

The first thing that needs to be sorted out is, "Can I weld, or learn to weld?" Alternatively, can I get my friend, relation, business partner to do the welding for me. Having decided who is going to do the work, what sort of welding equipment is needed.

I have been welding with gas since about 1968 so I am biased towards gas welding. I recognise that there are newer alternatives, so choose what you want to use from the following information.

Gas or MIG ?

If you are new to gas welding -- that is oxy-acetylene welding -- then again *"Panel Craft'"* has a section on this. For those more up to date than myself, I've asked Damian Halliwell of Frost Restoration Techniques Ltd to introduce us to MIG welding.

Introduction to MIG

Modern MIG welding equipment has made it possible for almost anyone with a mind to learn to become a reasonably proficient welder. Previously, oxyacetylene equipment was expensive, bulky and dangerous to keep anywhere but in an industrial workshop. Electric arc welding was relatively straightforward for heavier gauges of material (one eighth inch or thicker) but since most of us wanted to perform welding repair work on our cars this wasn't suitable either.

MIG is the abbreviation for Metal Inert Gas. The metal filler rod which also serves as the welding electrode is shielded at the weld area by a constant flow of inert gas to prevent oxygen entering the process and weakening the weld with oxidation. MIG welding has the advantage of being relatively inexpensive, portable, quick and easy to set up and use and its finely focused weld area uses the minimum amount of heat necessary and so prevents excessive distortion in your job. The notable disadvantages are that it can't be used as a heat source or as a cutting tool.

MIG Welding equipment

There are several companies marketing a range of low voltage MIG welders and it is worth shopping around before you buy. Take the time to learn about the various features different sets have in terms of capacity, versatility, and not least of all after-sales support. You don't want to buy this month's special offer only to find that after six months nobody stocks your particular spare parts any more. Consider your own application for your welding set and buy the one best suited to you.

The controls on most basic sets consist of an ON/OFF switch, variable voltage selector and variable wire feed speeds. The main voltage selection is usually by means of three buttons - LOW/MED/HIGH. This is sometimes multiplied by another high and low range button to give a total of six settings. The wire feed control is usually a dial with a scale 0 - 10. This enables you to "fine-tune" your current setting and welding speed.

Your reel of MIG wire will load into the welder behind a removable side panel. Each set will vary slightly but in the main you will find a spindle to carry your cable reel and wire inlet guide (nylon tube), leading to the drive rolls (one grooved and one plain). The fixed drive roll is powered by a small electric motor, while the other free roll is mounted on a hinged bracket secured by a spring and tension adjusting screw. After passing through the rolls another small bore tube (the outlet guide) steers the wire towards the main control cable and ultimately to the welding gun. The best general purpose wire for most car welding jobs on 18 to 24 gauge materials is 0.6 mm wire. From the exterior the control cable could be mistaken for a hollow rubber hose, but in fact it carries:

a) the MIG wire,

b) the inert gas supply,

c) the low voltage wiring from the trigger

DIAGRAM 1

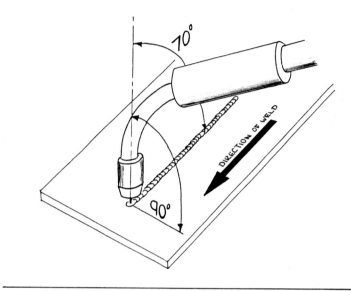

DIAGRAM 2   'T'- JOINT

switch to the wire feed motor and,

d) the high voltage wiring to the tip of the welding gun to complete the welding circuit.

Look after it! Don't drive over it, stand on it, drag it over sharp edges or across littered floors or otherwise risk damage.

The cylinder of inert gas is what makes a MIG welder more than just a fancy electric arc welder. It is only by excluding oxygen from the weld area that a non-porous strong weld can be produced. Two types of gas are used with MIG sets. Pure Argon is best suited to welding aluminium, while for mild steel and general purpose welding, a mix of Argon/CO_2 is used.

Safety

Now that you've been out and bought your welder, brought it home and unpacked all the bits and pieces, we should say a few words about safety. Boring, I know, but necessary all the same.

The first point might seem obvious but take your time as you set up and read your instruction manual from cover to cover. You'll find everything you need to know in there and most manuals give you enough tips on welding techniques to get you well started.

Protect Yourself! You'll need a full face helmet, gloves and overalls that button up to the neck and have long sleeves. Apart from the obvious risk of burning yourself with hot metal or flying sparks, a MIG welder gives off ultraviolet light and infrared radiation which can lead to mild sunburn. Your mask should have a Number 9 lens. Leather gauntlets will permit you to handle your job and the torch confidently and steadily, leading to better finished welds.

Prepare Your Work Area! Whilst I'm sure you wouldn't be careless enough to start welding in the vicinity of flammable objects such as paint, petrol, oily rags etc. there are many who have and paid the price. Teach yourself the habit of identifying potential fire risks and avoid them at all costs. If you have one, keep a fire extinguisher within easy reach. If you don't have one keep a bucket of sand or even a squeezy bottle full of water and some damp rags handy. If a small fire does start how else will you put it out before it becomes a big fire.

Protect your Vehicle! MIG welding is an electrical process so before letting it loose on your car disconnect the battery and the alternator and if it has any computerized systems, disconnect these too. Whenever you are about to weld, check the other side of the panel you are working on for flammable materials such as trim and wiring harnesses. Wiring can be neatly fused into a useless crispy strip in just a moment of carelessness.

Protect Others (including children and pets). It is quite probable that once you start welding you'll call on the assistance of family and friends to hold things in place or pass pieces to you under your car, so consider them by providing them with some form of protection from burns and from painful arc-eye by warning them to look away before you strike an arc. For your own good whenever possible you should keep your work area well ventilated. Work outdoors or keep garage doors and windows open to keep a flow of fresh air to carry away fumes from your welding. However, children and pets are fascinated by the bright light of a welder so check that they are not standing nearby watching you.

Setting up

Setting up your particular welding set will depend largely on you following the instructions laid out in your manual but

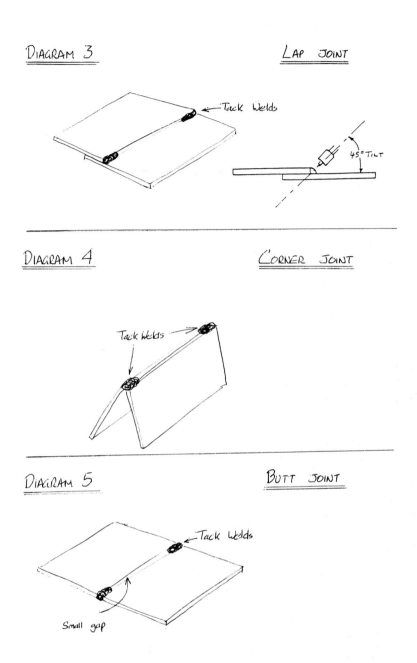

should follow these basic steps-

Load the spool of MIG wire and feed the wire through the drive rolls and up to the gun. Adjust the drive roll tension. Snip the wire off, leaving about 3/8 inch protruding from the nozzle. Turn the wire feed control down to zero to avoid wasting further wire while you adjust the gas flow meter. There are a few different flow meters - adjust according to instructions.

Now is a good time to prepare some practice pieces on which to get used to the variable adjustments on your welder. A dozen pieces of 20 gauge mild steel cut into 5 inch X 2 inch strips should suffice.

Set your current to LOW and the wire feed on 5 (on a scale 0 -10). Ensure you have a good earth connection by cleaning the point of contact down to bare metal.

Try to run a straight bead on the surface of one of your sample pieces. If the welder behaves and sounds erratic and produces an irregular bead with poor penetration, you need to increase the current. Do this by switching to the MEDIUM setting, while leaving the wire feed alone. Try again.

This time if the weld flows smoother and the sound is a more constant, even crackling you know you are close. The

Diagram 6   Plug welding

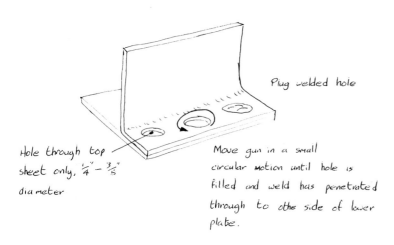

Plug welded hole

Hole through top sheet only, 1/4" – 3/8" diameter

Move gun in a small circular motion until hole is filled and weld has penetrated through to othe side of lower plate.

result should be a fairly even bead with visible weld penetration through to the back of the plate.

Now is the time to fine tune by either increasing or decreasing the wire feed control until you can run a smooth, even weld bead with good penetration.

Repeat this procedure on two or three thicknesses of material until you get to know how to set your controls for the material thicknesses you are likely to use on your car.

And finally, welding

After you've spent an hour or two setting up and making a mess of various bits of scrap metal you should be starting to develop a feel for the welding technique and in particular for the settings on your set, and you ought to be able to achieve a fairly presentable weld bead on the surface of a piece of 18 gauge mild steel. This is all very well but you don't want to run beads on the surface of your car you want to go one step further and actually stick two or more pieces together. There are only really four types of joint to master and then all welds you come across should fall into one or another category.

It is probably easiest to start with a simple T - joint (diagram 2). Check the edges are clean and fit together flush. Start by tack welding the pieces together at the ends. This will hold them securely in place and help prevent heat distortion. Then run a steady even bead from one end to the other ensuring you penetrate both pieces thoroughly. When you have finished, clean the weld with a wire brush and visually inspect it. Test it properly by clamping the bottom plate in the vice and hitting the vertical piece with a hammer. If you've completed a good weld it should hold while the plate bends all the way round.

Next try a lap joint (diagram 3). Again begin by tack welding the ends together then run a complete weld along the joint. Check the underside of the lower plate for thorough penetration but watch out for burning too much of the upper plate away. Try to break the weld in the vice again to

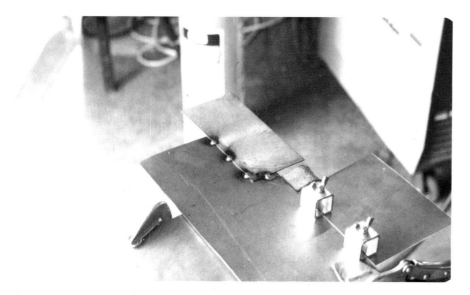

Middle photo: Tack weld the pieces together before running a bead. This helps keep everything in place and reduces distortion problems.

Bottom photo: Work in an uncluttered, well ventilated, area. Wear full protective clothing and observe all fire precautions.

Body and Chassis

Above, Left: Top weld shows a good weld bead on surface of 20 gauge sheet steel. Middle weld's voltage was too low, showing inconsistent and lumpy weld. In the lower weld the voltage was too high, burning away the steel. Above, Right: From the underside of the steel the top weld shows good penetration. Middle weld shows poor penetration. The bottom weld has nothing left to penetrate!

ensure full weld penetration.

If everything is okay so far move on to a corner joint (diagram 4). Use the same routine of tacking the ends, running the full weld then destructively testing.

Finally practice a butt joint (diagram 5). You will find a set of Intergrip clamps from Frost Auto Restoration Techniques particularly useful at this stage for clamping the two separate pieces of metal firmly together while you tack weld them. Then remove the Intergrips and proceed as before, weld, clean up and test to destruction.

One other type of joint is well worth noting and practising and that is a plug weld (diagram 6). It is really a small circular lap joint formed by punching a hole about 1/4 inch to 3/8 inch in the top plate and welding in a circular motion through to the bottom plate filling the hole with weld. The end result is very similar in appearance to a spot weld but should correctly be referred to as a plug weld.

If you have succeeded so far you are well on your way to handling almost any welding job on your car but as with passing

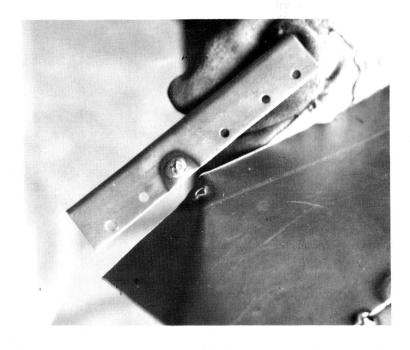

Test your practice pieces to destruction. Note that the weld has remained intact, while the metal has torn around it. This is what should happen!

your driving test, it is only after you've passed the test that you really learn to drive! Similarly now that you begin to tackle some real welding jobs you'll find all kinds of awkward situations will arise that no welding manual or book will have an answer for. Now it is up to you to master welding vertically, welding materials of unequal thickness, welding upside down underneath your car and so on. However, once you start to get the hang of it you will also find welding one of the most useful and rewarding skills you ever taught yourself. It won't be long before your MIG welder has paid for itself several times over, and you need never worry about your small Ford failing another M.O.T. test on corrosion! *(And now, back to Tommy).*

Tools

I won't bore you with great long lists of tools. The single most important item required apart from your welding equipment is an angle grinder. Although I find the idea of an exposed grinding disc spinning at 10,500 rpm extremely dangerous, the tool itself is indispensable.

Take great care when using an angle grinder. You need gloves and eye shields or goggles. Sparks from the grinder will damage glass such as windscreens. The spark or hot particle burns into the glass leaving a tiny black lump which you cannot get rid of. Be warned!

I once had a grinding disc disintegrate and it caught the back of my hand as it flew off. I still have a scar five years on, and at the time of the accident my hand swelled up to twice its size. You cannot be too careful with angle grinders.

Having sorted out your welding tactics it is now time to look at the various panels and how they can be made good.

FRONT END

Starting from the front of the car, the front panel is very important. Your whole car will be judged on the condition of the front panel, wings and bonnet. If you don't believe me, watch a group of people looking at a car. They always stand at the front for a long time -- just staring. Make a good impression and they get excited about your car. Make a mess of the front end restoration and you mess up the whole car.

Front panels tend to be very hard to obtain and hence very expensive. I've seen brand new front panels offered for the Cortina at over 450 pounds. I don't believe

Above: A well-rusted lower front panel on this early Cortina. It is also badly rusted round the left headlamp and this will require some delicate work if the purchase of an entire front panel is to be avoided.

Below: The rusty outer panel has been cut away and a new piece will be "let in." A new front chassis crossmember has been bought and welded in. This rebuilding of a panel can be very time-consuming but will save you an awful lot of money!

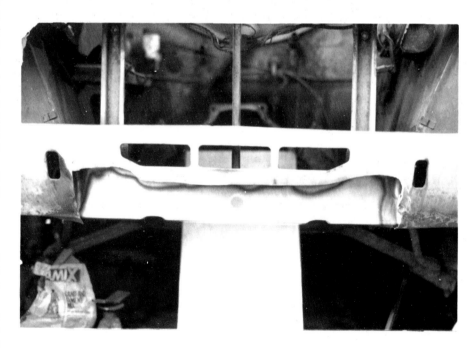

they are worth that sort of money so I always repair the one on the car. You can get a lower front valance for around 40 to 50 pounds and can patch any other damaged areas. Even quite difficult jobs can be tackled if you have the time and patience.

The photographs illustrate several front panels being repaired. The technique of fitting together lots of small pieces of steel to make up a complicated shape is known as "jig-sawing" and can be learnt. Once you have welded all the pieces into place use the angle grinder or a grinding wheel to

Body and Chassis

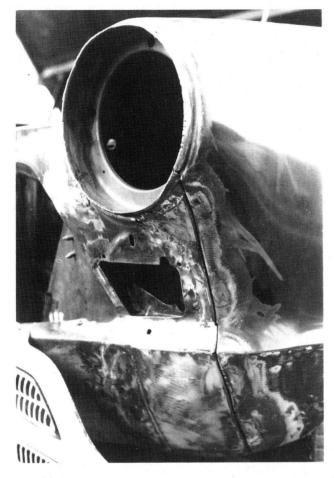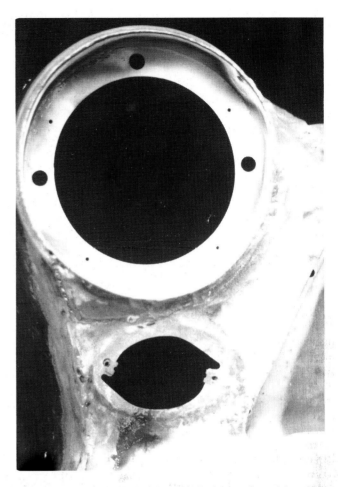

Left: This late type Cortina has had the outer six inches of the lower front panel replaced. Above that, small pieces of steel have been welded together to replace the rusted area below the headlamp. Right: A similar job on an early front panel. A new headlamp ring has been welded in. Some further work is needed with the angle grinder to smooth off the welds. I've been criticised for showing this type of job, but if you are working to a budget, as most people will be, you need to be aware of all the options. New panels are great if you can afford them, if you can't then try this "jig-sawing" method.

smooth off the working surface.

Lower front valances can be cut out and repaired with patches. These normally rust at the outside ends, where they meet the front wing, or in the centre. The corrosion at the centre is caused by the box section filling up with wet mud and rusting through. At the centre of the front valance (at the back of it) you will find a front panel closing plate which should have some holes in it. These holes are to allow the box-section to breath, but they are just the right size to let in mud and water. At the bottom there should be several drain slots, but these often become overloaded by dirt and just block up. It would pay you to keep these drain slots clear once you have repaired your front panel.

On later model Cortinas there is a complicated little box section used to mount the front sidelamps. This looks simple until you try to make one up. They

have little bits cut out and holes here and there. I don't know of anyone who makes these now, although Terry Burville of Panelcraft (Magor) made a batch some time ago. Because they are complicated they tend to very expensive for what they are. I'm sure if someone had a fresh look at the problem there would be a simple way round it. Some cars seem to rust around there while others don't.

Headlamp Panels

The Classic and Capri are notorious for rust around the front corners and head-lamp panel. Luckily there are a number of repair panels available through the owners club for these areas on the cars. Just above the lower part of the front panel is a small panel known as the headlamp panel shelf. On top of this panel sits the headlamp panel. Although at first glance these headlamp panels might seem easy to make,

they are really quite complicated. I've seen these being made for the owners club and they take a number of hours to make each panel. There are curves, changes of direction, little cut out bits for the shiny headlamp ring to locate to - they take a lot of making. If you are good with sheet metal you may be able to make a passable replica. If I tell you that Terry Burville has been making these for some six years and finds them a problem, don't say I didn't warn you. This is one of those panels you buy, leaving yourself time to tackle something you are capable of!

Sidelamp Panels

Again the Classic and Capri cause problems! The inner part of the sidelamp mounting is really an extension of the front quarter panel. The lamp is fixed to the front, then a sidelamp panel outer is fixed on. There are plenty of places where water

can get trapped and rust can form. Again all these panels are available through the club. Don't try to make these.

Body Front Crossmember

The body front crossmember can be bought from some of the suppliers listed in the Addresses section. You could try to make one, but it is yet again one of these jobs which look quite straightforward until you try to carry it out. The flat section of the panel can be made quite easily, as can the 90 degree lips at each end. The difficulty is in the folded-over part at the top and bottom. This would be easy enough if it were straight, but it isn't. It is shaped just enough to confuse the amateur restorer. I would elect to buy this panel and save some money elsewhere! Having bought it, it is then a relatively simple matter to clamp it in place and weld.

Headlamp Rings

These are the simple ring panels which weld into the front of the wing on Cortinas. As part of the headlamp bowl assembly they just rust away. Original ones are still available from time to time, and several people make replacement ones. At under ten pounds per side they are well worth replacing if you are doing any work in that area of the car. If you are handy with sheet metal then you could easily make these. Copy the old one!

Headlamp Bowls

These are included under the body chapter as they are originally made of steel and are fixed to the headlamp rings on Cortinas by self-tapping screws. If you fit new steel ones you need your head examining as plastic ones are freely available, certainly in the 7 inch sizes as used on all cars bar the Classic and Capri. There is no point fitting another steel one and have it rust again.

Top: The old crossmember has been partly cut away, as has the lower front valance.

Middle: The new crossmember welded in place. This panel should be well painted before fitting the new front valance. Note that the top strip of the old front valance has been left in place.

Bottom: The new lower front valance clamped in position prior to welding. In this example a continuous weld will be run across the sharp leading edge of the valance.

Above: The late type Cortina front panel has this curious assembly for mounting the sidelight cluster.

Below: These new sidelight mounting panels cost almost 20 pounds each, due to the work involved in making them.

A Classic gets a front-end rework. The headlamp panels are available through the owners club. The old headlamp panels are shown on top of the front panel. This area of the Classic and Capri are notorious for rust! (Photo: Maureen Salmon).

Above: The rusty old steel headlamp bowl and the plastic replacement. No further problems in that area!

A new headlamp panel for the Classic and Capri range. This is quite a complicated panel to make (correctly!) so it is better to buy these from the owners club and save some money elsewhere on the restoration.

Front Wings

Steel wings are now regularly available for the MK1 Cortina, as the owners club have had them re-manufactured. Other cars may have a problem. If you don't need a new wing then you may be able to repair the existing one. Rust is common at the front, round the headlamp, and at the bottom of the rear of the wing. Repair panels are available for both areas.

Wings can be repaired. There are a number of repair sections offered by clubs and suppliers. Care is needed with the welding as distortion can make a mess of a good repair. This then needs dollops of body filler to put right. The idea is maximum preparation and care and minimum filler! Specifically, the Cortina wing can have the front six inches replaced, and at the bottom, rear of the wing the lower six or so inches is available as a repair section.

Anglia wings in steel are in short supply, and I do not know of any source of re-manufactured wings. Repairs may be the only way out.

Classic and Capri wings were available as new ``oldstock'' but most of these have now been snapped up. Terry Burville made some for the owners club but while there was a stated demand for these they took a long time to sell.

The owners club now offer front of wing repair sections which extend about six inches from the front of the wing. These repair sections are then welded in place.

Corsair wings could be a big problem, as I know of no source of replacements. The owners club only re-manufacture a few items - but not wings - so owners will have to resort to looking around for a good second hand one or repairing the one on their car. One alternative is glass fibre. See below.

Prefect wings are also very scarce. Repair is going to be the only way to get this job done.

Making Wings

Wings can be made. As long as you have a good one to use as a pattern they can be made. The problem with making replacement wings commercially is two-fold. If the original die can be obtained then the wings can be stamped out quite easily on a big press. When I say "big" I mean something in the region of 50 to 200 tons. Not the sort of thing you will have in the shed. The MK1 Cortina Owners club were

Prior to fitting a new front panel and wing on his Anglia, Jeremy Tallett removed the old panel with hammer and chisel. What was underneath proves how well these cars were built. A bit of surface rust was cleaned off and repainted before the new front was welded on. (Photo: Jeremy Tallett).

A new Anglia front panel ready to be fitted. Note that the headlamp fixing ring forms part of the front wing. See photo above. New panels such as this are going to be harder and harder to find as time goes on. A cheaper alternative would be to repair your existing panel. (Photo: Jeremy Tallett).

able to have their wings made this way.

If no die is available they have to be built up by hand -- in other words a craftsman cuts large sections of flat panel steel, shapes them and welds them together to form a wing. More than twenty hours work is required by a skilled man to make one wing. So unless someone makes up a sizeable order of say, 10 pairs of wings, the individual is going to have to pay a high price for a new steel wing. Having helped to have Classic and Capri wings made I can tell you that not all the original ones were the same sizes! We measured a wing and worked out all the dimensions required. Later when we had a prototype wing we tried it on my car. It did not fit. We then measured some half a dozen assorted wings lying around in various stages of rust and decay and they were all different! There were also some "thick" ones and some "thin" ones, either indicating that they were made at different places or that tolerances were very lax. We finally arrived at a compromise figure and ten sets were successfully made.

NOTE: Only the Classic, Capri and Prefect have bolt-on wings. All the other cars covered by this book are welded on! This is important to remember as the design of the car will reflect how much strength is obtained from the wings. Where the wings bolt on, the remainder of the car must be stronger.

Glass Fibre Wings

Glass fibre wings are still available for the Classic, Capri Cortina, Corsair and Anglia. Some rear valances are also available. Look in the UK's weekly "Exchange & Mart" for advertisers of glass fibre. Some people swear by glass fibre. I never had much success with it. The problem is in fitting. I found that glass fibre wings would not fit whatever I did. I also had a rear valance which looked okay but I then found a second hand steel one and fitted that instead. The wings are still decorating the back of my shed somewhere from five years ago!

If you are tempted by glass fibre, make sure you check out the supplier. Ask around within the owners club. Make sure the supplier is offering a money-back guarantee.

I knew someone who had glass fibre wings on an old Morris Minor. It was a fabulous looking car and he used it every day. He had bought the wings from a local

Just one corner of Terry Burville's workshop. The bits of metal hanging on hooks are templates for various panels which Terry makes. There is a wing and a Lancia rear panel to the right of the photo. Dozens of metal profiles may have to be made during the development of a panel to be "re-manufactured." This costs time and money...

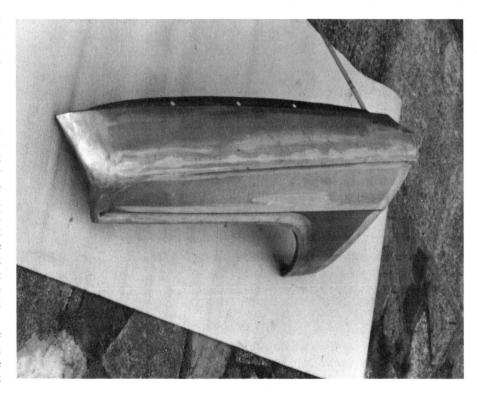

A re-manufactured wing for the Classic and Capri. Problems were encountered trying to find correct measurements for these wings as all the available samples were different!

manufacturer and they fitted perfectly. My friend had then stiffened the wings by using rolled up newspaper and lots of glass fibre resin to make stiffening "bars." He was delighted with his four wings.

INNER WINGS

Inner wings on all these cars can suffer badly from rust. I well remember seeing a smart-looking Classic in a scrap yard. I looked at it carefully yet could see nothing wrong with it. Thinking I had found a bargain, I asked the yard manager about it and he said it had been an M.O.T. failure, had been advertised in the local paper at 35 pounds and when no-one took it on, it ended up scrapped. The reason? The inner wings were completely rusted through! An enthusiast could have unbolted the outer wings, welded up the inner wings either by fabricating new patch-panels, or by purchasing some of the repair sections available through the owner's club, and had a really nice car. I plundered the car for spares for my Capri!

Anyway, inner wings can be repaired. Some repair panels and sections are available, see the lists at the end of the book.

Remember if welding inner wings that you have to be very careful of fire risks. What is on the inside of the panel you are welding?

Inner wing repair sections or re-manufactured inner wings are available for the Classic/Capri and the MK1 and MK2 Cortinas. The other cars in the range are going to have to be repaired, unless you have a fat wallet and are prepared to search around for new items. Repair seems the sensible course of action to me.

Sills

Ford sills tend to be nice and simple. There is an almost flat steel inner sill which runs the length of the outer sill. This often rusts so you should be expecting additional problems when you chisel off the outer sill.

This inner sill can be repaired locally (that is, in one or two small areas). If the problem is more widespread you will have to try and find a replacement. When that fails, as it probably will, you then measure up the inner sill and get your local sheet metal shop to make you one.

NOTE: The sills on the Classic, Capri and Corsair are not completely straight from front to back. They have a very slight

A front of wing repair section for the Cortina. These are available from several sources. Similar repair panels are available for the Classic and Capri. One of these panels is shown on the front cover of the book.

This sort of corrosion on the inner wing will almost certainly attract an M.O.T. fail. This example has already been plated -- but all that will have to be removed and a new top fitted with some extra steel between the existing patch and inner wing.

bow to them, so if you make up your own sills they will be difficult to fit. The sills available from the Classic and Capri club have this bow built into them.

There is also a reinforcing piece welded into the Classic/Capri sills, which is located at the bottom of the B-post. Some drain tubes also exist on the original Ford sill. Make sure any replacements you buy or make have plenty of drain holes drilled.

Here are some hot tips for working on sills, some of them found out the hard way.

over the last twenty-five years;

Only work on one sill at a time. Don't remove both sills in a burst of enthusiasm. Although small Fords are very strong and have an inner sill, you still run the risk of weakening or distorting the entire bodyshell.

Support the car with axle stands, as the sill provides a lot of strength.

Match the new sill against the old sill BEFORE cutting any steel. Make sure you have been sold the correct sill or that you know what modifications have to be done to make the sill fit correctly. When you are completely happy about the sill, carry on. Measure the gap between the bottom of the door and the sill for reference. You will need this measurement when you fit the new sill.

Remove the old sill. After you do this use a power tool such as an angle grinder to remove all the little welding tags on the inner sill which are left over from the chiselling operation. These tags are EXTREMELY sharp and can cause con-

Rotten A-post, rot in the inner wing flitch panel, rot along the top where the inner joins the outer wing, rot at the front end of the sill, and probable rot around the MacPherson strut tops. There's a couple of weekends of hard welding ahead!

Another Terry Burville special for the Cortina. This top of inner wing repair section has a generous four inches of inner wing -- enough to suit most cars already repaired in this area.

siderable damage to unprotected hands or arms.

Inspect the inner sill and all edges where the sill meets the floor, door pillar, etc. and where the sill meets the rear wheel arch. Allow plenty of time to do this repair work.

It pays off in the long run if you paint or protect the inner surface of the sill against future rust damage. Use a proprietary rust prevention compound. Finally finish off with a nice thick layer of underseal. Remember some of it will burn off during welding but you can always apply some more through suitable holes.

(If you have seat belt mountings, now is the time to check the threads of the big captive nuts welded into the inner sill. Make sure they are cleaned up and lightly lubricated to prevent future seizure).

Fasten the new sill in place with clamps, pop rivets or Mole Grips. Use as many clamps as possible. When you are absolutely sure that the sill is correctly located, go on to the next step.

Tack weld the sill in place. This involves welding the sill to the body every three or four inches. When you have tacked the sill in place, remove the clamps and try opening and closing the door. Now is the time to decide if the sill does not fit. Check the gap between the bottom of the door and the sill. If something is wrong -- fix it NOW!

When you are satisfied that the sill is fitted correctly, weld the rest of the sill in place.

When welding is complete, grind down any visible welds to tidy up the job.

Prime the sill as soon as you finish welding otherwise it will start to rust.

That only took a minute or two to read, but the actual job can take a very long time. I have never replaced a sill in the time I thought it would take me. There is always an unforeseen problem. Be warned!

If you fit new sills it pays to make drain holes in them to prevent any further build up of rust. You can drill a hole every so often to act as a drain, but I prefer the following method. If you have seam-welded the lower half of the sill, leave gaps of about half an inch every nine inches or so. Get your 1/4 inch blade, flat screwdriver and tap it in between the inner and outer sill. When you get the blade in about 1/4 inch twist the handle to force the two sheets of metal apart. If you repeat this process you will make slots just like on the original sills. Every six months or so, just stick a welding rod into the slots to make

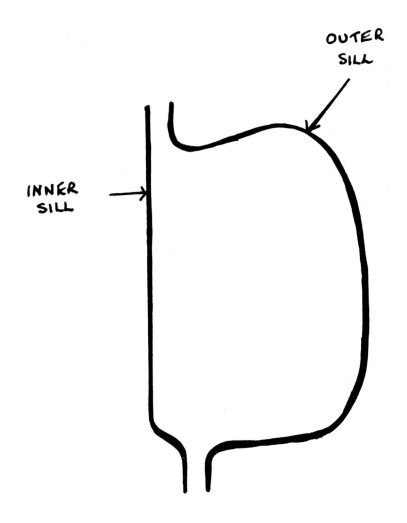

The inner and outer sills sketched to show their relative shapes. Note that the inner sill is basically a flat panel with a joggle or joddle at the bottom edge. This provides a lip for joining to the outer sill. On some outer sills, such as the Capri, there is a strengthening piece which bridges between the top and bottom of the outer sill.

sure they are clear. If the design of the car allows, you can drill holes at either end of the sill which can be closed off with rubber bungs. You can then take the bungs out once or twice a year, unblock the sill and apply new rust inhibitor.

INNER SILLS

If you find extensive rot in an inner sill there is little choice but to replace the entire section. This may sound daunting but can be accomplished with care and patience.

Measure the depth of the inner sill, and note that there is a joggle or ridge along the bottom edge. (See above diagram). Next measure the length of sill required. Don't measure and end up with something like 4 feet 6 and 7/8th inches. Get it made to 5 feet and cut off the extra! If you ask for an exact measurement you can be guaranteed that you have measured it wrongly and it will be too short! Well, that's what would happen to me!

This new length of inner sill can then be welded to the floor pan. It takes a lot of time and effort to do this job, but it can be done. I have done it at home on two cars. Remember a job like that could have been the reason the car was scrapped or sold off as an M.O.T. failure in the first place. If you got it cheap you should find out, why?

Floors

If there is one job I always make a mess of it is welding-in a floor pan section. If you think of a flat plate with a 90 degree lip on one side that is the sort of thing I'm talking about. Insert the above piece into a hole in the floor and clamp in place. Now the correct procedure is then to weld the lip onto the inner sill FIRST. I know that's what you are supposed to do but I always get it wrong for some reason and end up with a job I am less than satisfied with.

If you need large sections of floor pan, buy a new MK1 Escort floor pan. They currently cost under ten pounds from motor factors. With a bit of cutting and bending you can get them to fit. You might find if you are replacing a front floor pan section that there is an inconsiderate channel on the Escort floor pan which seems to foul the front outrigger. With a bit of metal bashing you can encourage this channel to flatten and allow the outrigger/jacking point to fit.

Never be afraid of a bit of vandalism. Most things can be achieved with sheet metal, and if this is your first attempt think how good things are going to turn out later as you build experience.

Boot and Bonnet

Boots and bonnets are normally available second-hand, and there are still some brand-new panels available. If your bonnet is rusted it will probably be along the front edge. If you cannot find a replacement, then you will have to weld (if you are very good) or fill with filler. The risk of distortion along the front edge of a boot or bonnet is very great. A cold repair using filler may be the best option. At the moment you may be able to acquire a better, or new panel. This situation will change rapidly over the next few years as all the old/new stock is used up.

For information about bonnet or boot badges, see the address section at the end of the book.

Spare Wheel Wells

The spare wheel well on all the small Fords tends to fill with water, so as you

This Anglia floor shows signs of requiring work! A couple of big holes decorate the floor while a lot of the paintwork looks discoloured due to rust. A new floor panel could be made up with the only difficulty being the X depression stamped into the panel. (Photo: Mark and Jill Bradbury).

carry a couple of pints around with you it helps the rust bug eat away at the well. When the panel gets so weakened from rust a hole develops and the water drains away. Then you have a period of time when the well rots slowly but does not fill with water.

When you repair or replace the well, make doubly sure that water can drain away.

Replacement wells are available for the Cortina, but they are not difficult to fabricate for any of the other models. Basically you have a large, almost flat sheet which has a straight top edge which meets the boot floor, and a curved lower edge which meets the bottom of the well. The bottom of the well is a flat sheet with a 90 degree lip which fastens onto the well side. Some other work is needed to blend the outer edge of the well bottom into the surrounding bodywork but this is not difficult. Since it is also not seen, you can afford to make a mistake here and get away with it!

MacPherson Strut Tops

Almost every small Ford around now will have had some welding done on the MacPherson strut tops on the inner wing. This is the favourite area for rust, but with a weekend set aside to do the repairs you

can chisel out all the old steelwork and weld in a new tower and inner wing top for around 25 to 30 pounds per side for parts plus welding materials.

The strut top will probably have already been plated. If not, you are very lucky. If it is already plated and has rusted again you may have a bigger problem than you think. The available inner wing tops for Cortinas, Corsairs, Classics and Capris have a certain amount of metal on the repair section. This is fine for first-time repairs, but for subsequent repairs there may not be enough steel to meet up with sound steel on your inner wing. In other words, the repair section is not large enough. On most of the small Fords you are going to have to make up some sort of bridging section to join the repair section with the inner wing. This need not be a problem if you think the job through.

Anglia owners are catered for by L.M.C. Panels of Westbury, Wilts. See the addresses section at the end of the book.

Cortina owners may still be able to purchase a special repair section made by Terry Burville of Panelcraft (Magor) which included a generous four inches of the top of the inner wing. (If you need five inches this can be stated at the time of ordering). These panels are shown in the photographs.

ABOVE: The type of inner wing repair panel shown on page 89 has been welded in position on this car. Great accuracy is needed in cutting away the old wing to get a close fit with the new panel. If you don't get it right you will be left with a gap between the old and the new which will be awkward to repair. Measure three times, cut once!

OPPOSITE PAGE, TOP: The MacPherson strut tower repair welded in place. The welding was done by gas in this example, but you could use MIG or even a spot welder if it had long enough arms! The welds now need to be ground down with an angle grinder. This stage of the job always looks worse than it is. The inner wing may need to be dressed with hammer and dolly after all the heat from a gas welding torch. It will look a lot better when it is painted.

OPPOSITE PAGE, BOTTOM: Looking up the tower the two verticals and the top are held in place with clamps, prior to welding. The car is on its side at the point. This makes jobs like this much easier to do. It is also easier because there is no outer wing to get in the way. This is the author's 1965 G.T. Cortina being restored.

These need a fair bit of fitting to get them lined up properly, but the photograph shows what can be achieved.

MacPherson Strut Towers

This section should be read in conjunction with the last section as one goes with the other. It will be an extremely rare car that has rust damage on the MacPherson strut top and no rust on the top of the underwing towers.

Replacements are available for the Cortina and Corsair. The Classic and Capri have a slightly different arrangement and panels are available from the owners club. Anglia and Prefect owners are going to have to fabricate panels for their cars.

The photographs show the problems being tackled on the Cortina. There is little choice but to totally remove the top of the strut tower. This means detaching it from the top panel and you will be very lucky indeed if you don't find rust on both. I use a four inch chisel and a two pound hammer. A sharp chisel soon makes "dismantling" easy.

You don't have to replace all of the vertical sections of the strut tower. Clean off all the paint, underseal and rust, and find where the rust stops, working from the top downwards. When you find clean sound steel, mark a line two inches below that point. That is your cutting point.

Chisel off or gas cut the top off the old verticals.

When all the old steel is removed, go over the area with an angle grinder if you have one or a grinding stone in an electric drill. Get rid of as many sharp edges as you can. Really spend some time getting the job tidy. It will pay off when you come to assemble all the new bits.

On the top pan you have three holes which will locate the pan with the original top panel. I use a couple of bolts to hold the two together. Next I align the verticals. I normally overlap the new vertical without cutting anything off it. I find this helps to get a better alignment.

Clamp things in place with as many clamps as you can lay hands on. You will need, at the very least, four. One for each vertical and one each side clamping the vertical to the top pan.

When you are satisfied with the line up -- and ONLY when you are fully satisfied, reach for the welding equipment.

I normally tack weld all the bits in place, so that I can remove the clamps. This gives you more room to see what you are doing plus gives you a second chance to confirm that everything is aligned properly.

NOTE: You have a choice at this point. Rush on and weld without being happy about the alignment. If you have a conscience it will bother you for all the time you own the car. The alternative is to take five minutes and satisfy yourself that it is properly aligned. It is a major suspension component after all and you don't want to have an accident.

When you are happy with everything, seam weld all the joints. Yes, I know it is a lot of work, but it can be done quite quickly, certainly within an hour or so.

One point that most people overlook is the reinforcing ring welded on to the underneath of the pan on the Cortina and on the top on the Corsair, Classic, Capri and Anglia.

It takes a bit of effort to remove this from the original top pan, as it is spot welded on in about a dozen places. A hammer and sharp chisel is the best way, followed by a session of hammering the ring flat again. You may be able to tackle this job by drilling out the spot welds. This will be easier than the hammer and chisel method, but you then have to weld up the holes again. Whichever way you tackle it, it is well worth the effort to get the job right. When all is completed, spend some time dressing the inner wing with hammer and dolly. You will have caused some distortion when welding the vertical to the inner wing. This needs to be put right. A small amount of body filler may be needed in extreme cases, but normally with a little time and effort you can dress away most of the lumps and dips.

One last note about MacPherson strut towers. If buying these parts, for example at an autojumble, remember that the MK2 Cortina's strut towers are very similar to the MK1 (I believe they can be interchanged) but the pan has a much larger hole on the MK2. The larger hole is for the larger suspension unit top mounting. It is very easy to buy parts which look right until you get them home and make comparisons.

Continued on Page 96.

ABOVE: The Classic and Capri's MacPherson strut is a bit different to the Cortina. This one has rusted where the MacPherson strut shroud meets the inner wing. Both parts can be repaired with panels usually available through the owners club. (Photo: Maureen Salmon).

BELOW: This is a new (re-manufactured) MacPherson strut shroud for the Classic and Capri. This one is a "near-side" panel, but you should be able to see how they fit into the inner wing by referring to the photo above.

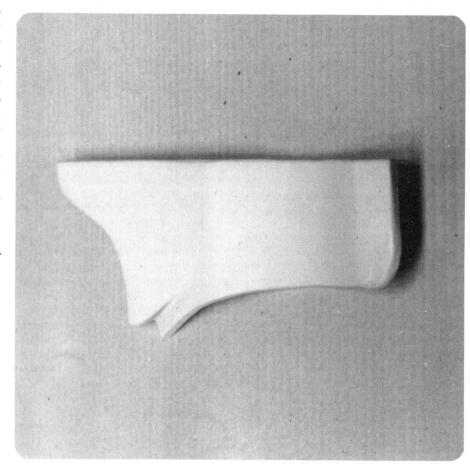

RIGHT: This is the rear wheel well, looking forwards. Rust often makes a hole here, and this patch is being clamped in place prior to welding. An outer wheel arch repair panel will be fitted next.

BELOW: This area of the inner wing often develops a rust hole. In this photo I have used a drilling technique to find the extent of the rust. I expand the area with drilled holes until I find sound steel. Then chisel from hole to hole. Cut a patch to fit and you will find that the patch will sit almost flush with the remaining panel, while being supported by the little tags of steel left by the chiselling. It is then a simple job to weld it in place, then grind off excess welds.

Rear Valances

Rear valances can be patched so that you will not know a repair has been done. Cut out the damaged area and weld in some new. Remember that you do not have to weld all the repair in at once. In other words you can make up a complicated shape from several smaller pieces.

Rear valances are regularly available in steel or glass fibre for Cortinas, Anglias, Classics and Capris. Corsair owners are not so lucky.

If you are working with steel valances, there is a difficult section where the rear bumper bracket bolts onto the rear chassis leg. This is quite a complex little area and foxed me for quite some time. The best way I have found to tackle this is to do a little bit at a time. So for example I would do the large flat area against which the bumper bracket fits, first. When this is done, let in small strips of steel to form the shaped part of the valance. The photographs should make this clear.

When everything is welded, go over all the joins with an angle grinder to finish off. It should be possible to achieve an invisible mend.

ABOVE: Rear valance rust damage can be seen at the right hand side of this car. The rust has eaten the valance away as far as the petrol tank filler. This damaged area can be cut out and repaired as described in the text and following photos.

This panel may be a candidate for buying, thus saving you a lot of time and frustration trying to make something you are not yet capable of.

Doors

There are basically three choices for door repairs. Either acquire a newer, better door than the one you have, or acquire a new door skin (they're getting quite scarce now), or patch the bottom of the door skin. This could be done "cold" with glass fibre, or "hot" by welding.

There are still a few new doors around. You have to seek them out at autojumbles or through the owners club magazine.

Door skins tend to be quite scarce but if you can get them they will often provide the best answer to the problem. It means the door has to be resprayed but you have the satisfaction of knowing that the job has been done well and should last a long time with some sensible protection like paint and underseal.

Patching a door skin is fraught with difficulties. The problem is that the bottom of a door is really a large, unsupported area of flat steel. This will tend to distort quite badly if you heat it by welding. Let's look at a cold repair first.

Clean off all the rust and flaky paint from the damaged area. This area will probably grow as you work! When you are certain that you have worked back to sound steel examine the area you are left to repair. If it is an excessively large area you are going to have to consider a replacement door, new skin or a welded patch.

If the job can be tackled with glass fibre, buy a glass fibre repair kit. The sort of kit you want contains a tin of resin, powder and sheets of glass fibre mat. You will also need a small paint brush to apply resin with.

Clean and roughen the inside of the area to be repaired. This means rub off any surface rust and score the area with the sharp end of a file or screwdriver. You need

Body and Chassis

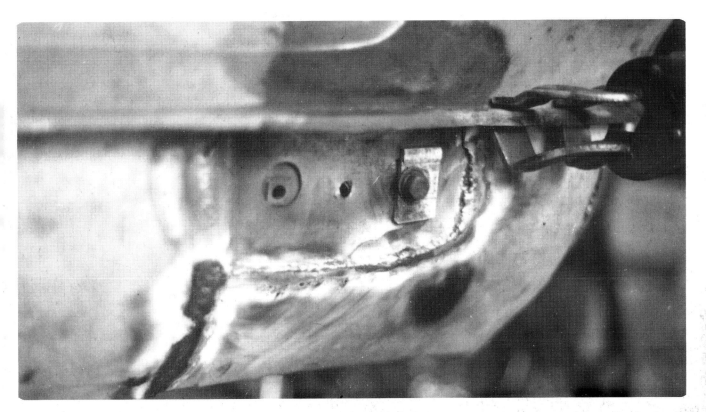

ABOVE: A new piece of steel has been welded in from the middle of the valance to a convenient point at the bumper mounting bracket. This only needs the welds smoothing off with an angle grinder. The next biggest piece of steel runs from the extreme right hand edge, where it meets the rear corner, to the new piece in the middle. Where it meets the bumper bracket shape, it has to be coaxed into the required shape with hammer and welding torch.

BELOW: A close-up shot of the same area, showing more detail of the welding. Note the panel is located by the welding clamp, while the piece on the bumper bracket is held by a bolt, washer and piece of scrap. Finish with angle grinder, undercoat and paint. In a year or so you will have forgotten you had a problem in this area!

to provide a good key for the resin to bond to.

Apply resin to the area to be patched. It needs to be at least a couple of inches wider all round than the damaged area.

Soak a piece of matting in resin. Apply the matting to the resin on the door. If the matting shows signs of bulging out, push it back in place and ensure that there is plenty of resin to keep it bonded to the steel. Leave to set.

Next mix up some glass fibre filler and apply it to the front of the repair area. Smooth it off with a plastic strip. If required, build up a deep area with several layers of filler, allowing each to set before applying the next.

When all this has set, smooth it off, first with a coarse body file if you have one, or a sanding machine with coarse paper in. The idea is to get the shape approximately right as quickly as possible, followed by a lot of effort to get a smooth finished surface which matches the contour of the door being repaired.

There are usually some instructions in these glass fibre repair kits, so if in doubt read these instructions.

When all is complete, spray over the area

ABOVE: Another car, another rear valance. This one has had the left hand end of the rear valance replaced. It has been repaired in conjunction with a new spare wheel well which has been fabricated. The plug welds will be ground, then the groove filled with body filler. Note the aircraft-type fasteners (available from Frost Restoration Techniques Ltd) holding the new rear wing panel in position.

BELOW: A similar rear valance on the Corsair can be dealt with in the same way. This one has been repaired, finished with the grinder and spray painted. (Photo: Alex Gooding).

with a tin of aerosol grey primer. This will show up any faults in your repair (if you need to do any more filling, do it now!) and will protect any bare metal on the repaired area. The door should now be ready for respraying.

Door Corner Repair

Terry Burville has experimented with door patch panels which aim to reduce distortion. His repair panel has a pre-formed half inch lip on the bottom and front (or rear) edge of the patch and a wide groove is sunk in the patch panel. This tends to stiffen the panel and will reduce distortion. Take care to align the bottom and side edges correctly. Great care must be taken to get this right. When they are aligned, clamp in place then braze them in a couple of places to the door frame. I made a mistake on the first one I tried and just clamped the edge to the door frame. During the welding the panel "crept" away from the correct alignment and needed a lot of work to correct. Make sure you braze or spot weld this bit FIRST! When you are happy with that edge, turn your attention to the join with the door skin.

This needs to be clamped too, and the best thing for an overlap join are some aircraft-type fasteners which need a small hole drilled through both pieces of steel.

When this is done, make a few welds along the seam. Leave to cool, and I mean leave to cool, for five minutes or so, then make some more short welds. No more than half an inch at a time. Leave to cool. Repeat the process until the seam is welded. Finish with an angle grinder and dress with hammer and dolly if required.

Any competent sheet metal shop can make this "Burville panel" up for you. The photograph shows you what you need.

Door Skins

I hesitate to advise you to fit your own door skins. The problems are many. First, if you have got one it has probably cost you 50 pounds or more. Secondly, if you try to fit it yourself and make a mess of it you will be pretty unhappy, and thirdly it is not as simple as it might appear!

You can quite happily remove most of the old door skin. Use an angle grinder and grind along the edges of the skin. This will separate the skin from the folds over the door frame and most of the skin will then be loose.

At the top of the skin it may be brazed to

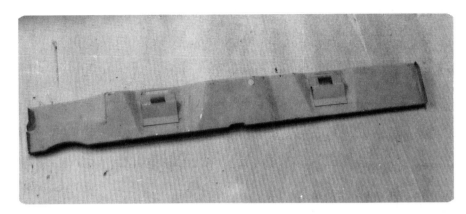

ABOVE, This odd-shaped panel is the inner rear valance for the Classic and Capri. One of the main functions of this part is to locate the ends of the petrol tank supporting straps which run under the tank. This is a club re-manufactured item.

ABOVE: An experimental repair panel for door corners. The bottom and front edges have a half inch lip which folds over the door frame. The curved portion has a half inch wide surface for joining, (underneath), the existing door skin. This should be held by aircraft-type fasteners prior to welding. There is also a half inch wide groove to stiffen the repair section where it will be welded. This aims to reduce distortion.

the door frame. This is where it starts to get tricky. Before removing any braze on the old skin look closely at the NEW skin to see what arrangements have been made for fitting in this area. If you are sure that the new skin can be fitted, then remove the braze either by angle grinder if you can get access to it, or by heat from a welding torch.

If you get all the old skin off, be extremely careful fitting the new one. It can easily be damaged and you are going to be very unhappy if you fit the new skin only to find a dent due to your mistake.

My advice is, find an expert prepared to fit the skin for you and do something else which you can do without getting into trouble!

Wheel Arches

Wheel arch repairs present their own problems, the main one being that you have to form a simple curve in the steel. To do this, use any sort of round former which will help you create the shape. Telephone poles, dustbins, beer barrels etc. all have useful shapes. Don't forget that an old

Chapter Six

wheel and tyre might have a very similar shape to the required wheel arch! Try to get the shape as near correct as possible, as it will result in a neater job. Once again weld only clean steel, and do not risk distortion by welding too long in one area.

Wheel arch repair panels are available for the Cortina, and may be available for some of the other cars in the range. Ring round the suppliers listed at the back of the book.

When fitting a wheel arch panel you can either use a butt weld, where the old and new panels are cut so that there is a gap of about a sixteenth of an inch. This gap is where the weld goes. You can also arrange for an overlap joint. Make sure that the new panel goes UNDER the old one otherwise the repair will attract water and just rust out again.

If you can't find a repair panel for your model, refer to the L.M.C. Panels' illustration showing the curved sections they make. You may be able to adapt something from their range to fit your car.

Chassis Patching

If you decide that you have to apply a patch to a section of chassis, there are some very old, established guidelines available for this type of job. Bear in mind that these were intended for very heavy, old fashioned chassis, and not 1960s Fords. They are worth repeating, though.

The patch should not be cut out as a rectangle. Instead, the top edge of the patch should be shorter than the bottom. The recommended angle between the bottom edge and the side edge is 60 degrees. Only the top and bottom edges of the patch should be welded otherwise a stress is built into the area and cracks could result later.

Repairing a crack in a chassis section is not too difficult. Try to establish the cause of the crack though, to avoid it happening again. Some small Fords, such as the MK1 Cortina, used to crack where the steering box was mounted. I know, one of them was mine!

Anyway, the crack will often start from a bolt hole or some other fitment. Clean off the entire area so that you can see the extent of the damage. Next, drill a small (say 1/8th inch) hole at the end of the crack. This will stop it spreading any further.

When you are sure of the extent of the crack, weld the hole and the crack. Finish off the job by grinding the weld to tidy it up. Rust proof the area, prime and paint.

The Burville panel, described on the previous page, welded to a door. The main problem encounted on this first, experimental panel was that I did not fasten the panel to the door frame tightly enough. It probably should have been brazed just to keep it in place. Otherwise the repair panel should be successful.

ABOVE: These wheel arch repair sections are available for several small Fords. This one has been modified by setting a half inch "joggle" along the edge indicated. A joggle or joddle is a lip formed to go under or over another panel. In this case the lip MUST go under to keep water and rust out. The panel will then be fastened in place by a number of aircraft-type fasteners. (See photo, page 98). Doing this will minimise distortion.

Gutters

Gutters tend to give trouble on the Classic and Capri. On my Capri they rotted out at several points. It is probably to do with the heavy chrome strips which go over the gutter. These trap moisture in between the surfaces and the result is inevitable.

Pic 645

ABOVE: A common problem is rusting at the front of the inner wing, caused by the bumper brackets trapping water. In this shot the rust has been cut away, the area is about to be painted, and some oil will be applied to the captive nuts which locate the anti-roll bar. (Make sure the threads are okay before welding a patch in place!).

LEFT: The patch held in place by a bolt and a welding clamp. Some tack welds will next be applied before dressing the patch to match the ridges on the inner wing. When this job is complete and the bumper bracket bolted in place, make sure the rust cannot begin again!

PAGES 102 AND 103.

Page 102 shows the panels which make up the engine compartment of the Corsair. In the lower illustration the floor and members are shown. These drawings are useful in that they show how all the bits fit together if you are new to the vehicle.

Page 103 shows the same panels for the Anglia. If you can buy a parts book on the second-hand market all these drawings will be available to you during your restoration.

(Both illustrations courtesy of the Ford Motor Company).

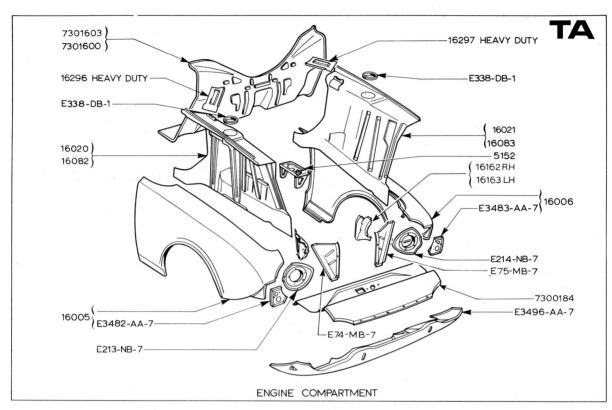

7301603
7301600

16296 HEAVY DUTY

E338-DB-1

16020
16082

16005
E3482-AA-7

E213-NB-7

16297 HEAVY DUTY

E338-DB-1

16021
16083

5152

16162 RH
16163 LH

E3483-AA-7   16006

E214-NB-7
E75-MB-7

7300184

E3496-AA-7

E74-MB-7

ENGINE COMPARTMENT

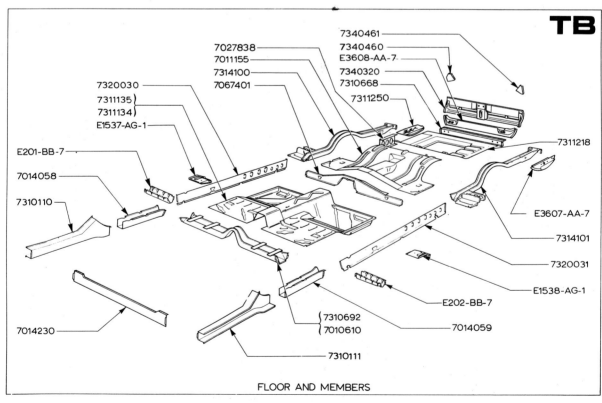

7027838
7011155
7314100
7067401

7320030
7311135
7311134
E1537-AG-1

E201-BB-7

7014058

7310110

7014230

7340461
7340460
E3608-AA-7
7340320
7310668
7311250

7311218

7310692
7010610

7310111

7311218

E3607-AA-7

7314101

7320031

E1538-AG-1

E202-BB-7

7014059

FLOOR AND MEMBERS

Body and Chassis

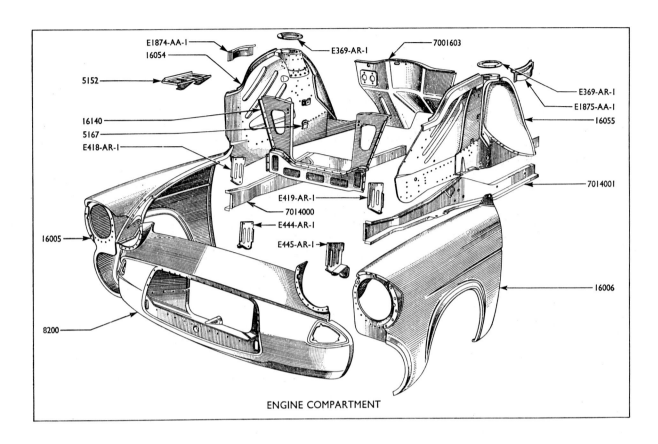

E1874-AA-1
16054
5152
16140
5167
E418-AR-1
16005
8200

E369-AR-1
7001603
E369-AR-1
E1875-AA-1
16055
7014001
E419-AR-1
7014000
E444-AR-1
E445-AR-1
16006

ENGINE COMPARTMENT

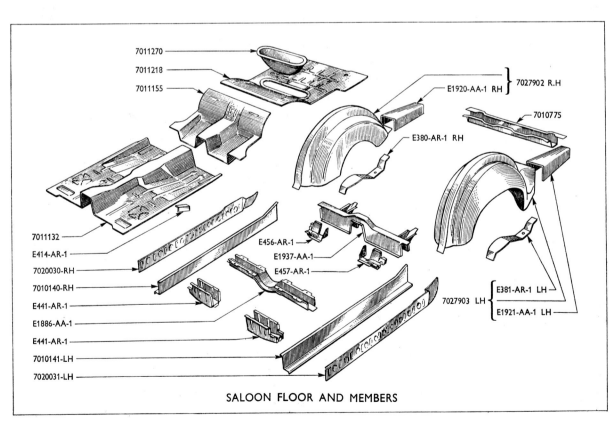

7011270
7011218
7011155
7011132
E414-AR-1
7020030-RH
7010140-RH
E441-AR-1
E1886-AA-1
E441-AR-1
7010141-LH
7020031-LH

E1920-AA-1 RH
7027902 R.H
7010775
E380-AR-1 RH
E456-AR-1
E1937-AA-1
E457-AR-1
7027903 LH
E381-AR-1 LH
E1921-AA-1 LH

SALOON FLOOR AND MEMBERS

It is quite a simple job to get a strip of guttering made up. Ask your sheet metal shop to make a length of U-shaped steel to the required length. Measure your gutter to get the dimensions of the sides of the "U".

The "U" shape has to be slightly spread open to match the gutter on the car. This can be done once the welding has been done. Grind off all the old gutter, leaving just the bald roof. Locate one end of the gutter against the roof and get an assistant to hold in position while you apply a couple of small tack welds.

The problem is welding it in place. Pay very careful attention the line of the gutter. Once you have ground the old gutter off it is very easy to make a mistake and get this job completely wrong. I know, because I did! Remember too that when you weld the roof section you must take steps to protect or remove the headlining material which can easily catch fire.

The sketches show what you need to get made up by the local sheet metal shop. There should be no great difficulty with this item. When the gutter is welded on you then need some flat steel to make up

the chrome mounting part of the gutter. I made this from about three different pieces, welded them in place and then smoothed everything off with the angle grinder.

On my car there was an added complication of a rust hole in the roof, just above the gutter. This had to be patched. Having done that job I then filled the area with glass fibre filler and smoothed everything off. However a few weeks later all the filler fell out! No, I don't know why and I have not got round to sorting it all out again. These things happen sometimes.

REAR CHASSIS LEGS

Rear chassis legs are available for the Cortina, Anglia and Corsair. The Classic and Capri owners' club also had a batch of these made up. There is quite a bit of work

involved in welding these in, as you have to remove the rear spring shackle. Then some hammer and chisel work is involved, after making doubly sure you have measured the joining point on the original chassis leg.

With the old chassis leg removed, clean up all the surfaces with an angle grinder or grinding stone. One little tag of steel or one spot weld not rubbed down can cause the new panel to fit badly. Spend some time getting this stage right.

Offer up the new chassis leg. With a bit of luck and some wiggling around it should fit into place. When you are satisfied that it is correctly aligned (make sure!) make some tack welds to hold the leg in position. Make another check to ensure alignment, then weld the leg in.

That only took a minute or two to read. The reality is a bit different. Allow at least four or five hours for this task. Unless you

Body and Chassis

ABOVE: A Corsair Cabriolet having its sills attended to. On this conversion an extra box section is welded-in against the inner sill, inside the car to strengthen the bodyshell. In this shot the new outer sill has been welded in place and is awaiting final welding and finishing. Note that some welding is usually required round the bottom of the A-post when fitting a sill.

BELOW: The old outer sill has been removed and the damage is surveyed. The edge which can be seen above the line of the bottom of the sill is actually the floor panel. The floor panel has a half inch lip used for welding to the inner sill. This is no five minute job so don't get carried away with enthusiasm if the job is beyond you! (Photos: Liz and Ray Checkley).

ABOVE: Mike Pratt's Crayford converted MK1 Cortina in the process of being restored. Here the convertable's roof mechanism can be seen. The near-side rear wheel arch appears to show signs of rust and a repair may well be needed in this area. Other body panels appear to be in good condition. In the background is Mike's Lotus Cortina under wraps.

BELOW: Mike's Crayford again, this time showing the common rust problem where the driver's side floor meets the front chassis outrigger. This area will need repairing and one solution may be to fit a modified Escort floorpan. The outrigger/jacking point is available from several sources. The photo also shows the re-inforcing box section welded in on the inside of the inner sill. This strengthens the bodyshell which is now minus a roof!

Curved Angle Section

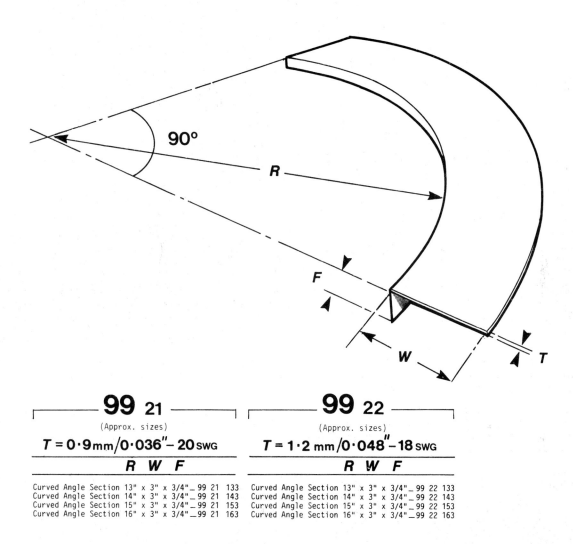

99 21				99 22		
(Approx. sizes)				(Approx. sizes)		
$T = 0.9$ mm/$0.036''$ – 20 SWG				$T = 1.2$ mm/$0.048''$ – 18 SWG		
R	**W**	**F**		**R**	**W**	**F**

Curved Angle Section 13" x 3" x 3/4"– 99 21 133		Curved Angle Section 13" x 3" x 3/4"– 99 22 133
Curved Angle Section 14" x 3" x 3/4"– 99 21 143		Curved Angle Section 14" x 3" x 3/4"– 99 22 143
Curved Angle Section 15" x 3" x 3/4"– 99 21 153		Curved Angle Section 15" x 3" x 3/4"– 99 22 153
Curved Angle Section 16" x 3" x 3/4"–99 21 163		Curved Angle Section 16" x 3" x 3/4"–99 22 163

ABOVE: Another brilliant idea from LMC Panels. These pieces of curved angle section could be adapted for all sorts of repairs such as wheel arch sections. Also in the LMC catalogue are channel (chassis) sections, straight angle sections, sheet steel and plastic headlamp bowls in 7 inch size. Steel bowls in 5-3/4 inch size are also available. (Copyright illustration reproduced by kind permission of LMC Panels).

have the car on its side, you are lying underneath working above your head. This is uncomfortable, dirty and unpleasant. Few people enjoy it. However, doing a job like this yourself and getting it right is a major confidence booster during a restoration. It is also a major test of your welding skills.

If you think it is beyond you, do the labouring work and get someone else to weld it in.

Chassis Outriggers

Front chassis outriggers which include the jacking point are available for the Cortina, Corsair, Classic and Capri.

On the Cortina and Corsair they consist of a piece of top hat (three sided box section) where the fourth side is made up of the floor of the car. The jacking point consists simply of a hole. The jack locates into the hole when jacking up the car. Some internal reinforcing of the chassis section may be included.

On the Classic, Capri and Anglia the box section is much bigger, and the jacking point consists of a steel tube parallel to the road. The jack is inserted into this hole. An MGB jacking point can be adapted to fit Classics and Capris (I know because I have done it) and it is probable that it can be made to fit the Anglia, although I have not tried this myself.

Centre outriggers usually consist of a section of ``Top Hat''. That is a ``U''shaped section of steel with half inch mounting flanges on both legs of the ``U''. You can buy these from motor factors or get any sheet metal shop to fold up a length if you supply a sample or accurate measurements.

Much of the advice given above for the rear chassis leg fitting applies to outriggers also.

Spring Mountings

The rear spring mountings on the Cortina are really box sections with rein-

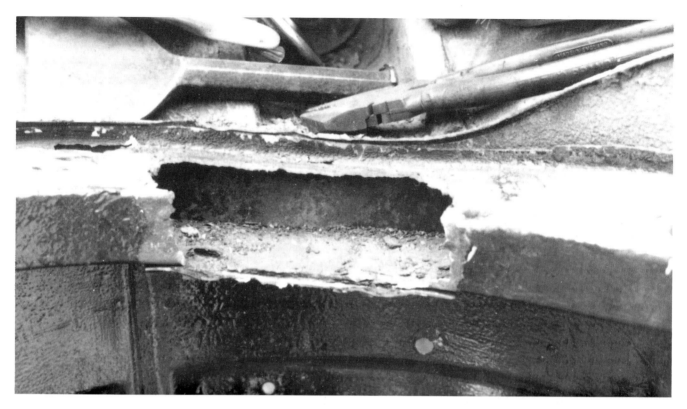

ABOVE: This is the rear chassis, above the rear axle. The re-inforcing box has rusted away and taken a section of the chassis with it. Here the chassis is being cut back to sound metal. Because there is only localised damage to the chassis on the left of the big hole, it was decided to fit an overlapping patch. A copy of the shape required was cut out of paper, transferred to card and then to steel.

BELOW: The steel patch is offered up to the car for a trial fitting. At the front (right hand side of the photo) there is an overlap of about an inch. On the other side the overlap extends about four or five inches. Because the steel is curved the hammered-over lip has these distinctive kinks. These will disappear as welding is done and they are encouraged away with a small hammer!

forced holes in them. They can be repaired conventionally. However, the Classic and Capri have different mountings which consist of ``ears'' welded onto the chassis. That's the best description I can come up with! See the photograph. No-one makes these (to the best of my knowledge) but they could mean the difference between a car being scrapped and a car being restored and kept alive. You could make new ones!

The technique involves making paper patterns of the mountings, then when you have got these right make cardboard patterns, then steel ones. The mounting itself needs lots of steel in the areas where it meets the floor of the car.

This is no simple job. The car has to be jacked up and supported, the carpets lifted to avoid fire when welding underneath and the springs either removed or undone at the front mounting. I have done this job, but was not happy with the result. If I ever weld on the floorpan of this car again I will re-do this part of the work. I recommend you get some help.

One last word on this. A problem like this could be the reason the car is being scrapped. The previous owner might have had a fright when he asked for an estimate for doing the job. It might be an opportunity for you to get an otherwise good car very cheaply. However, don't go into this with your eyes shut. Be well aware of the problems involved and weigh up all the angles before you jump in. Be warned!

Fabricating

Occasionally, you will need to make up a repair section from several pieces of steel. If the shape is complex, and cannot be folded in a machine, then cut out a paper template for each part of the repair panel. Measure up and when the paper shape is correct, transfer to card, then steel.

Cut out the steel pieces and try them against the original. Next, tack weld the pieces together in the required shape, and offer them up to the car. If the shape is correct, complete the welding operation off the vehicle. Take your time and don't concentrate too much heat on any one area, otherwise distortion will result.

Miscellaneous Patching

If you patch an area which might be seen, or if you are very particular and want to disguise a line of weld, then you can sink it. This is done with a hammer and a special dolly known as a shrinking dolly.

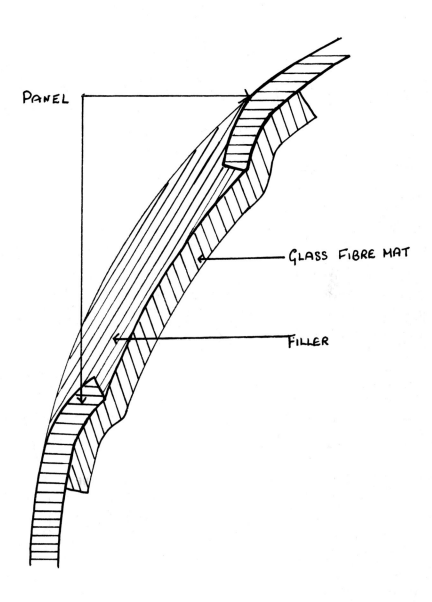

The basic "cold" repair, using glass fibre mat, resin and body filler. If the area of the repair is too large, then the mat will tend to sag under the weight of the resin. You may need to support the matting until the resin sets hard. Follow the instructions supplied with the glass fibre repair kit.

This type of dolly consists of a block of steel with a groove cut in one face. If the groove is placed below the steel with the weld in the middle of the groove and parallel to it, the weld can be hammered down below the level of the panels. The depth to sink is about 3/16 inch. The groove formed can be filled with lead or plastic filler depending on your skill.

Small to medium sized patches should be dished if possible, so that their centres are at a slightly lower level than the edges. This is because the welding process, even if carried out to avoid distortion, will cause the patch to ``rise'' and expand. The result will be a patch which is much neater and does not bulge.

Curved Patches

So far, we have only looked at straight line repair panels. But what happens if you need a curve? For example you might want to weld in a patch between the wheel arch and the floor. For this you need a piece of steel bent at 90 degrees. One side is welded to the floor, the other to the wheel arch. But the wheel arch is curved. What can you do? The simple, time-honoured way is to cut some ``Vs''in the side to be welded to the floor. This allows the other side to be bent to the required shape. However there is another way. Spread the metal with a hammer as described below for the compound curve. If you want to bend the vertical side, hammer the horizontal side and vice versa.

This will give you a nice smooth curve. Try it on a piece of scrap and you will get the idea in just a few minutes. Once you have tried it this way, you will find it makes a neater job than using ``Vs''. The nice smooth curve is the one to use.

It is also quite easy to make a compound curve. If you hammer a piece of steel it will expand and get thinner. Rolling can be done with expensive equipment, but for our purposes we are going to hammer. Try the following experiment. Take a small piece of scrap steel about three or four inches square. Fold a 90 degree lip of about 1/4 inch. Now, with your panel beating hammer repeatedly strike the area of the 1/4 inch lip. After a time, depending on how hard and how frequent your blows are, the lip will expand and get thinner, but the larger area of the steel will start to bend. If you kept on hammering you could almost make a semi-circle. Once again this is difficult to put into words, but it only takes a few minutes to learn.

Now having proved to you that you can do it, the next step is to appreciate that you have made a curve in one direction only. What you want is a piece of steel with a shape like the curves on a football. From any point on the surface, each curve moves in many directions, to give you a ball-shape. The rear valance has a compound curve at each end. It is difficult to make this shape unless you make it in two (or even three) pieces. Cut the required piece of steel. Make a right angled turn of about 1/4 inch. Start to hammer the lip with your panel hammer. As the metal stretches, a curve will form. Keep on checking the shape of the curve against the original or pattern. (Once again, let me remind you -

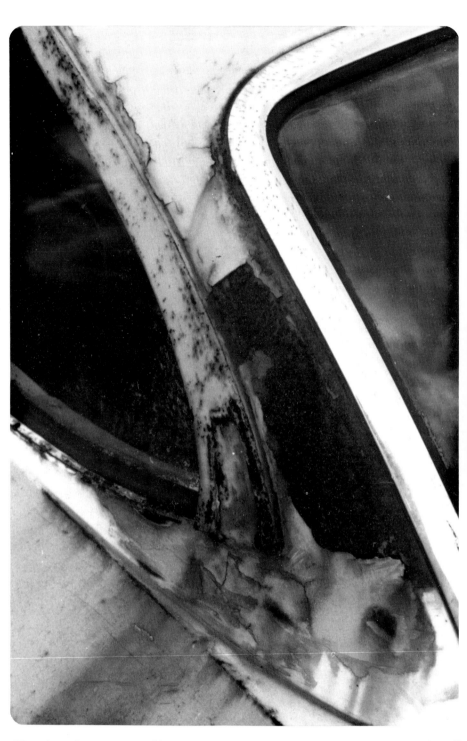

Attempt number one at repairing the gutters on my Capri. The welding went okay, but all the aluminium-based body filler fell out leaving this ugly mess. Must get round to finishing it off again...

NEVER throw away any body parts, no matter how rusty, until you have completed the repair or replaced the part with a new one).

Keep on checking until you have got the curve right. Once you have got the first part of the curve right, make up another

OPPOSITE PAGE: LMC Panels of Westbury, Wiltshire offer a good range of pressed-steel replacement panels for small Fords. Shown is the range for the Corsair, and MK1 and MK2 Cortinas. (Copyright Illustration reproduced by kind permission of LMC Panels).

Body **and** Chassis

Ford
Corsair

30 30

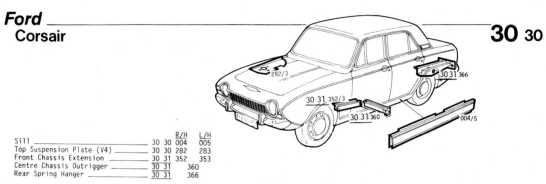

Sill		R/H	L/H
Sill	30 30	004	005
Top Suspension Plate (V4)	30 30	282	283
Front Chassis Extension	30 31	352	353
Centre Chassis Outrigger	30 31	360	
Rear Spring Hanger	30 31	366	

Cortina Mk1
1962-66

30 31

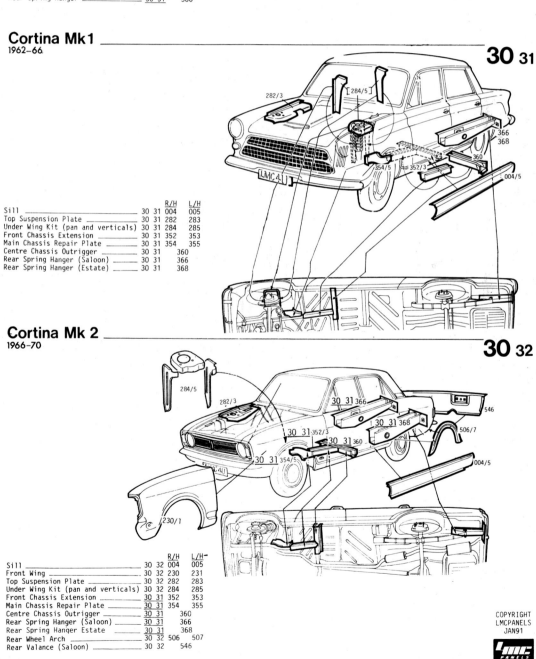

Sill		R/H	L/H
Sill	30 31	004	005
Top Suspension Plate	30 31	282	283
Under Wing Kit (pan and verticals)	30 31	284	285
Front Chassis Extension	30 31	352	353
Main Chassis Repair Plate	30 31	354	355
Centre Chassis Outrigger	30 31	360	
Rear Spring Hanger (Saloon)	30 31	366	
Rear Spring Hanger (Estate)	30 31	368	

Cortina Mk 2
1966-70

30 32

Sill		R/H	L/H
Sill	30 32	004	005
Front Wing	30 32	230	231
Top Suspension Plate	30 32	282	283
Under Wing Kit (pan and verticals)	30 32	284	285
Front Chassis Extension	30 31	352	353
Main Chassis Repair Plate	30 31	354	355
Centre Chassis Outrigger	30 31	360	
Rear Spring Hanger (Saloon)	30 31	366	
Rear Spring Hanger Estate	30 31	368	
Rear Wheel Arch	30 32	506	507
Rear Valance (Saloon)	30 32	546	

Major surgery has been carried out on this Cortina A-post. The lower section of the windscreen pillar had rotted and other bits of the A-post were not too good either! A better A-post was removed from a scrap car and welded in. This is a big job and not for the faint-hearted. The inside section of the windscreen pillar was cut through (just at the top of the photo) and this needs careful replacement. Remember a cable runs up this hollow windscreen pillar section. The wire serves the interior light. More importantly, if welding at the bottom of this pillar (which is really a hollow tube) could set fire to the headlining at the top. Be VERY careful never to set fire to the car when welding. Most of the work has been done and the new front wing has been welded in place.

The rust damaged section of the windscreen pillar can be seen on the opposite page.

paper template for the next part of the curve. You will have to make a part like a corner piece out of two or three separate pieces which you have to weld together.

This technique is useful in that it teaches you to line up two or more parts accurately and should also improve your welding techniques. The finished article will be in a prominent place being an outer panel.

Grooving

To make your own strengthening grooves, you need either a shrinking dolly or a small piece of steel pipe, say about 1 inch in diameter. Place the dolly or the open end of the tube under the steel where you want the groove. Hammer the steel with the round face of a hammer. The steel will be stretched and pushed down into the unsupported area. Move the dolly or tube along the line you want the groove to take. Do not strike the steel too hard. A slow controlled stretch is what you want.

Seat Belt Mountings

If you are restoring a pre-1965 car you might decide to fit seat belts. (Cars registered before January 1st, 1965 do not need seat belts to be fitted, but if they are fitted they must be worn by the driver and passenger).

Belt mountings will have to be fitted to the floor and a general requirement is that the mounting should pass through a piece of steel about 1/4 inch thick and about 4 square inches in area. This plate is fitted on the outside of the car and you can weld it in position if required. Plates are often supplied by the seat belt manufacturer, but if you have to make your own do not use anything thinner than 1/4 inch or smaller than 4 square inches. When welding the plate in position, do not damage the seat belt with heat. Remember to work safely. Similarly, if you are fitting non-standard seats, you may have to make up new seat mounting plates. Follow the same rules for size and thickness as described for seat belts.

If the seat belts are fitted to a pre-January 1965 car they will be tested as part of the M.O.T. test.

Conclusion

In this Chapter I have tried to show what can be done to restore body and chassis sections. Many panels are available, either from the owners club or other sources. If you can't find the panel you need, there are

The over-axle re-inforcing boxes from the Cortina. These must have been designed to trap water! Repair is possible, but can take time. These repair sections may still be available but if not you will have to make your own. Note that the sections are "handed" -- that is there is a left hand one and a right hand one. The chassis is curved at the point these attach.

people who can make it for you. Again you are trading time versus money. If you can't make it yourself, you have to pay for the expert to do it for you.

Don't be afraid to try making repair panels for your small Ford. Steel is relatively cheap, so have a go. Remember, the second attempt is always ten times better than the first attempt!

The following pages show various jobs being carried out in "photo and extended caption" format.

RIGHT: The windscreen pillar on the author's Cortina Super has rusted out. The repaired section is shown on the facing page. The A-post was so weakened by rust that the door started to move about! The car cost 75 pounds in 1983 and gave reliable daily service for three years before being laid up for restoration.

OPPOSITE, TOP: The anti-tramp bar mounting point on the 1965 G.T. Cortina has rusted. Here the damage has been cut away and some welding done on the inside of the box section. A large repair section is being prepared, with a hole in it to locate the mounting bolt's tube.

OPPOSITE, BOTTOM: The repair section offered up and about to be clamped in position. When everything is lined up correctly it will be welded in position. The bolt tube will be brazed to the repair plate. A nice tight fit between the tube and plate is recommended.

THIS PAGE, TOP: The main repair plate welded in place and the remaining closing plate being offered up. Again, when everything is correctly lined up and clamped in position, welding will begin. Remember that you need a lot of confidence before you tackle a job as difficult as this.

RIGHT: The first of several photos of Jim Norman's 107E being repaired. Here, part of the front panel, known as the radiator panel is being fitted. The flanges are being tapped down so that they are flush before welding begins. This is important if there is to be any strength in the weld. Note the clamp at the lower part of the panel, locating things until welding begins.

ABOVE: The closing panel is of less structural importance so is being spot welded in place. The plug welds from the previous MIG operation can be seen.

LEFT: The A-post can rust at the bottom where it meets the sill. This one was okay and all the work was done forwards of it.

OPPOSITE PAGE, TOP: The offside front wheel arch. This panel corrodes just above the hole (next to the battery terminals when all is fitted up), and along the bottom edge. Repairs are straightforward. The front of sill, at the extreme bottom, left of this photo is very prone to corrosion which spreads from the outer wing. The outer wings are bolted onto this car.

OPPOSITE PAGE, BOTTOM. Fitting the outer panels. It is essential to get all the joins correct and the car must be standing on its wheels, preferably with all the major parts, for example engine, glass, seats and so on, in situ. Although this was not the case here, Jim got away with it! These early shells are extremely rigid and distortion is less of a problem than on later cars. The car was put back on the road in December, 1989 and being too cold for spraying the painting was done the following year. Having the car back on the road is a great morale booster!

All The Other Bits...

Mike Wilkins' Classic being prepared for the Pirelli Classic Rally. Note the petrol pipe on top of the transmission tunnel, floor mounted handbrake, different steering wheel and a lot of extra switches under the dashboard. The big switch is a battery cut-off switch. On the inside of the inner wing there are signs of welding. (photo: Mike Wilkins).

Rebuilding a car seems to follow a certain pattern. There is the initial surge of enthusiasm when you start to dismantle all the bits to be restored. The second phase is when you lose the initial urge, but settle down to the long slog. The final phase is perhaps the most important, putting it all back together again.

Just as a ship is moved from its slipway to a fitting out dock, so should a car. I find it a tremendous boost just to start the engine, put it into gear and move it a few feet. It means that the car is now living, breathing, coming to life!

This also allows you to clear up the accumulated mess of the last six months, including that time when you spilled half a pint of dirty oil from the sump all over the garage floor.

Let's have a look at what happens in the final stages of a rebuild. You have completed all the bodywork repairs, rebuilt the mechanical assemblies and have a rolling vehicle sitting in the garage perhaps looking a bit blind, without its headlamps.

Various jobs must now be done to complete the restoration. Many of these jobs seem to be the "5-minute" variety (at least on paper they do) but when you get down to it they can take forever.

There is also the question - to what standard do you carry out the final fitting up?. None of my cars will ever win prizes at shows, but they are functional, reasonably presentable, and above all, reliable. I use as a guide-line the owners handbook. If a two speed heater is fitted, then both speeds must work. A few minutes thought will

show you that many of these things are NOT working on second-hand cars. They are bodged, until you come along and try to sort things out. What is the point of having a thing if it does not work.

Recently I was finishing off the front panel of my restoration. I fitted the headlamps and began to sort out the wiring at the "chocolate block". A quick reference to the wiring diagram refreshed my memory and I connected up what should have been dipped headlamps. Nothing! Out came the bulb and cord tester and I started to break down the circuit. The feed wire produced a voltage and the bulb lit. I connected the headlamp cable and its earth directly across the battery and it lit. The answer had to be the chocolate block. On careful examination I found that the

118

Starting to clear up the mess after the restoration. Months of dust lies on the windscreen and all sorts of bit and pieces decorate the floor. It can take a good few hours to clear up all the mess you made! Here Alex (Corsair Fanatic!) Gooding's V4 Corsair nears the end of the work period and starts the fitting up. Now is the time you discover how well you stored and labelled all the bits you took off all that time ago. (Photo: Alex Gooding).

connectors were rusty, having been lying about for over a year. I rubbed each connector and the block with a sharp screwdriver to remove the muck. Hey presto the headlamps work.

I followed a similar sequence to coax the side-lamps into life. Next, I had a look at the rear lamps. Why would the nearside rear indicator not flash? Then I remembered a day six months ago when we borrowed the bulb to sort out another car. A quick remove of the lens, pop in a new bulb and instant flashes.

Not all your fitting out problems will be electrical. I fitted a "new" carburettor which I bought at an autojumble. When I tried to blip the throttle it stuck. On closer examination I found that there were some extra washers fitted to the spindle, effectively locking the movement of the spindle. A look at the Parts Book provided the correct assembly and within a few minutes everything was ticking over nicely again.

You will find surprises at every turn when you start to fit-out a car. I tried to refit the drivers seat after a seven month rebuild. No matter how I tried to fit it, it would not go on. Perhaps I have the

passenger seat. Yes, that it. Try to fit the other seat. At this point I discover that the car I had paid 30 pounds for, had been fitted with two passenger front seats. I ``encouraged'' one of the seats to fit but will now have to comb the local scrapyards for a driver side seat. The moral is, no matter how careful you think you are, you will always come unstuck on something. Instruments can also cause problems. For example, you may have fitted a new oil pressure switch to the engine block. When the motor runs for the first time after six months and an oil change you can be excused a moments panic if the oil light does not go off right away. A few second's thought will bring the answer that the oil has to pump through the filter before building up pressure -- so it can take up to a minute or two before the light goes out. A tip here is to look into the oil filler hole at the nearest rocker. If the oil is circulating,

it will dribble out through a hole in the rocker.

Another fairly common problem is a sticking solenoid. This is actually a relay which is activated when you turn the ignition switch. The relay activates and connects the heavy load of the starter motor across the battery. Often the solenoid will stick but it can sometimes be brought to life by tapping it with a heavy screwdriver. Alternatively, it may be the type which can be operated by hand, by pressing on the rubber-covered end. Be sure to keep your hands clear of the fan blades.

In this chapter I will try to highlight various problem areas and how you can overcome them.

Trim

Trim panels often give the restorer a lot of trouble. The trim seemed to change so often on a 1960's car. There were so many different colours available then that the problem now is to ensure you have the correct colour or combination of colours for your car.

Luckily, the manufacturer helps you with this. Locate the chassis plate on the chassis of the car. It should be on the top of the inner wing, normally on the driver's side. On this plate you should find a number of code letters. Most of these items are described in Chapter One. Amongst other things the plate will tell you the trim code. Look in the factory parts list and you should be able to match the code number against a colour. There are too many codes to list here.

If you find you have the wrong trim or a mixture or correct and incorrect trim panels, there are a few things you can do.

Firstly, advertise in the owners club magazine. This way you are telling all other enthusiasts what you are looking for. This often brings surprising results.

The second thing you can do is to clean the trim panels you have, then dye them to the correct colour.

Cleaning Vinyl Trim

If you acquire a mouldy old set of trim panels which look as though they belong on a bonfire, don't give up hope. There is a quick simple way to clean even the most disgusting trim panel. Incidentally, mould is caused by dampness and is often found on cars which have been left for years in some old garage.

Get a handful of Swarfega and rub it onto an area of the trim. Spend a few minutes, working the Swarfega into all the pores of the material. When it turns a dirty brown colour, wipe it off with some rag or a piece of newspaper. You will be surprised how much muck and mould can be removed this way. If necessary repeat the process.

I often use a couple of old toothbrushes for this, as well as the best tool ever invented, your fingers.

Swarfega is also good for removing oil stains from trim. Many an old car is used by a mechanic as cheap transport, before being discarded. If you have bought an ex-mechanics car you will find that he has left you a legacy of oily stains on the drivers side door panel and the drivers seat. (Why bother to change out of oily overalls just to drive home in the "banger"). Half an hour's work with the Swarfega will remove months of dirt, oil and mould.

ABOVE: Trim can be cleaned with Swarfega if oily or moldy. This Cortina Super needs the dashboard top cleaned with a damp cloth, and the chrome on the dials with a cotton bud dipped in Swarfega if dirty or just some chrome cleaner. (For those keen to fit extra instruments this type of instrument pod was used on the 1964 G.T. works rally cars to house the special trip meter and extra switches and knobs. It was mounted alongside the existing instrument pod, and looked quite at home!)

ABOVE: This 1966 dashboard is generally a bit tatty but quite good enough for an every day drive to work car. The parcel shelf shows signs of scuffing, but if this was repainted it must be done correctly otherwise it will look worse than the "fair wear and tear" version. This car provided reliable transport for two years after being dragged out of a field and 25 pounds changing hands.

Other items which can be cleaned in this way are sun visors, which often suffer from years of cigarette smoke. Swarfega can work wonders on these too. The green slime is excellent for all these jobs and in case you did not know is great for cleaning soiled floor tiles too.

Windscreens

One way to remove a windscreen is to push it out with your feet. If this sounds a bit drastic, it needn't be.

Try to get comfortable on the floor of the car, and place both feet flat against the windscreen, near the corners. Gently, but firmly, push the glass to see if it is "willing" to move. If you cannot feel any give in the rubber surround, DO NOT continue. Have a look at the rubber windscreen rubber and check the workshop manual to see if any chrome trim has to be removed before the glass can be got out.

Try pushing again. You will need an assistant on the outside. Make sure you brief him or her on what to do when the windscreen starts to come loose. The glass is not unduly heavy, but normally it is the size that causes the problem. So long as the assistant knows that he is there to steady the glass rather than snatch it away, all should be well.

Once the glass starts to move, gently change the position of your feet and encourage it further. I have used this method many times over the years without any problem. It is yet another of these jobs that the amateur can tackle if only he has the courage to try it.

Rubber Windscreen Surrounds

Rubber surrounds are available for most of the cars covered by this book. You may have to phone round a few places to locate one, but I have seen them advertised in two or three places. The going rate seems to be around 30 pounds.

Damaged Glass

Angle grinders can damage glass beyond repair. The little hot sparks burn their way into the glass. If you run your fingers over the glass you can feel the little lumps. Think what this will do to windscreen wipers.

There are only a couple of choices. The first is protect the glass at every opportunity. The second is find a new glass which is undamaged and fit that. You can always keep the damaged one as a spare. The third choice is to try one of the glass reconditioning products available. However, while scratches can be removed from glass, angle grinder damage is probably terminal.

Water leaks can be cured by using some of the many sealers available from motor

The windscreen surround on this Cortina suffered from the rust bug and the lower half of it had to be replaced. A new rubber windscreen surround will be fitted, together with plenty of sealer to keep water out. As outlined in the text below, a leak now can mean welding later!

factors. Curing a water leak can also save a lot of welding later on. If the screen leaks, the water will fall to the floor, and rust will start.

Instrument Faults

One of my cars had a fuel gauge which always read high. Even when the tank was half full, the gauge registered full. After restoring this car I put it back on the road and drove it just 15 miles to the nearest town. On the way back it ran out of petrol, because I had forgotten about the gauge reading incorrectly and had let the tank run dry. Luckily I was able to get petrol within a few hundred yards, but it was an embarrassing lesson to learn.

If you knew about a problem such as the above, you should write a sticky label and stick it on the dashboard somewhere. Years later when you finish the rebuild you will have forgotten all about the problem until you find the sticky label. Alternatively, follow the advice given in Chapter Ten.

Exhaust Blown

If the exhaust pipe has rusted away then there is little you can do about a blown exhaust except replace the system or part of it. Stainless steel may be an option. If the exhaust manifold gasket has blown that can be cured by fitting a new gasket and tightening the studs correctly.

One little tip (I've never tried this by the way!) that may extend the life of an exhaust pipe is to drill a 1/8 inch hole at the lowest part of the silencer system. It is claimed that this will allow water to drain away and hence prevent the silencer rusting from the inside out. It sounds good to me but I'm not sure if the M.O.T. people would count this as a "leak". They probably wouldn't notice.

Disc Rust

Disc brakes can cause problems after a lengthy rebuild. The disc surface attracts rust which very often looks worse than it is. A good method to clean up a disc is to use an electric drill with a wire brush. If you apply the wire brush to the disc there is very often enough drive to start the disc turning. This means that the wire brush removes the rust from the front face of the disc, while the brake pad will do a reasonable job of cleaning up the other face. This saves you removing the brake caliper. It does not always work, but if it does, can save you a fair bit of time. You should get a few miles on the discs and pads before they will work at their best.

Steering Wheel

If you intend to change steering wheels make sure you get one you can live with. What I mean is that if you drive the car around town all day, then a small steering wheel will not be all that practical. The extra effort needed to turn the wheels, park and so on will make the car less enjoyable.

Blown bulbs

Bulbs have a curious habit of working for years then when they are left for a long time the solder inside the bulb seems to

ABOVE: An interior view of Mike Pratt's Lotus Cortina. Mike has stuck a reminder note on the rev-counter, probably to remind him not to over-rev the engine during running in. (Photo: Mike Pratt).

BELOW: Wyn Evans exibits BEJ 555 C at Pembroke Castle Vintage and Classic Show in 1981. This is the same car bought by the author as a dismantled shell in May 1991. Wyn bought the car in January 1974 for £220, kept it in beautiful condition for eight years (used every day), and sold it in 1982 for £300. (Photo: Wyn Evans).

The dashboard of the Capri, showing signs of wear and tear. Notice the cracks in the plastic dashboard material at the extreme right, and to the left and above the heater. The only real answer to these cracks is to find a better trim panel. This car has a Yazaki rev-counter from the 1960s and the G.T. remote gear change. No horn ring is fitted, the horn being operated from the end of the indicator stalk. (That used to be the headlamp flasher!) The owners club can now provide horn rings.

dry out and the bulb fails. Just because all the bulbs were working when you laid the car up does not mean that they will work two years later when you power up. Be prepared to fit new bulbs. You may also find that some bulbs might fail shortly after powering up.

Rubber Weatherstrip

Lots of problems are caused by leaking weatherstrip. This can be bought from the suppliers mention at the end of the book. They will also be able to supply clips to hold the strip in place. Some of the Capri weatherstrip is different to everything else (it would be!) but very close matches can be made from other weatherstrip.

Windscreen Wipers

Windscreen wipers really should be changed every year. Be sure that you have the correct wipers and wiper arms before you start restoring them or replacing them. All too often you will find that the previous owner, to whom the car was a banger,

would fit anything he could get away with. You then come along and spend good money replacing the wrong parts. Don't be caught.

Carpets

Carpets can make the final touches to a restored car. Read the monthly magazines and find some carpet suppliers. Phone round and get some prices. Generally, you get what you pay for, so if you want 20 pound carpets, pay 20 pounds. More likely you are going to have to spend nearer 100 pounds to get good quality carpets which fit.

Stitching Seats

A few loose stitches in a seat can be repaired by the amateur but anything more than this may require expert attention. It may pay you to keep your eyes and ears open for some better seats from someone else breaking a car. Various seat colours seem to be in short supply now, so if anyone has a set of black seats for a 1965 G.T. Cortina which they don't want...

Headlining

Headlining for some of the small Fords are very hard to find. I know of several people who have been forced to sew up a headlining from several damaged ones. The headlining comes in several panels, so if one panel is damaged you may be able to have a new panel sewn in rather than replace the whole thing.

ABOVE: An interior view of Bert Wiesfeld's 100E, showing the roof panel with the headlining removed. Just above the front windscreen surround is some surface rust on the panel, and this is typical of what you can expect. Headlinings are tricky this to remove and fit and great patience is required with them. Bert seems to have very comfortable surroundings to work in -- note the sink and water heater, visible through the door aperture. (Photo: Bert Wiesfeld).

BELOW: If you are lucky enough to find a car in original condition, such as this beautiful Anglia 105E, then you will have less work to do! (Photo: Mark and Jill Bradbury).

Make sure you get the same type of material, as there were several different patterns made.

Rather than repeat fitting instructions, I again refer you to the workshop manual. However, I have found headlining to be very fragile things. Look at them the wrong way and they tear. Unless you are good with material, I would either try to persuade your wife/girlfriend to get her needles out, or hand this one over to an expert.

DOOR OPENING MECHANISM

Door opening mechanisms only require to be oiled now and again for them to work perfectly. If yours have been lying for years unused, they may need some time spent getting the levers and links free from rust.

TOP, RIGHT: Re-manufactured headlamp bezels are available for the Mk1 Cortina, while grills, such as this late type which wraps round the sidelamp are going to get harder to find in good condition.

MIDDLE, RIGHT: A refurbished heater unit for the Anglia. Sprayed with shiny black paint this heater looks as good as new. Take care to check that the electric motor works before rebuilding the heater assembly! (Photo: Mark and Jill Bradbury).

LOWER, RIGHT: The late Cortina heater, showing the outlet pipes for the Aeroflow ventilation system. This is a two speed heater, and the author was careful to check that the motor worked before starting to recondition the assembly! This assembly hides under the dashboard, unlike the Anglia unit above which is in full view when the bonnet is lifted.

Remove the operating handles from the door opening mechanism and the window winder. Remove the two screws holding the door pull to the door. Next remove the trim panel, carefully. Underneath you should find a sheet of plastic which is supposed to keep dampness off the underside of the hardboard trim panel.

Remove the plastic and you should have access to the mechanisms. An oil can with a long spout, or a spray can of WD40, can work wonders here. Keep operating the mechanisms until they work freely without any sticking.

If one part is found to be truly seized up, disconnect it from the other parts. You don't want to bend or strain a working part trying to free off a seized part. If a part is broken you will have to find a second hand part to replace it, as trim panels and parts are often the hardest bits to find.

Window Winder Mechanism

Window mechanisms generally follow the pattern of door opening mechanisms, but there may be problems with weatherstrip. The glass is located in felt or rubber runners and these can actually weld themselves to the glass after a time. You will have to keep exercising the glass to free it off, otherwise dismantle the entire assembly. If you do this, you might as well fit new runners. These are still available, refer to the address section at the end of the book.

Seat Belts

Early Fords did not have seat belt

anchorages, but later ones did as legislation loomed. For example my 1963 Super does not have anchorage bolts fitted, but my 1965 car does. You used to be able to buy fitting kits which consisted of a steel plate, and the necessary bolts and fittings to mount seatbelts. Generally the rule is that if you make up your own mounting then the reinforcing plate wants to be at least 4 square inches in area. For those cars with seat belt anchorage points, make sure the threads are free from rust or damage. This is particularly true when welding new sills on. You are going to look a bit foolish if you discover a problem in your lower seat belt anchor point after you weld the new sill on!

Wheel Refurbishment

Nothing sets off a restored car as much as a nice set of wheels. However, painting wheels is fraught with problems as nothing looks worse than hand-painted wheels in the wrong colour.

Cleaning a wheel which is rusty and discoloured takes a lot of time. It is akin to preparing a panel for respraying -- preparation is all-important.

Spend a lot of time with a wire brush mounted in an electric drill. Get into every corner and get all the rust and flaky paint removed. Then take advice from you local motor factor about the current range of paints available for wheels. If you use very silver-looking paint, then the wheels look tatty and hand-painted. Try to get a good colour match as this will repay you later when the wheel looks "right".

Weber 28/36 Carburettor

Although this carburettor was mentioned in Chapter Two, it may be worth looking a little closer at it here. It is a downdraught unit with two chokes. It also has two throttle valves, with a clever arrangement whereby the secondary throttle is not opened until the primary one is 2/3 open. This helps economy. It is the most common carburettor for the 4-cylinder Ford engine and is the one fitted to the G.T. models.

The illustrations show the unit in exploded form, together with both the Weber part numbers and the old Ford part numbers. Haynes of Sparkford also do a book entitled, "Weber Carburettors" which provides masses of information including tuning and overhauling information.

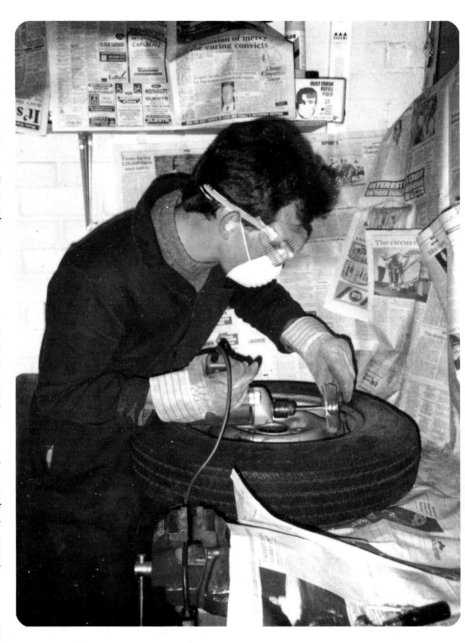

Wearing all the right protective equipment, including goggles, gloves and a face-mask, Mark Bradbury removes all the old paint from a wheel. In the drill is a rotating wire brush, while his left hand holds a screwdriver, useful for scraping off stubborn paint. This sort of job can be extremely messy, hence all the newspapers. (Photo: Mark and Jill Bradbury).

Tow Bars

Some people seem to find it amusing when you fit a tow bar to a 25 year old car. However, these are strong cars and well able to tow a caravan, as indeed they did in the 1960s. Tow bars are still available for these cars. Look in the monthly magazines for names and addresses. You may be able to find one second-hand, but make sure it is safe. You don't want to be overtaken by your trailer due to a fault on a second-hand tow bar.

PAGES 127 AND 128: All you ever need to know about the Weber 28/36 carburettor.

For further details contact, Weber Concessionaires Ltd, Dolphin Road, Sunbury, Middlesex, TW16 7HE, United Kingdom. Telehone 0932 788805.

(Illustrations courtesy of Weber Concessionaires Ltd).

All The Other Bits...

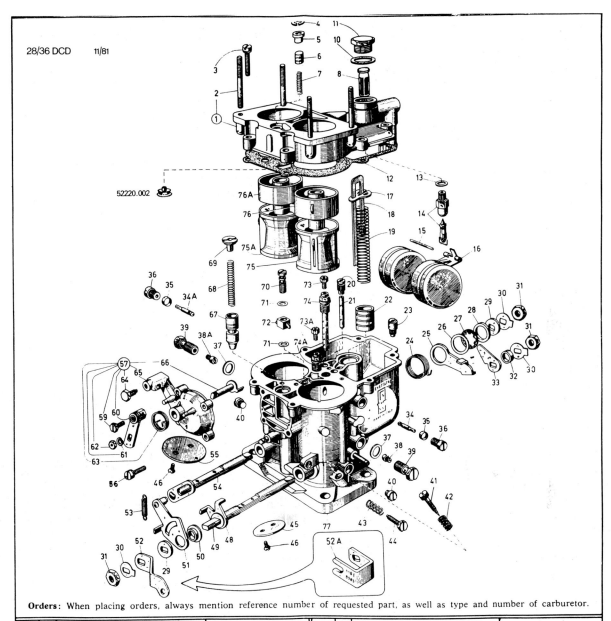

28/36 DCD   11/81

52220.002

Orders: When placing orders, always mention reference number of requested part, as well as type and number of carburetor.

Key. Nr.	Q.ty	PART NAME	Ref. number WEBER	Ref. number FORD	Key. Nr.	Q.ty	PART NAME	Ref. number WEBER	Ref. number FORD
1	1	**Carburetor cover, including:** . . .	31716.054	116E-9524-B	24	1	Loose lever return spring	47610.050	116E-9B564
2	4	Stud bolt	64955.007	116E-9A659	25	1	Loose lever for pump control . . .	45039.018	116E-9D591
3	6	Carb. cover fixing screw	64700.005	113022-ES	26	1	Spring ring washer	55510.041	113430-ES
4	1	Lock washer, starter plunger seat .	10140.010	113426-ES	27	1	Toothed spring ring	10140.401	113429-ES
5	1	Starter plunger seat	12775.037	116E-9K505	28	1	Spring ring washer	55510.040	113427-ES
6	1	Starter plunger	58600.007	116E-9K506	29	2	Shafts distance washer	55555.016	113428-ES
7	1	Starter plunger spring	47600.108	116E-9K507	30	3	Lock washer	55520.002	113431-ES
8	1	**Strainer**	37022.002	2725E-9L541-A	31	3	Shafts fixing nut	34715.014	114212-ES
10	1	Filter plug gasket	41530.024 †	116E-99722	32	1	Shaft distance bushing	12750.058	116E-9715
11	1	Filter plug	61002.010	116E-9A540	33	1	Pump control cam	14850.009	116E-9529
12	1	Carb. cover gasket	41705.002 †	116E-9519	34	1	Primary idling jet	74401. •	116E-9596-A
13	1	Needle valve gasket	41535.015 †	116E-9B539	34 A	1	Secondary idling jet	74401. •	116E-9596-B
14	1	**Needle valve**	79507. •†	116E-9564	35	2	Idling jets-holder sealing ring . .	41555.004 †	116E-9K508
15	1	Float fulcrum pin	52000.001	116E-9558	36	2	Idling jet-holder	52570.005	116E-9K509
16	1	**Float**	41030.011	116E-9555	37	2	Main jets-holder gasket	41540.001 †	113438-ES
17	1	Plunger spring retaining plate . . .	52140.002	116E-9688	38	1	Primary main jet	73801. •	116E-9533-A
18	1	Pump control rod	10400.024	116E-9B512	38 A	1	Secondary main jet	73801. •	116E-9533-B
19	1	Pump plunger spring	47600.106	116E-9D598	39	2	Main jet-holder	52590.001	116E-9K510
20	1	Starting air adjusting jet	77506. •	116E-9K511	40	2	Progression orifices inspection screw	61015.001	113024-ES
21	1	Starting jet	75504. •	116E-9971 B	41	1	Idling mixture adjusting screw . .	64750.001 †	116E-9541
22	1	**Pump plunger**	58602.005	116E-9B544	42	1	Spring for idling mixture adj. screw	47600.007 †	116E-9578
23	1	**Intake valve with exhaust orifice** . .	79701. •	116E-9573-B	43	1	Spring for throttle adjusting screw .	47600.084	116E-9B896

Key. Nr.	Q.ty	PART NAME	Ref. number WEBER	Ref. number FORD	Key. Nr.	Q.ty	PART NAME	Ref. number WEBER	Ref. number FORD
44	1	Throttle adjusting screw	64625.002	116E-9B538	62	1	— Starting lever fixing nut	34715.010	114214-ES
45	1	Primary throttle	64005.017	116E-9585-B	63	1	— Lever return spring	47610.004	116E-9C513
46	4	Throttles fixing screw	64570.008	116E-9E519	64	1	— Screw securing sheath	64605.017	113027-ES
48	1	Stop sector	45039.017	116E-9B792	65	1	— Sheath support cover	32534.003	116E-9849
49	1	Primary shaft	10000.439	116E-9582	66	1	— Starting valve control shaft	10085.004	116E-9A753
49	1	Primary shaft, oversize	10001.430	—	67	1	Starting valve	64330.001	116E-9K502
50	1	Primary sector bushing	12775.027	116E-9B508	68	1	Spring for starting valve	47600.061	116E-9K503
51	1	Primary sector	45131.002	116E-99602	69	1	Spring guide and retainer	52030.001	116E-9K504
52	1	Throttles control lever (28/36 DCD22)	45025.052	116E-9583-C	70	1	Pump delivery valve	64290.003 †	116E-9A096
52 A	1	Throttles control lever (28/36 DCD23)	45136.016	118E-9583	71	2	Pump jet gasket	41530.012 †	116E-9926
53	1	Primary sector return spring	47605.011	116E-9B848	72	1	Pump jet	76203. *	116E-9940
54	1	Secondary shaft	10015.436	116E-9581	73	1	Primary air corrector jet	77502. *	116E-9K512-A
54	1	Secondary shaft, oversize	10016.422	—	73 A	1	Secondary air corrector jet	77502. *	116E-9K512-B
55	1	Secondary throttle	64005.088	116E-9A598	74	1	Primary emulsioning tube	61455. *	116E-9991
56	4	Starting control fixing screw	64700.004	113025-ES	74 A	1	Secondary emulsioning tube	61455. *	116E-9991
57	1	Starting control, including:	32536.013	—	75	1	Primary choke	71702. *	116E-9E514-A
					75 A	1	Secondary choke	71701. *	116E-9E514-B
59	1	— Screw securing wire	64615.004	113026-ES	76	1	Primary Auxiliary Venturi	69001. *	116E-9586-B
60	1	— Starting control lever	45027.050	116E-9E523	76 A	1	Secondary Auxiliary Venturi	69001. *	116E-9586-B
61	1	— Spring washer	55525.010	113474-ES	77	—	Carburetor body	NOT SUPPLIED	

(*) Calibrated parts
† Parts supplied in Service Kit No. 93.0027.05

	WEBER	FORD
Master repair kit	92.2028.05	—
Tune up kit	92.1033.05	
Gasket kit	92.0027.05	

FORD 1500 G.T. SETTING

Key Nr.	Q.ty	PART NAME	Ref. number WEBER	Ref. number FORD	Setting in mm.
75	1	Primary choke	71702.260	116E-9E514-A	26
75A	1	Secondary choke	71701.270	116E-9E514-B	27
76	1	Primary Auxiliary Venturi	69001.450	116E-9586-B	4.50
76A	1	Secondary Auxiliary Venturi	69001.450	116E-9586-B	4.50
38	1	Primary main jet	73801.140	116E-9533-A	1.40
38A	1	Secondary main jet	73801.155	116E-9533-B	1.55
34	1	Primary idling jet	74401.050	116E-9596-A	0.50
34A	1	Secondary idling jet	74401.070	116E-9596-B	0.70
72	1	Pump jet	76203.070	116E-9940	0.70
21	1	Starting jet	75504.205	116E-9971-B	F1/2.05
74	1	Primary emulsioning tube	61455.152	116E-9991	F 30
74A	1	Secondary emulsioning tube	61455.152	116E-9991	F 30
73	1	Primary air corrector jet	77502.230	116E-9K512-A	2.30
73A	1	Secondary air corrector jet	77502.180	116E-9K512-B	1.80
20	1	Air starting jet	77505.100	116E-9K511	1.00
14	1	Needle valve	79607.175	116E-9564	1.75
23	1	Intake valve with exhaust orifice	79701.060	116E-9573-B	0.50
	—	Float levelling	—	—	5 (**)

Messrs. E. WEBER do not answer for eventual working anomalies due to arbitrary modifications introduced into the above setting.

(**) DIRECTIONS FOR LEVELLING THE FLOAT

It is essential that the following directions be complied with in order to obtain correct levelling of the float:

- Make sure that the **weight of the float (G)** is the correct one **(gr. 18)**, that float can freely slide on the axis and does not show any pit.
- Make sure that needle valve **(V)** is tightly screwed in its housing and that pin ball **(Sf)** of the dampening device, incorporated in the needle **(S)**, is not jammed.

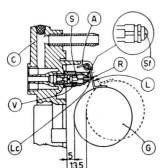

- Keep the carburetor cover **(C)** in vertical position as indicated in the figure since the weight of float **(G)** could lower the pin ball **(Sf)** fitted on the needle **(S)**.
- With carburetor cover **(C)** in vertical position and float clip **(Lc)** in light contact with the pin ball **(Sf)** of the needle **(S)**, the distance of both half-floats **(G)** from upper surface of carburetor cover **(C)**, without gasket, must measure **5 mm. (Weber gauge 9620.175.3419/2)**.
- After the levelling has been done, check that the stroke of float **(G)** is **8,5 mm.** if necessary adjust the position of the lug **(A)**.
- Check that the return hook **(R)** of the needle **(S)** allows its free movement in its seat.
- Should the float **(G)** not be correctly placed, modify the position of the tabs **(L)** of the float until the required point is reached, taking care that the tab **(Lc)** is perpendicular to the needle axis **(S)** and that it does not have any indentations on the contact surface which might affect the free movement of the needle itself.
- Fit up the carburetor cover making sure that float can move without any hindrance or friction.

NOTE - The operations of levelling of float must be carried out whenever it is necessary to replace float or needle valve: in this last case it is advisable to replace also the sealing gasket, making sure that the new needle valve is tightly screwed in its housing.

The M.O.T. Test

An Anglia, or any small Ford, as neat and tidy as this one is half way through the M.O.T. test already. The examiner will be impressed and will probably take a keen interest in the car. (Photo: Mark and Jill Bradbury).

The M.O.T. (Ministry of Transport) test in the United Kingdom is an annual problem for all cars over three years old. It has become the aim of every car restorer to get his or her restored vehicle through the test. It generally marks the end of the rebuild and the start of enjoying the car. That means your restored Ford must submit to the test. This chapter aims to help you pass that test without too many headaches.

The test was first introduced in 1960. Those first tests drastically reduced the number of older cars still running at that time. Those cars which were otherwise just about legal were subjected to the test and failed. Many were deemed not worth repairing having soldiered on since the war. The pool of old cars for restoring dwindled overnight.

General

The first thing to state is that the advice given here is not how to bend the rules to get a certificate -- rather to make you aware of what is required and why.

The Department of Transport produce an excellent book entitled "Vehicle Testing, The M.O.T. Tester's Manual." This is available from HMSO Bookshops or can be ordered from High Street bookshops. If in any doubt about information given in this Chapter, refer to the Tester's Manual or seek advice from the Department of Transport.

Remember that the M.O.T. test is just an indication that the car was in a satisfactory condition at the time it was tested. It is NOT a guarantee of the car's condition. Two minutes after leaving the test centre it could have its nice new tyres removed and four bald ones substituted. It would still have a current, valid M.O.T. certificate but would be dangerous to drive. The driver would also be liable to prosecution for failing to keep a vehicle in a roadworthy condition.

The M.O.T. Inspection Report shows all the items the examiner will be looking at. You are given a copy of this form VT30 when your car is M.O.T. tested, so if there was an item that the examiner thought was borderline, but he passed you on it, he would note it down on the Inspection Report. If a certain item does not apply to you then you will not be tested on it and so cannot be failed on it. For example, if your car does not have power-assisted steering you will not be tested on that item and so cannot be failed. If this is the case, the examiner will write N/A for "Not Applicable". A similar checklist is provided at the end of this Chapter so that you can carry out your own pre-M.O.T. test.

If there is a problem with an M.O.T. test you can always appeal. Details of how to do this are marked on the VT30.

If we start at the top of the list and work through, it will save you problems later. Armed with this check list you can do your own pre-M.O.T. test and save 90% of problems. Many garages now offer pre-M.O.T. tests as well.

The M.O.T. tester will examine your car with the aid of an assistant. However, he need not even begin the test if the vehicle is not capable of being moved under its own power during the test. In other words, if your car does not start when he tries to drive it into the testing station, then he can refuse to carry out the test.

Normally the M.O.T. test does not involve a road test. However the examiner can carry out a road test if he wishes.

Lighting Equipment

Two sidelights showing a white light to the front and two rear lamps showing a red light to the rear are required. Cracked, broken or missing lenses will fail the test. Broken bulbs will fail, as will a lamp which does not light immediately it is switched on, for example if there is a faulty electrical connection. Check before you go for the test by a visual inspection.

Headlamps must be white or yellow, be correctly aimed and be capable of illuminating the road ahead. You can't have a white one and a yellow one. Headlamps must work on both main and dipped settings. As with sidelamps, cracked, broken, or missing lenses will fail. Check before you go by visual inspection. For Classic and Capri owners with twin head-

Check that your headlamps work before submitting the car to the M.O.T. test. Check also for cracked or broken lenses. Headlamp aim should be set by a garage with the correct equipment. Check that indicators flash at between 60 and 120 flashes per minute.

lamps the requirement is that each pair (either the two outer lamps or the two inner lamps) must be of the same colour. So the outers could be yellow and the inners white. The only other requirement (apart from them working immediately they are switched on), is that they should be of adequate brightness to do their intended job.

Stop lamps need to be red, work when the footbrake is applied (with the ignition switch ON) and must not have damaged or missing lenses. For most of the small Fords the "before September 1st 1965" proviso applies. This says that the rear brake lamp can be combined with a rear direction indicator.

Two rear reflectors are required. They must be red and be undamaged. Check by inspection.

Front and Rear Lamps

You can test these yourself simply by switching them on! You will fail if a lens is missing or if a lens is badly cracked. Discoloured lenses, or the wrong lens may also result in a fail. One point to note here is that front indicator lenses changed colour from white to amber, so your older car may have a white lens on the front indicator. The tester should be aware that this was correct at the time of manufacture.

Headlamps

Again, test by switching them on! Make sure they dip properly. If they are wired incorrectly, and one is on main and the other on dip, then you will fail, and presumable only have yourself to blame for not wiring them properly. Look out for poor earth connections. These could cause a headlamp to appear dim, which might also attract a fail certificate.

If you have fitted two "odd" headlamps, such as one high power unit and one normal power unit, this may also attract a fail certificate.

Headlamp Aim

Not much you can do about this except have the job done professionally before you take the car for an M.O.T. You may find that the same workshop can perform beam-setting as well as M.O.T. tests. Refer to the appropriate workshop manual for correct headlamp aim information.

Stop Lamps

Test by getting a helper to press the brake pedal (you will probably need the ignition switched on!) and looking for both lamps. You may be failed if you have the wrong bulb fitted. For example, if you fitted a 6 watt bulb instead of the normal 21 watt. You should not really be able to get these mixed up unless you have forced the bulb into the holder the wrong way.

Direction Indicators.

Lenses must be white or amber at the front, and either red or amber at the rear.

Check by inspection. Note this little gem though! You could be failed if the rate of flash is not between 60 and 120 flashes per minute! That is, too fast or too slow and you fail. Note that if the dashboard indicator bulb is blown it could upset the rate of flash. If one or more of the dashboard "tell-tale" lamps are blown, this will also result in a test failure. Remember too that if your battery is a bit flat then when the engine is run the indicators may run at a different speed. Check all these points before you submit to the test.

Steering and Suspension

The tester will check the amount of steering play at the steering wheel. "Play" is the amount of movement of the steering wheel before anything happens to the wheels or steering linkages. The requirement is that 3 inches of movement on a non-rack and pinion steering system is excessive. Small Fords don't have rack and pinion, so check steering wheel movement for less than 3 inches of play.

I was failed once for excessive play in the steering column, between the column and the steering tube. In small Fords there is a felt seal, consisting of a piece of felt about two inches long by an inch wide. This must be soaked in heavy grease for a couple of hours. The only way to do this is to heat the grease in a small, shallow tin until it is just melted, put the felt seal in and let it soak. Gently heat may be needed to keep the grease liquid. If you can't find a new seal, gently remove the old one and re-soak it in grease. The chances are it has never been touched since it left the factory!

Steering Wheel

The steering wheel must be securely fixed to the steering column and not have any loose or fractured spokes. Note that cracks or bits missing from the covering skin of the wheel will not normally result in a fail.

Steering Mechanism

Wear in the steering box may attract a fail. Also, all the ball joints and their respective securing nuts will be checked for wear or looseness. If any parts of the

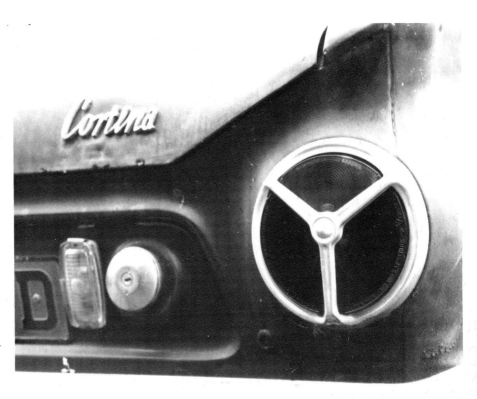

At the back of the car check again for cracked or broken lenses. Get a helper to press the brake pedal and ensure that the brake lights work. The reversing lamp is NOT part of the test, but the number plate lamp is, so check it when you test the lights.

steering assembly are loose relative to the vehicle chassis this will attract a fail.

Any corrosion, damage or fracture in the chassis or body within 12 inches (30 cms) of a steering box, idler arm mounting or other fixing point will fail the car.

The steering stop locks must be in place, and tight. If these were not in place the wheels could be turned beyond their safe angle and come into contact with the body or chassis.

Power Steering

Power steering was never available on any of the Small Fords covered by this book. If you have done any such conversion you are on your own!

Wheel Bearings

Wheel bearings will be checked by the tester jacking up the car and holding the top and bottom of the tyre. He will try rocking the tyre relative to the axle. Some little play is expected here, but if the wheel rocks excessively, then you could be failed. Remember that you can try this yourself before you submit to the test.

If any roughness or tightness is detected which might indicate an impending bear-

ing failure this may either be noted, or result in a fail depending on the severity and the judgement of the tester.

One little cautionary word. I was failed for excessive play in the front wheel bearings of my Capri. I fitted new bearings are re-submitted the car. I was told that the bearings were even worse than before! The tester demonstrated the problem to me.

What had happened was that I had been over-cautious because of the very fine thread on the Classic / Capri stub axle. It is very easy to damage. (See Chapter Three). I had fitted the bearings, but they had not seated properly. When I tested them after fitting they were fine. After driving six miles to the test centre they had seated themselves and required adjustment. The tester was able to do this work and the car received its certificate. Don't get caught out like I did!

MacPherson Struts

The tester will bounce the car up and down and look for "rebound". How many times does the car bounce up and down after he lets go? If the dampers are working correctly it should only bounce once.

Needless to say, if you have a broken coil

spring or one so sad that the car leans to one side, you will also fail.

The tester will also look for leaking fluid in the MacPherson struts. If there are signs of a fluid leak you will fail. Yet again, you can check this before you submit to the test.

What does "leaking" mean? A slight dampness may be noted on the VT30, while suspension fluid running down the strut will result in a fail.

The suspension must not foul any brake pipes or hoses.

The top suspension mounts will be checked for wear in the bearings and any signs of deterioration between the rubber and steel parts of the mounting. If the rubber is showing signs of becoming detached from the metal you may fail, depending on the severity.

The bottom ball joint will be tested for excessive wear.

The front anti-roll bar will be examined for secure fitting and the bar itself will be checked for corrosion or distortion. My first reaction on reading this in the "Tester's Manual" was that it would be unlikely for the anti-roll bar to corrode on a Ford! Then I remembered seeing a dismantled car in a scrapyard where the anti-roll bar had rusted to about half thickness at the point where it is enclosed in the rubber mounting bush. Water in there over the years could do damage. I think this is just a point to be noted rather than worried about.

The top of the inner wing will be examined for rust or damage. This is probably the best-known point of failure for small Fords. See Chapter Six for all the necessary information to restore this area. Note that any rust or damage within 12 inches (30 cms) of the top mounting will be under scrutiny.

Rear Suspension

Leaf springs are fitted to all the small Fords covered by this book. Look out for broken leaves, damaged rubber mounting bushes or saggy old springs which won't support the car.

Loose or missing mounting bolts will attract a fail, as will odd springs, or rust or damage to the chassis within 12 inches of a spring mounting.

Bushes at the front of the spring are in short supply for some small Fords (check with your owner's club) but generally the bushes at the rear of the spring are freely

The thread on the Classic and Capri's stub axle is extremely fine. It is also a very peculiar thread type, so spare spindle nuts are hard to make. Take particular care when adjusting the wheel bearings on these cars. And take great care not to strip the threads! (Photo: Mike Watkins).

available.

G.T. cars with rear radius arms will have them examined for corrosion, sloppy bushes or loose or missing mounting bolts or nuts.

Shock Absorbers

On the Classic, Capri, Anglia, and the Cortina estate there are lever type shock absorbers fitted. The tester will look for fluid leaks or damage to the links between the shock absorber body and the axle.

He will also look to see if the car goes on bouncing up and down after he depresses each rear corner.

You can do the same before you take the car to the centre.

Service Brake System

The service brake is M.O.T. language for the foot brake, or the main braking system. The tester will examine the handbrake lever to make sure it can be set in the ON position and will not be released accidentally. It must be securely fixed to the bodywork and the tester will look for any rust or damage to the bodywork within 12 inches of the lever mountings. This is

unlikely (though not impossible!) on small Fords as the floor mounted handbrake is in the centre of the car and subject to protection from oil from the engine's lower breather pipe or from the gearbox.

On cars with dashboard mounted handbrakes the tester may wish to open the bonnet to examine cables, linkages and pivot levers. Frayed or damaged cables will fail.

If you have fitted the wrong handbrake cable (one too long for the car) you will not get away with putting a knot in the cable to shorten it. There are recognised cable adjusters available for this.

Service Brake

The tester will look for leaking brake fluid, test for a spongy brake pedal, and also check that when force is applied to the brake pedal it does not slowly sink to the floor.

Under the car he will check for corrosion in any of the brake pipes (not very likely if you have fitted copper pipes -- see the Address section at the end of the book) and will also look for flexible hoses which bulge under pressure.

Brake discs, drums, shoes and pads will be checked as far as possible without dismantling any part of the car.

Service Brake Performance

The foot brake needs to achieve a minimum result of 50 per cent efficiency, when measure on the rolling road. This does not mean very much to you and I, but is a measure of how well the brakes will stop the car. All you can do here is keep the brakes well maintained, perhaps try an emergency stop on a quiet road prior to the test, and trust that the magic figure will be achieved.

If brakes operate unevenly, or stick, this will show up in the test.

Parking Brake Performance

For small Fords which do not have "dual" system brakes the handbrake must achieve a minimum result of 25 per cent efficiency. See comments above.

Tyres and Wheels

Damaged wheels, either buckles or cracks, will fail the test. Missing or loose wheel nuts and studs will also fail.

Note that many people think that the spare wheel is included in the test. It isn't. However if a problem is spotted, you will be advised on the VT30 form.

Tyre Type

Are the correct type of tyres fitted? By this the tester means are crossply or radial fitted, and if so are they in a legal combination? I would avoid any possible controversy here and take all crossply tyres and throw them away as far as you can. That removes a host of possible M.O.T. problems and makes your car much safer to drive.

Too wide tyres squeezed onto the wrong rims (or the opposite, too narrow onto the wrong rim) will result in a fail. If the tyre fouls any of the bodywork or the suspension you can also expect a fail. All of this can be checked before you set out to the test centre.

Tyre Condition

The tester is looking for bad cuts to the tyre wall or tread, blisters, or other weak or damaged areas on the tyre, plus the condition that everyone knows about -- tread depth. The new tread depth minimum will shortly be 1.6 mm. See New Tests and Checks later in this Chapter.

The tester will be looking at your wheels and tyres. Cuts or other damage to the tyre could cost you a Pass certificate. The wheel on the right has been thoroughly cleaned and inspected so there should be no problem with damage to the road wheel. The wheel on the left is about to undergo the same treatment. (Photo: Mark and Jill Bradbury).

Ford's MacPherson struts are a favourite fail on many cars. That top mounting point will be checked for corrosion, as will the condition of the strut itself. (Photo: Mark and Jill Bradbury)

Seatbelts

Most of the Small Fords covered by this book would not have had seatbelts fitted as standard. They became law on 1st January 1965 and if the car is registered on or after this date, then they must be fitted and are tested.

Generally the situation is this. If seatbelts are fitted they will be tested. If your car was registered before January 1965 then you do

This is the interior of MK1 Cortina Owners Club Chairman Mike Pratt's Crayford convertible Cortina. Obviously, the roof is removed in creating a convertible, so where does the strength in the bodyshell come from? The answer is these "internal" sills and strengthening pieces at the bottom and front of the door. (Photo: Mike Pratt).

not need to have them fitted and you will not be failed for not having them.

Seatbelt Mountings

Seat belt mountings could include the inner sill, where the bottom mounting is located. If the sill is rotten and judged to be a load-bearing member you will fail on that. If the sill is rotten within 12 inches of the seat belt mounting you may then fail in two categories.

Seatbelt Condition

Seat belts must not be cut or damaged or show signs of repair.

Seatbelt Operation

If you have inertia reel seat belts the tester will want to see that they will lock if tugged sharply. If they do not then you will fail. Check before you go.

Windscreen Washers

Make sure you fill the washer bottle or bottles. Some detergent or proprietary liquid helps to keep the glass clear and will also prevent it freezing in winter. (Alternatively, you can always add a little methylated spirit to the water to achieve the same result). Test before you go!

Windscreen Wipers

Wipers fail a lot of cars, as their condition deteriorates gradually and the driver may not be aware of a problem. The safest course of action is to fit new units each year.

Remember that they must be the correct size for the vehicle and move over an adequate area of the screen.

Horn

Does the horn work? Test by operating

it. If you car fails on the horn then you are poorer by the test fee and could have easily saved yourself the time, trouble, cost and inconvenience. Remember that two-tone horns on passenger cars are illegal.

Classic and Capri owners BEWARE. Up until recently, the horn rings on these cars were as scarce as droppings from a rocking-horse. My M.O.T. tester broke mine a few years ago trying to get the horn to work. If necessary, advise the tester of this problem. Luckily, the owners club are now seeking to have this item re-manufactured.

Exhaust System

If there is a leak you will certainly fail. If the exhaust system is not secured properly you will also fail. Many cars fail on the condition of the exhaust system.

The M.O.T. Test

A MacPherson strut top in this sort of state will certainly bring an M.O.T. fail. Vehicle structure problems such as this need urgent attention before they get to this condition. However, to put this into perspective, the car cost the author 25 pounds and after a few months part-time welding provided daily transport to work for more than two years!

Vehicle Structure

The tester is interested primarily in load bearing structures. What does this mean? How does it apply to the small Ford range?

Basically it means all the main chassis members, including the outriggers. Inner sills are load bearing while outer sills may not be considered load bearing. Some corrosion may be allowed on an outer sill, but the question then becomes a matter of degree. How much corrosion is too much?

All the suspension mounting points and steering mounting points are definite areas for inspecting for corrosion. To quote from the "M.O.T. Tester's Manual", "Excessive corrosion, serious distortion or fracture in a load bearing member or surrounding panelling of the chassis or body structure within 30 cm (12 inches) of any spring mounting..." etc. would result in a fail.

New Tests and Checks

From November 1st 1991 a special purpose tool to improve M.O.T. testing corrosion assessment will be introduced. This is described as a combined tapping hammer, blunt scraper and short lever which bears the three triangles logo as a mark of authenticity.

These will be available from equipment and tool suppliers and instructions regarding their use will be issued.

As this is a very new introduction it is not yet clear how it will be used. It is understood that the tester will now be able to tap the chassis or bodywork with the special tool to assess its condition while prior to this the tester had to rely on finger pressure.

Tyre Tread Depth

From January 1st 1992 all passenger carrying vehicles including cars must have tyres conforming to a legal minimum of 1.6 mm tread depth. This applies to all vehicles used after January 2nd 1933.

This change from 1 mm tread depth should cause few problems to conscientious drivers and brings the requirement closer to European standards.

Exhaust Emission Testing

From November 1st 1991 an exhaust emission test will be introduced to the M.O.T. test. This will check carbon monoxide and hydrocarbon emissions by means of an approved exhaust gas analyser which will itself be subject to regular calibration. The new rules will be applied as follows:

For vehicles first used between August 1st 1975 and July 31st 1983, a maximum of

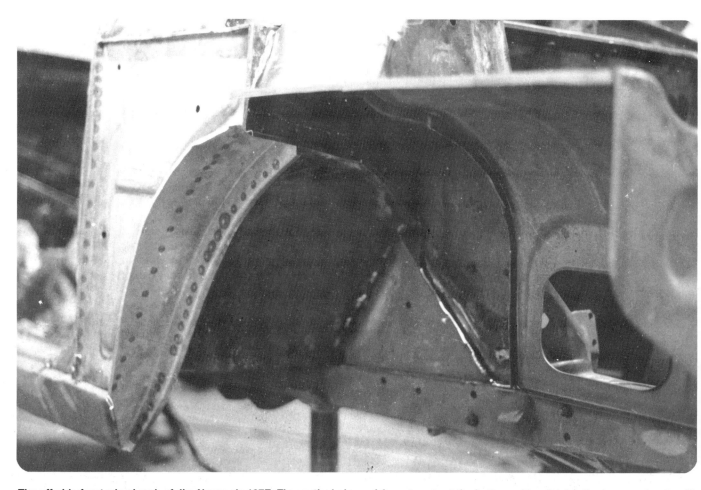

The off-side front wheel arch of Jim Norman's 107E. The vertical piece of A-post rusts at the bottom where it joins the inner and outer sill. All the metalwork here is new, following a complete front end rebuild. Jim obviously has access to a spot-welder -- just look at all those spots! (Photo: Jim Norman).

6 per cent carbon monoxide in the exhaust gas.

For vehicles first used on or after August 1st 1983, a maximum of 4.5 per cent carbon monoxide in the exhaust gas.

For vehicles first used on or after August 1st 1975, a maximum of 1200 parts per million hydrocarbons in the exhaust gas.

While these dates will not directly affect small Fords of the age discussed in this book, there are some further requirements which might:

All vehicles will be checked to ensure that there is not excessive smoke from the exhaust, and,

"For all vehicles carbon monoxide emission levels will not be required to be reduced below the manufacturer's specification for the engine fitted to the vehicle. Vehicle owners will be encouraged to have their vehicles tuned to the manufacturer's specification wherever possible."

Conclusion

Having tested your pride and joy, the examiner will then issue a pass or fail certificate and sign the Inspection Report VT30.

If the vehicle is too dangerous to drive on the road, the examiner will state this in section D in which case you should make alternative arrangements to get the vehicle safely home. That means get a trailer!

Throughout this section I have continuously emphasised that you can perform almost all the tests involved before you even set out to the test centre. I have had cars fail on things I thought were okay, things that I had inspected and thought they were all right. Generally the examiner has taken the trouble to point out the problem to me.

I have also been failed over the last 25 years on things I have neglected. My own fault, but you can always find an excuse to account for your car not being properly maintained -- too busy at work, no time,

The author's G.T. Cortina getting a new MacPherson strut tower. No more M.O.T. problems here.

Will your small Ford look as good at the M.O.T. test station? This is Mike Watkins' very tidy looking Classic which took part in the 1991 Pirelli Classic Marathon. Various photos of this car appear in this book. (Photo: Mike Watkins).

don't use the car very much -- fill in your own excuse.

On every occasion the test has been fair. I might not have been happy at the time, but on reflection the tests have always been fair. Problems are few and far between, but if you feel badly treated, fill in an appeal form and air your grievance.

Whatever the situation the M.O.T. test is with us to stay and it comes round every year. Don't be put in the position where you get a fail certificate and are forced off the road while looking for spares. Keep on top of the situation, submit the car for the test before the old certificate expires and you will have a hassle-free M.O.T.

Remember if you do fail and need spares the best source is the owner's club. This is run by part time enthusiasts for no reward. Don't expect main dealer service from them. You owe it to yourself and to the club to take the test in plenty of time to allow spares to be delivered should there be a problem. Better still, ensure there is no problem!

On page 139 is a checklist which you can photocopy and use for your car. Five minutes spent checking off the various items will be time well spent!

PHOTO ON PAGE 138. The author gets down to some serious welding on one of his three MK1 Cortinas. This car has just had a new centre outrigger welded in place and the author is making good some small holes in the floor. Lying underneath a car welding is quite difficult, but a job can often be tidied up from above. Note the wiring tied up out of the way. (Photo: Derek Thow).

M.O.T. CHECKLIST

LIGHTING EQUIPMENT

✔ Front & Rear Lamps   `TICK`

✔ Headlamps   `TICK`

✔ Headlamp Aim   `TICK`

✔ Stop Lamps   `TICK`

✔ Rear Reflectors   `TICK`

✔ Direction Indicators   `TICK`

STEERING AND SUSPENSION

✔ Steering Control   `TICK`

✔ Steering Mechanism/ system   `TICK`

✔ Power Steering   `TICK`

✔ Transmission Shafts   `TICK`

✔ Stub Axle Assemblies   `TICK`

✔ Wheel Bearings   `TICK`

✔ Front Suspension   `TICK`

✔ Rear Suspension   `TICK`

✔ Shock Absorbers   `TICK`

BRAKES

✔ Service Brake System Condition   `TICK`

✔ Parking Brake System Condition   `TICK`

✔ Service Brake Performance   `TICK`

✔ Parking Brake Performance   `TICK`

✔ Service Brake Balance   `TICK`

TYRES AND WHEELS

✔ Tyre Type   `TICK`

✔ Tyre Condition   `TICK`

✔ Tread Depth   `TICK`

✔ Roadwheels   `TICK`

SEATBELTS

✔ Mountings   `TICK`

✔ Condition   `TICK`

✔ Operation   `TICK`

GENERAL

✔ Windscreen Wipers & Washers   `TICK`

✔ Horn   `TICK`

✔ Exhaust system/ Silencer   `TICK`

VEHICLE STRUCTURE

`TICK`

Expert Required

Steering parts need to be checked for wear during any restoration. Here the track rods have had new track rod ends fitted and are about to be re-fitted to the car. Twisting the rod will lengthen or shorten the distance between the ends. This is because one track rod end has a right handed thread while the opposite end has a left handed thread. Although initial settings can be "guestimated" final setting should be done by an expert with the correct equipment to ensure correct wheel tracking.

Whilst there are hundreds of jobs the amateur restorer can successfully tackle, there are a few jobs which MUST be left to the experts. Either some special equipment is needed, or some special skill is required. There may be a short cut, but my advice is to get the experts to carry out the jobs described in the following section. One advantage of this is that it leaves you free to get on with something else!

Wheel Tracking

When you come to restore the steering system, you may need to fit new track rod ends. Once you fit the new track rod ends, you can never be quite sure that they have been fitted in EXACTLY the same position as the ones that came out. Indeed, you can never be sure that the original ones were right either!

The safest way to cure this problem is to take the finished car along to one of the many tyre service depots around the country. They have the special equipment which will ensure that the tracking is set correctly. The equipment consists of a small turntable onto which the front wheels are placed. Then, by carefully twisting the track rods the length of the rod is increased or reduced by very small amounts. This results in the front wheels either running exactly parallel to each other, or the front edges of the wheels facing out, or facing in. You will find a figure for your car in the workshop manual. When you have the job done it is nice to supply this figure to the fitter, who may be more familiar with more modern vehicles than the one you have. Look in the appropriate workshop manual.

If you don't have this job done, you can suffer from faulty steering which is dangerous, or at the other extreme suffer excessive tyre wear which is costly.

Wheel Balancing

When a wheel rotates slowly it does not matter too much if the tyre or wheel is out of balance. When it rotates quickly, any out-of-balance can be very dangerous.

An out-of-balance can occur if there is a slight heavy spot on one part of the tyre. Alternatively, the wheel itself may not be absolutely true, or it could have a heavy spot or a light spot on the rim. Any of these can cause the wheel to be out of balance.

This job must be left to the experts. The wheel is mounted on a special machine and any heavy spots are detected. These are marked, and exactly opposite the mark some lead weights are attached to the wheel. Using the machine plus the experience of the operator, the wheel is adjusted until the balance is considered to be acceptable. Obviously, if you have a high performance G.T. then balancing is more important than if you have a round-the-town saloon.

Out of balance wheels can cause steering problems and excessive tyre wear. A very bad wheel could cause excessive wear on the suspension too. Balancing is quite cheap to do, and you will probably find that if you have a new set of tyres fitted the suppliers will usually balance the wheels for you. They might ask if you want it done, and my recommendation is that you have it done. If money is very tight, just have it done on the front wheels. Remember then that you cannot swap wheels from front to back if you've only had the two front ones balanced!

Drive Shaft Balancing

As described above for wheels, a similar situation can occur with the drive shaft or prop shaft as it is often called. In top gear the prop shaft rotates at the same speed as the engine, so if the engine is doing 5000 rpm, so is the prop shaft. Any out of balance factor can cause the whole car to vibrate and be noisy and uncomfortable to drive. This job requires an expert. It is better if you have new universal joints fitted and have the prop shaft balanced at the same time. The shaft will be mounted in a machine and rotated. Any high or heavy spots will be located and compensated for by adding a weight opposite the problem area. A cheap and cheerful way of tackling this yourself is to use a jubilee clip. It will take some time and effort to get it in the right place but you may wish to try it. Prop shafts are balanced when they leave the factory but in some cases the balancing weight may have come off during the last 30 years, so it pays to check this before you fit your prop shaft in place.

Reboring

What is a rebore? The term is bandied around freely but many people, even quite knowledgeable enthusiasts, don't really know what it means.

Reboring a cylinder block demands special equipment, not the sort of thing the restorer has in the shed! Here a Ford block is being rebored as part of a Lotus 1558cc engine rebuild. Go to a recommended engine reconditioner for this sort of job. Back street cowboys could ruin the block for you. (Photo: Belinda Wilkins).

Quite simply it means an engineer bores out (or enlarges) the hole that the piston slides up and down in. The reason is that the action of the piston moving up and down will create wear, and the bore (the hole where the piston moves up and down) will wear unevenly. To get the bore clean and even, the engineer enlarges it very slightly. This machining action must be done very accurately.

When a rebore is carried out, a new set of pistons must be fitted. The bore is now bigger, so larger pistons are required to form a good seal and provide good compression. Compression makes the engine develop power.

This reboring process can only be carried out a certain number of times before the cylinder wall becomes too thin to contain the compression. If the bore wall becomes

Regrinding a crankshaft demands heavy, expensive equipment which the amateur is not going to have. Here a Ford crankshaft is reground. The shaft is mounted in the jaws at either end of the machine and rotated. The large grinding wheel in the middle of the photograph does all the work. Once ground and polished, the shaft will be returned to you with a set of thicker (oversize) bearings. (Photo: Belinda Wilkins).

too thin the engineer will advise you. How does he know? He will measure the internal diameter of the bore using an internal micrometer. This measures very accurately. He will know what pistons are available for your engine.

Oversize pistons are often available in plus 20 thou, plus 40, and plus 60 thousandth of an inch. (See next page).

If the bore wall is too thin to rebore, the engineer may be able to re-sleeve the bore. This means he bores out the hole even more and inserts a special tube which forms the new bore. This is much more expensive than a rebore, but could save an engine from the scrapheap. If you have no spare engine block available, your only choice may be to have the bores re-sleeved.

Regrinding

Regrinding a crankshaft follows the same principle as a rebore.

The bearing surface is ground down until a new, clean, and even layer of metal is exposed. When this is done the bearing that the shaft runs in must be made thicker to accommodate the thinner shaft.

Bearings are often available in plus 10, plus 20, plus 30, plus 40, plus 50 and plus

Tuning an engine may mean fitting a re-ground camshaft. Grinding the round part of the cam means that the cam follower will be that much closer to the centre-line of the camshaft. So when the cam follower rises on the "lumpy" bit, known as the lobe, it will rise higher so opening the valve more. Cam modification is complicated. Leave it to the experts!

60 thou. What is "thou"? It is the shortened term for thousandth of an inch. In these days of metric measurement there must be an equivalent, but it will be a long time before ``thou''stops being used. ``Take a few thou off'' means remove a very small amount.

Main bearings are supplied in packets of 10 for a five-bearing engine, or 6 for a three-bearing engine.

Remember that big end bearings also need to be replaced if the big end part of the shaft is reground. These are also available in sizes mentioned above.

Prior to installing a reground crankshaft, make absolutely sure that any swarf or metal filings have been removed. To do this push a thin welding rod into all the oilways. Alternatively, blow the oilways through with compressed air.

Complete cleanliness is essential. I have been guilty of making a mistake in this area and it meant I had to re-build an engine at considerable cost. When I assembled the main bearing and big end bearing caps I neglected to clean them properly. I should have used emery paper to clean off all the contaminants. When I bolted up the bearing caps the extra thickness of these contaminants, slight though it was, meant that the bearing shells were distorted and clamped the crankshaft tightly to the bearings.

I just thought it was a tight engine. I got the engine to run, but it was very rough, hard to start and ran very hot. When I later stripped it down again (and just think of the time and inconvenience of this!) my local motor engineer examined the crankshaft and bearing caps and pointed out my mistake. Don't get caught the same way.

Bearing caps should be clean, almost to the extent of being polished.

Flywheel Skimming

There are probably just two reasons why you would want your flywheel skimmed -- to lighten it, or to remove scoring caused by a worn out clutch. But what is skimming?

The flywheel disc is mounted in a machine, which may be a lathe or a more specialised machine, and a sharp tool is applied to the surface. The machine rotates the flywheel and the tool then removes small amounts of metal from the face of the flywheel.

If you are having the flywheel skimmed to reduce the weight, be aware of several things. First the Anglia 105E flywheel is already lighter than that fitted to the other Fords covered by this book. Secondly, having removed this weight the car may not be as pleasant to drive. The engine will accelerate faster, but tickover will have to be higher and gearchanging may be slightly more difficult. Look at all the pros and cons before having this work done.

Remember that there are already two flywheel weights. See Chapter Two.

Brake Disc Skimming

Disc skimming is the same as flywheel

These rusty brake discs can easily be saved by having them skimmed in a lathe. You'll have to undo four bolts which fasten the disc to the bearing hub and give the engineer the discs only. Shop around to get the best price for this work.

Unless you are a dab hand with a soldering iron a leaking radiator will have to be handed-in to a specialist for repair. Radiators can be re-cored, and if the top and bottom are leaking can be repaired too. Don't scrap a radiator until you have had an estimate!

Jim Norman's Prefect suffered severe front-end accident damage. During a long rebuild Jim took a number of photographs to illustrate the work being done. Here the bonnet has been fitted to ensure alignment with the scuttle panel. At this stage, with little serious welding completed -- only tacks -- it would still be easy to adjust the front panel if required. Note that vice-grips hold the various parts together. (Photo: Jim Norman).

skimming but without all the discussion about removing weight! You want to remove as little as possible if you have a disc skimmed. Consider replacing it with a new one.

I recently had this job costed in a machine shop doing general engineering. They said 20 pounds per brake disc. When I pointed out I could buy a new one for 16 or so the engineer recommended that I buy new ones. He was good enough to point out what was involved in doing the job. The disc has to be mounted in the jaws of a lathe, centred and checked for run out. This means is the disc flat, or does it have any unevenness in it? When all this is sorted out the engineer decides how much material needs to be removed from each side of the disc. He then sets up a tool and starts the machine. The process is largely automatic once set up, but it can take half an hour per side to machine. So for two brake discs the machine shop has to spend

some two hours of machine time. That time could be spent doing a much more profitable job.

The footnote to this story is that I then telephoned another machine shop specialising in rebores, regrinds and so on. They quoted 12 pounds per disc, since they were geared up to do that sort of work regularly. It pays to shop around.

HEADLAMP BEAM SETTING

Headlamp beam setting information is usually given in the workshop manual for your car. It can be done by shining the lights onto a wall which has been marked to show the correct aiming points, but it is much better to have it done professionally on the correct equipment.

If you do want to tackle it yourself the workshop manual gives all the measurements for height and so on, so you can mark out a wall or wallboard and set the headlamps against it.

CHASSIS ALIGNMENT

If you have reason to suspect that your chassis or body is misaligned you MUST have the car checked by experts. A body shop specialising in accident damage will have the necessary measuring equipment. Ford do provide body drawings in their workshop manuals, so you could try measuring all the reference points, but you would need a very accurate measuring device. My advice is look in the manual, decide if you can measure accurately enough, then when you decide you can't - have the car examined by experts.

ACCIDENT DAMAGE

Accident damage is really outside the scope of this book. We have tackled a number of jobs, some of which are quite complicated and may be beyond the ability of the newcomer to car restoration. Most can be learnt. Accident damage means the

Another view of Jim's Prefect. The new front end has been painted with a good finish being achieved because everything was removed before spraying. This bulkhead contains more holes than Ford intended. They were left this way as filling them successfully would have taken too long. The two large holes on the passenger side were later hidden by the washer bottle. (Photo: Jim Norman).

body shell or chassis rails are bent or otherwise damaged. It is VITAL that you get expert guidance if your small Ford is involved in an accident. The first words your expert will probably say are, "Is it really worth repairing?" Only you can decide that. Extensive damage means stripping out a lot of the car and fixing it to a body alignment jig. Bits of the chassis are then pulled or pushed back into place by means of hydraulic jacks. All of this work is beyond the ability of the amateur, if only because he does not have access to the necessary equipment. What you can do is the dismantling work. You can be the mechanic while the expert does his job and re-aligns your bodyshell. If damage is limited to a bent wing, then you can happily follow the advice given in the Body and Chassis Chapter. If in doubt -- seek assistance.

Paint

I don't get on well with paint. Only once did I do a spray job I was pleased with. I then went on to spoil it by putting on another coat before the first was properly dry. The result was sags and runs!

Paint mixing is an art. Go to a specialist and quote the paint code number on your car's chassis plate. If you can then quote the actual colour, for example "Caribbean Turquoise" the paint specialist should be able to mix the required paint from stock. The specialist will probably refer to a list or catalogue giving him the required ingredients for the paint colour.

Unless you are confident about spraying a car, I would tend to leave this job to an expert. It does no harm to try out your spraying skills where possible. If you get good results then by all means consider spraying the whole car. I am not so confident about paint so I'll be looking to the expert for this job.

Engine Building

Throughout this book I have assumed that you will be building your own engine from reconditioned parts. This may be beyond your ability or you may wish to put this job out to an expert, leaving you free to tackle something else.

When choosing an expert try to establish his knowledge of the Ford pre-crossflow engine. Remember that these engines were used between 1959 and 1969 so a lot of time has passed and much of the expertise may have moved on to later models. There is nothing particularly difficult about assembling a Ford engine, the only special tool you really need is a torque wrench. However it pays to check out the expert to save yourself grief later. He should also be sympathetic to your type of car. If the expert sees your restoration project as a chance to make a quick and easy pound then you will be the sorry one.

ABOVE: Respraying your own car can be tackled by the amateur restorer provided you have the time, confidence and a good helping of ability. Alex Gooding's Corsair was sprayed in a small garage but the results are excellent. A considerable amount of preparation work is required for a full body respray with lots of rubbing-down and a plentiful supply of newspapers needed for masking.

BELOW: Another view of Alex's Corsair. The doors, bootlid and bonnet were sprayed off the car and are stored in another shed until they can be refitted. Care needs to be taken, if doing the job this way, that the paint is mixed exactly the same way otherwise a mis-match may occur. If painted at different times with a different batch of paint slight differences in colour may be detected. No such problem arose on this excellent spray job. (Photos: Alex Gooding).

Expert Required

ABOVE: Building an engine may not be your forte, so you might have to put the job out to an expert. Make sure that the expert is sympathetic to old Ford engines, or he might just put together any old rubbish to make some easy money. This well put together engine is in Mike Watkins' Classic, entered in the 1991 Pirelli Classic Rally. (Photo: Mike Watkins).

BELOW: If you have not built an engine before don't start with the Lotus unit! Great care is needed in the assembly of these engines if long life and reliability is to be achieved. The beautiful engine bay belongs to Mike Pratt's MK1 Lotus Cortina. If you are rebuilding a Lotus engine you'll need Miles Wilkins' book, Lotus Twin Cam Engines, as a reference. (Photo: Mike Pratt).

ABOVE: Refurbishing a leaf spring is another job which the amateur cannot tackle. A forge or furnace may be needed to heat the leaves so that they can be re-set and tempered. Old, saggy springs can be given a new lease of life but new springs are available for many of the small Fords. If necessary a spring specialist could make a new set of springs for you. These new springs are on Mike Watkins' Classic and they appear to have been built to increase the ride height of the car. (Photo: Mike Watkins).

BELOW: One of Terry Burville's merry men welds a valance for a customer. If you can't weld you will have to call in an expert. Note the number of clamps used to maintain accuracy during welding.

Keeping Records

It is said that many small businesses fail because they do not keep good records. The same could be true of car restorations.

As indicated way back in Chapter One, when you rush off to dismantle your new toy, will you remember where everything goes in two or three years time?

If you think that it will not take you two or three years, but it will only take six months, then you are kidding yourself. It is extremely rare for any sort of restoration to be completed in such a short time. Invariably, the project gets side-lined for some reason or other. It could be illness, unemployment, a house move, divorce(!), another car coming on the scene -- fill in your own excuse. Certainly I never expected my Capri to be running round like a dog's dinner after 11 years, but it is!

Keep as many records as you can. You can make notes in a book, and for this I recommend a child's scrapbook with big pages. Then you can stick in photos, make notes etc. Also, keep every receipt for parts bought or services paid for.

The following section is offered if you have access to a computer. Don't worry if you don't. The important thing is to keep records. The more you keep the easier the job will be.

Computer-Aided Restoration

I believe this is the first time the phrase computer-aided restoration has been used. Computer buffs will immediately abbreviate that to CAR, while others will look at this section and quickly turn the page. Wait!

This section may not be of any interest to you! If this is the case I apologise. However, I have found the use of a simple computer to be of great help in carrying out car restoration. You may have access to a computer at work. Read on, give the subject a chance, then decide if it is of any use to you.

You can follow all of this advice and use a pencil and paper. However there are several things that you cannot easily do with pencil and paper, which the computer is really good at!

With any computer which has a word

```
                                    HTB 148 B

Replace/repair rear valance

Repair o/s wheel arch

weld n/s door

clonk from n/s steering

o/s and n/s headlamps

clean/repaint front outriggers

wire brush/paint front chassis

judder from rear propshaft

front disc brakes sticking

adjust handbrake

spare wheel well corroded

finish strut-top repair

fuel gauge reads high

rear wheel arch holes

change screen and rubber

seat covers

replace front wings

rust on front panel + headlamps

replace felt and rubber mats/carpets

repair front of sills

repair inner wings both sides

repair windscreen pillar/ both sides

repair A post

replace braid round doors + clean headlining

fix wiper/washer switch + fix chrome trim
```

This is a print out of the computer file I made up when I laid up my Cortina Super HTB 148B a few years ago. Things like the clonk from the n/s steering may well be fixed during the overhaul of the steering gear, but the item which says fuel gauge reads high could be a very valuable reminder that the gauge or sender unit needs attention.

processing package on it, you can open a file and make a list of all the parts you need to buy to complete the job. Another file could act as a sort of diary of the work. If you have the will-power to keep it up to date (just like a real paper diary!) you will be rewarded in years to come when you read about all the problems you had and how you overcame them.

Illustrated is a copy of a list I made up some years ago when I laid-up a car. It consists of the things which would require attention before the car could be put back on the road. You may think you will remember that the steering "clonked" when you turned left, but in six months time or a year, you will have forgotten and that list will become extremely valuable.

More advanced computer users might like to consider a spreadsheet package to cost-out the complete restoration. You can also use the same spreadsheet to log your hours.

The way I use it is this;

Down the left hand side I made up a long list of all the parts I thought I would have to purchase to restore my car. In the next column I put in some prices. They were guesses of how much I thought an item would cost. So for example, I had RES-PRAY down as 400 pounds, while BRAKES was budgeted at 50 pounds. All the figures in the second column can be added up by the spreadsheet and a total produced in another column, marked TOTAL COST.

My first estimates showed that I would need to spend some 2385 pounds to restore my car fully. Then I remembered that I had spent over 200 pounds of that already to purchase the vehicle itself.

As prices change, say when you actual purchase parts, you can enter the exact amount spent against its title. The spreadsheet will alter the total for you.

You might like to put a marker, such as an asterisk in the next column to indicate that the cost is an actual one.

When the job is done you will have a complete breakdown of all expenses involved.

Looking at this another way, you set yourself a budget, then try to work within it. This involves a few more calculations to be set up within the spreadsheet, but they are not too difficult to do. You would need to decide on a total budget for the project. Then add up all the jobs you think you need to have done. If budget exceeds jobs, then you are okay. If not, then you are going to have to make some adjustments to the project to keep within budget, or go back to your wife/girlfriend and try to get an increase on your allowance!

A few hours spent tapping away on the computer can quickly pay for itself, as it

ITEM	COST		Hours	TOTAL COST		2385
car	200	*	20			
t/port	10	*	3	TOTAL HOURS		83.5
gas	44	*	2			
drills	7	*	0.5			
panels	53	*	1			
t/rod/end	36	*				
t/c/arm	12	*				
a/rollbush	12	*				
rearbuskit	14	*				
battray	30					
respray	400					
coreplug	5					
timinchain	5					
cam	40					
followers	30					
gaskets	15					
rearspring	70		2			
struts	70		5			
struttops	50					

My spreadsheet for the G.T. Cortina project. I have spent 200 pounds on the car, 44 pounds on welding gas, 53 pounds for panels and so on. Total estimate for the whole job is 2385 pounds and I have so far spent 83.5 hours on the car. The asterisk means an actual cost rather than an estimate.

provides so much information.

Under the hours column I log the number of hours I spend on a given job title. For example, under CAR I know I spent some 15 hours getting all the bits of the car moved from where they were stored to my house.

This computer-aided restoration may become more and more popular as time goes on. More people have personal computers at home than ever before. The disc on which you stored your information could become a valuable part of the car if you ever came to sell it.

Without going into too much technical detail if a file can be converted to ASCII format, then it can be moved between computers. Refer to the manufacturers manual for details of ASCII conversions.

One word of warning. Don't let the computer take over your restoration. If you would prefer to sit in warmth and comfort and play with your computer, rather than spend countless evenings in a draughty garage, then sell the car! The computer is just another tool. Use it as you think best.

SWANSEA DVLC

The Driver and Vehicle Licensing Centre at Swansea in South Wales contains the records of most cars and changes of ownership.

You are allowed to contact Swansea by letter and ask for all available details of previous owners. As discussed in Chapter One this can provide many benefits, as previous owners often have spare parts hidden away in their garages. Often for twenty years or more!

RESTORATION CHECKLIST

The following pages are offered as a check list for your restoration. You can photocopy these pages, as long as the Willow Publishing (Magor) logo is not removed. Removal of the logo or other alteration to these forms without written permission is not allowed.

RECORDS FOR VEHICLE:
BOUGHT: /   /
M.O.T. TEST DATE:

ENGINE

Crankshaft Re-ground by/ Date:
Undersize:
Oversize shells size:
Oversize shells supplied by
Shells/Part Number
Crankshaft Thrust Washers size

Block Rebored by/ Date:
Piston oversize:
Pistons Supplied by:
Pistons/Part Number:

Gasket Set Part Number:
Gaskets Supplied by:

Clutch Supplied by:
Make / Part number:

Camshaft type / Part number:
Supplied by/ Date:
Cam Followers:
Cam Followers supplied by:
Cam Followers Part Number:
Timing chain fitted / Part Number:

Core plugs replaced / Date:
Core Plugs supplied by / Part number:

Cylinder Head overhauled / Date:

Carburettor overhauled / Date:
Carburettor type / Part Number:
Air filter supplied by:
Air Filter type / Part Number:

Water pump type / Part Number:
Water pump supplied by:

Dynamo overhauled / Supplied by:
Dynamo / Part Number:
Fan belt type / Part Number:
Fan belt length:
Fan belt supplied by:

Distributor overhauled / Replaced / Date:
Distributor Type / Part Number:
New points fitted / Date:
New condenser fitted / Date:

Oil pump fitted / Type:
Oil Filter type / Part Number:
Oil added / Date:
Oil type / Manufacturer:

Petrol Pump Overhauled / Date:
Petrol Pump supplied by:
Petrol Pump Type / Part Number:

Engine First Run / Date:
Car Mileage/ Date:

Gearbox

Gearbox Type / Part Number:
Gearbox supplied by:
Gearbox Overhauled:
Gearbox Oil Filled:
Gearbox Oil Type:
Gearbox Speedometer Drive Installed / Teeth =

Clutch Slave Cylinder Overhauled / Date:
Clutch Slave Cylinder supplied by:
Clutch Slave Cylinder type / Part Number:

Prop Shaft

Prop Shaft overhauled:
Prop Shaft Universal Joints fitted / Date:
Prop Shaft Universal Joints type / Part Number:

Willow Publishing (MAGOR)

© *Restoring Small Fords*

Final Drive

Final Drive Unit overhauled / Date:
Final Drive ratio fitted:
Final Drive Unit oil type:

Brakes, Front

Brake Shoes / Type:
Brake Shoes Supplied by / Part Number:
Brake Pads / Type:
Brake Pads supplied by / Part Number:
Brake Cylinders overhauled / Supplied by:
Brake Cylinder type / Part Number:
Brake Calliper overhauled / Supplied by:
Brake Calliper type / Part Number:

Brakes, Rear

Brake Shoes / Type:
Brake Shoes supplied by / Part Number:
Brake Cylinder overhauled / Supplied by:
Brake Cylinder type / Part Number:

Brake Master Cylinder supplied by:
Brake Master Cylinder overhauled:
Brake Master Cylinder type / Part Number:

Brake Pipes supplied by:
Brake Pipes type / Part Number:

Handbrake

Handbrake Cables supplied by:
Handbrake cable type / PartNumber:

Wheels, Tyres, Bearings

Tyres Fitted/ Date:
Tyre Type:

Tyres Supplied by:

Front Wheel Bearings fitted / Date:
Front Wheel Bearings supplied by:
Front Wheel Bearings type / Part Number:

Wheels Balanced:
Balanced by / Date:

Wheel Tracking done by / Date:
Wheel Tracking Settings:

Miscellaneous

Radiator Fitted / Date:
Radiator Supplied by:
Radiator Repaired by / Guarantee:

Antifreeze Installed / Date:
Antifreeze Type / Make:
Antifreeze Quantity:

Exhaust System Fitted / Date:
Exhaust System Supplied by:

Windscreen Wipers fitted / Date:
Windscreen Wiper Type / Part Number:

Battery Fitted / Date:
Battery Type / Part Number:
Battery Supplied by / Guarantee:

Bodywork

Panels supplied by:
Panels repaired:
Notes:

Willow Publishing (MAGOR)

© *Restoring Small Fords*

ABOVE: Ray Checkley's 1966 V4 G.T. Corsair is used every day and has over 140,000 miles on the clock. It is important to keep good records when parts are changed or when major work is done. If you were to buy a 1966 Corsair you would want to know as much as possible about the car, wouldn't you? Here Liz and Ray are about to set off on a tour of the Lake District in 1991. (Photo: Liz and Ray Checkley).

BELOW: Why does BEJ 555 C have a battery tray in the boot? Why is the original battery tray in the engine bay missing? Who did it? Why? When? Owner for eight years, Wyn Evans didn't do it, so it must have been some-one after 1982. The author is currently tracking down all this information from previous owners. It will be restored with a battery in the boot.

Useful Addresses

Ford Motor Company Limited,
Press & Information, Public Affairs,
Eagle Way,
Brentwood,
Essex, CM13 3BW
United Kingdom.

Old Ford Spares Service,
Unit 4, 14 Paynes Lane,
Rugby, CV21 2UK,
United Kingdom.

Telephone: 0788 547642
Fax: 0788 547644

Old Ford Spares Service offer a full range of new and reconditioned spares for Anglia/Popular/Prefect 100E (1953-1962), Anglia 105E/123E Saloon/Estate/Van (1959-1968), 107E Prefect (1959-1962), Classic 315 and Consul Capri (1961-1964), Corsair (1963-1970) and MK1 Cortina (including Lotus) (1963-1966). They offer a full Mail Order service worldwide, and accept credit cards.

Edgware Motor Accessories,
94 High Street,
Edgware,
Middlesex, HA8 7BN,
United Kingdom.

Telephone: 081 952 4789 and 081 952 9311
Fax: 081 952 4752

Edgware Motor Accessories specialise in rubber and trim for all old cars and cover all the small Fords. Items include sponge rubber strips and mould sections, screen rubbers, exterior window weatherstrip, fasteners and fittings. They offer a full Mail Order service and accept credit cards.

Panelcraft (Magor),
2 Hollytree Bungalows,
Waenllapria,
Llanelly Hill,
nr Abergavenny,
Gwent, NP7 0PN,
United Kingdom.

Telephone: 0873 830966
Fax: 0873 830966

Panelcraft specialise in small runs of hard to get Ford panels. Individual panels can be made to order if you can provide an old panel as a pattern. Examples of Panelcraft's work are shown throughout this book. Father and son between them have over 40 years experience in the fabrication of high quality repair panels that really fit!

Automec Equipment & Parts Ltd,
36 Ballmoor,
Buckingham,
Buckinghamshire, MK18 1RT,
United Kingdom.

Telephone: 0280 822818
Fax: 0280 823140

Automec offer a wide range of products, but are probably best known for their range of copper brake pipes. Made up as a kit for most popular cars, the copper pipe is thick-walled, seamless and fitted with brass unions, making them maintenance free and non rusting!

Burton Performance Centre,
623/631 Eastern Avenue,
Barkingside,
Ilford,
Essex, IG2 6PN,
United Kingdom.

Telephone: 081 554 2281 and 081 554 8256
FAX: 081 554 4828

Ford specialists since 1963, Burton's can supply spares, service and tuning parts for all the Ford pre-crossflow engines, twin-cam engines and V4 and V6 motors. A full range of machining operations can be carried out. Burton's also carry stocks of high quality specialist equipment and accessories.

London Stainless Steel Exhaust Centre,
249-253 Queenstown Road,
Battersea,
London, SW8 3NP
United Kingdom.

Telephone: 071 627 2271
Fax: 071 627 0991

Manufacturers and suppliers of stainless steel exhaust systems for all the Fords covered in this book. Massive stocks and quick delivery on most orders. Dispatch from London, Heathrow to anywhere in the world. All systems have a "Lifetime Guarantee".

Addresses

Lotus Cortina Spares Centre,
North Street Trading Estate,
Crewkerne,
Somerset, TA18 7AW,
United Kingdom.

Telephone: 0460 73775
Fax: 0460 76855

Supplier of a wide range of spares for Lotus Cortina, including replacement alloy castings for the Lotus Twin Cam engine. A full range of spares and performance engine components for this engine are also available. A comprehensive list of suspension, bodywork, weather seals, electrics and lighting, transmissions, brakes, and interior parts are offered.

Ford 50 Spares,
69 Jolliffe Road,
Poole,
Dorset, BH15 2HA
United Kingdom.

Telephone: 0202 679258

Ford 50 Spares specialise in spares for 1951-1966 Zephyr, Zodiac and Consul models. However they are always worth a phone call for spares for Anglia, Cortina, Corsair, Classic and Capri. For these cars they stock re-manufactured windscreen rubbers, front suspension top mounts and some mechanical items. Other parts are available to special order.

Frost Auto Restoration Techniques Ltd,
Crawford Street,
Rochdale,
Lancs, OL16 5NU
United Kingdom.

Telephone: 0706 58619
Fax: 0706 860338

Frost Auto Restoration Techniques are Europe's leading suppliers of specialist tools and equipment for auto restoration and fabrication. Their full-colour catalogue displays an extensive range of specialist implements for the restorer, including welding equipment and metalworking hand tools.

Flairline Supplies,
124 Cricklewood Broadway,
London, NW2 3EE
United Kingdom.

Telephone: 081 450 4844

Flairline Supplies offer arc and Mig welding equipment, air compressors, air tools, and a comprehensive range of automotive tools and equipment, all at discount prices.

Five Star Ford,
Unit 6, Sylvan Industrial Estate,
Sylvan Grove,
London, SE15,
United Kingdom.

Telephone: 071 277 8143

Five Star Ford carry a large stock of new and second-hand spares for most Ford cars from 1955 to 1965. They also have a large workshop where they offer a "supply and fit" service and can carry out work ranging from routine servicing to full engine rebuilds. Occasionally they have cars for sale.

A.J.P. Emblems Ltd,
Unit 23 Crawford House,
West Avenue,
Wigston,
Leicester, LE8 2FB,
United Kingdom.

Telephone: 0533 813881
Fax: 0533 887429

A.J.P. manufacture the finest chromework, gold and enamelled badges for sports and classic cars the world over. If your emblem is no longer available A.J.P. can reproduce or restore your existing badge to its original condition. They offer a wide range of badges for small Fords.

LMC Panels,
Quartermaster Road,
West Wilts Trading Estate,
Westbury,
Wiltshire, BA13 4JT,
United Kingdom.

Telephone: 0373 865088
Fax: 0373 865464

LMC Panels are manufacturers of high quality replacement body panels and chassis repair sections. Order through distributors, or in case of difficulty contact them at the above address.

PUBLISHER'S NOTE: This is not intended to be a complete list. Look through the pages of the monthly magazines such as the "Practical Classics and Car Restorer" for other addresses.

Clubs and Spares

When writing to any owners club, don't forget to include a stamped, self-addressed envelope for the reply.

Ford Classic And Capri Owners Club,

Club Officially recognised by Ford Motor Company Ltd.

Membership Secretary, Maureen Salmon, 58 Dewey Road, Dagenham, Essex, RM10 8AR, United Kingdom.

The Ford Classic and Capri Owners Club have re-manufactured the following panels in steel:

Rear Valance, Inner rear apron chassis section, Headlamp panels, Front apron quarter panel, Sidelamp panel, outer, Sidelamp panel, inner, Sills, Headlamp panel shelf, Offside rear wing repair panel, Door pillar to inner wing repair panel, Inner wing in front of sill panel, Inner wing suspension shroud, Flitch panel, Suspension top plate, Door to wheel arch lower panel, Front of wing repair panel, Front outrigger/jacking point.

(Front wings and right hand boot floor pending)

Other panels available from time to time.
The club also have a large list of mechanical items available. As these vary in availability they are not listed here. Contact the club for details.
Club policy is that spares are available to members only.

Ford Sidevalve Owners Club

Club Officially recognised by Ford Motor Company Ltd.

Membership Secretary, Mick Crouch, 30 Earles Close, Bishopstoke, Eastleigh, Hants, SO5 6HY, United Kingdom.

For the 100E and 107E the following re-manufactured parts are available:

Radiator hoses (all types), Water pump (reconditioned), Engine core plug, Air filter rubber sleeve, Cylinder block water inlet tube (for bottom hose), Clutch driven plate (reconditioned), Front suspension leg (reconditioned), Handbrake cable, Anglia, Prefect & Popular bonnet script badges, Anglia, Prefect & Popular boot script badges, De Luxe boot script badge, Triangular wing motif, Bonnet Vee, De Luxe front & rear windscreen rubbers, Side window rubber (2-door models), Rubber floor grommets, Dimple hub caps, Stainless steel exhaust system (all saloons), Gear lever rubber gaiter, Door sill, Engine mountings (100E only), Gearbox mounting (100E and early 107E only), Front suspension top mountings, Front suspension top mounting bearings and cones.
There are a number of other parts being investigated, including several lenses, rear spring front eye bush, big end shells and gasket sets.
Club policy is that spares are available to members only.

Ford MK1 Cortina Owners Club

Club officially recognised by Ford Motor Company Ltd.

Membership Secretary, Roger Raisey, 51 Studley Rise, Trowbridge, Wiltshire, BA14 0PD, United Kingdom.

The Ford Cortina MK1 Owners Club have re-manufactured the following parts and panels;

Front wings, Front wing repair sections, Sills, Strut repairs, (under wings), Suspension top plates, Rear Wheel arches, Lower rear corners, Front & Rear lower valances, Chassis outriggers, A-posts, Suspension Top mounts (rubber), Bottom Ball Joints, Studs/bushes, Track Control Arms, Gearbox mounts, Dash-type handbrake cables, Headlamp bezels.
There are more than two pages of new or reconditioned spares listed in the owners club magazine. As these vary from time to time they are not listed here. Contact the club for details.
Club policy is that spares are available to members only.

Clubs and Spares

Ford 105E Anglia Owners Club

Club Officially recognised by Ford Motor Company Ltd.

Membership Secretary, Mr & Mrs M Lewis, 81 Compton Road, North End, Portsmouth, Hants, PO2 0SR, United Kingdom.

The Ford Anglia Owners club have available the following body panels:

Saloon rear spring hanger, Saloon rear valance, Saloon rear crossmember, Saloon rear jacking point, Saloon rear jacking point chassis extension, Saloon/Estate outer sill, Saloon/Estate inner sill repair panel, Front wing rear edge repair panel, Front jacking point, Door pillar outer skin repair panel, Saloon rear wing lower corner repair panel, Estate rear wing lower corner repair panel, Van rear wing lower corner repair panel.

The club have a considerable list of mechanical and electrical items available -- far too many to list here. There is a total of four pages (in small type!) of spares available for the Anglia 105E.

Club policy is that spares are available to members only.

Ford Corsair Owners Club

Membership Secretary, Liz Checkley, 7 Barnfield, New Malden, Surrey, KT3 5RH, United Kingdom.

The club have re-manufactured the grey plastic beading round the headlight unit surround, and are currently trying to find a source of rear windscreen rubbers.

Pre-67 Ford Owners Club,

Membership Secretary, Alison Miller, 100 Main Street, Cairneyhill, Fife, United Kingdom.

Th Pre-67 Owners Club caters for customised or standard Fords. You don't have to be an owner to join the club and they also have special rates for under-17 year olds who are encouraged within the club.

The Club do not re-manufacture any spares but have substantial stocks of new and second hand spares. When they locate an MOT failure, or other unwanted old Ford the club break it for spares.

The Lotus Cortina Register

Membership Secretary, Jeff Fenton, 10 Manor Farm Drive, Soothill, Batley, Yorks, WF17 6HE, United Kingdom.

The Register publish a regular magazine which includes spares for sale and wanted.

LMC Panels

LMC Panels, Quartermaster Road, West Wilts Trading Estate, Westbury, Wiltshire, BA13 4JT, United Kingdom, press the following panels for small Fords.

For the Anglia 105E they have outer sills, inner sills and inner wing sections which fit around the MacPherson strut suspension mounting. There are also centre crossmembers and saloon rear spring hangers.

For the 100E (1955-1962) outer sills are available.

Corsairs can have outer sills, top suspension plates (for the V4 model), front chassis extensions and centre chassis outriggers. At the back rear spring hangers are available.

The MK1 Cortina is offered outer sills, top suspension plates, under wing kit (pan and verticals), front chassis extension, main chassis repair plate, centre chassis outrigger, and rear spring hangers for saloon and estate.

A similar selection of panels is available for the MK2 Cortina. Also, a wide range of Escort panels is supplied. Many of these, can be adapted to fit other small Fords.

It is important to bear in mind when buying replacement body panels that they are not only of the correct gauge of metal but that they are also correctly shaped to fit the exact contours of the car.

Bibliography

Much of the literature relating to small Fords is freely available on the second-hand market. Try second hand-bookshops, autojumble or the owners' club magazines.

Books

"Panel Craft," by Tommy Sandham, published by Willow Publishing (Magor), Barecroft Common, Magor, Newport, Gwent, NP6 3EB, United Kingdom. Contains a large section on MK1 Cortina body restoration.

"How to Restore Chassis and Monocoque Bodywork," by Tommy Sandham. Published by Osprey (address below). Now out of Print.

"Guide to Do-it-Yourself Purchase and Restoration of the Ford Cortina and Escort," by Kim Henson. Published by Haynes Publishing Group, Sparkford, nr Yeovil, Somerset, BA22 7JJ, United Kingdom. Available from bookshops, car accessory shops or direct from Haynes.

"The Sporting Fords, Volume 1 - Cortinas," by Graham Robson. Published by Motor Racing Publications Ltd, Unit 6, The Pilton Estate, 46 Pitlake, Croydon, CR0 3RY, United Kingdom.

"Ford Cortina MK1," by Jonathan Wood. Published by Osprey as an Osprey Autohistory. Now Out of Print.

"Tuning Small Fords," by John Young. Published by Speed and Sports Publications Ltd, Acorn House, Victoria Road, Acton, London W3. Now out of Print. A later version of the same book, but entitled *"Tuning Anglias and Cortinas,"* was also available. Also out of print.

"The Theory & Practice of Cylinder Head Modification," by David Vizard, Published by Motor Racing Publications Ltd. Address above.

"Lotus Twin Cam Engine," by Miles Wilkins, published by Osprey. (Octopus Publishing Group Ltd, Michelin House, 81 Fulham Road, London, SW3 6RB, United Kingdom).

"Lotus Cortina Gold Portfolio 1963-1970"," published by Brooklands Books Ltd, PO Box 146, Cobham, Surrey, KT11 1LG, United Kingdom.

"Car Bodywork Repair Manual," by Lindsay Porter, published by Haynes (address above).

"Ford 100E: Anglia, Popular & Prefect Super Profile," by Melvyn Smith, published by G.T. Foulis. (For address see Haynes, above).

"Ford Cortina 1600E Super Profile," by Graham Robson, published by G.T. Foulis. (For address see Haynes, above).

"Anglia, Prefect, Popular From Ford Eight to 105E," by Michael Allen. Published by Motor Racing Publications. Address above.

"Consul, Zephyr, Zodiac, Executive: Fords MK1 to 4," by Michael Allen. Published by Motor Racing Publications. Address above.

Workshop Manuals

A range of Workshop Manuals and Owners Manuals are still available from Haynes of Sparkford, nr Yeovil, Somerset. Currently available from Haynes are:
Ford Anglia 105E Workshop Manual, Ford Cortina MK1 and Corsair 1500 Workshop Manual, Ford Cortina MK2 Workshop Manual, Ford Cortina MK1, MK2 and Corsair 1500 Car Handbook.

Road Test Books

The following Road Test books are available from Brooklands Books, address above.
Ford Consul, Zephyr & Zodiac MKI and MKII, 1950-1962,
Ford Zephyr, Zodiac, Exec. MKIII and MKIV, 1962-1971,
Ford Cortina 1600E & G.T. 1967-1970,
There is also a series of books on High Performance Escorts from 1968 to 1990, High Performance RS Escorts, and a High Performance Capri Gold Portfolio 1969-1987.

INDEX

Index